S0-AYQ-352

A History of the

FORT WORTH
MEDICAL
COMMUNITY

A History of the

FORT WORTH
MEDICAL
COMMUNITY

By
Ann Arnold

Grapevine Public Library
1201 Municipal Way
Grapevine, Texas 76051

Other Fort Worth Books by Ann Arnold

Gamblers and Gangsters:
Fort Worth's Jacksboro Highway in the 1940s and 1950s

History of the Fort Worth Legal Community

· ·

First Edition
Copyright © 2002
Published in the United States of America by Landa Press
P. O. Box 122336
Arlington, TX 76012

All Rights Reserved

Library of Congress Control Number: 2002093133

Library of Congress Cataloging-in-Publication Data

Arnold, Ann
A History of the Fort Worth Medical Community
Includes bibliographical references, index and photos

ISBN 0-9721297-0-7

1 2 3 4 5 6 7 8 9 0
1. Fort Worth   2. Physicians   3. Hospitals   4. Epidemics   5. Medical
Schools   6. Allopaths   7. Osteopaths

All inquiries for purchase or delivery of this book should be made to
LandaPress, P. O. Box 122336, Arlington, TX 76012; or call 817-451-0884.

Inside photograph courtesy UT Southwestern Moncrief Cancer Center

Cover and text design by Bill Maize; Duo Design Group

Table of Contents

PART THREE

THE PAST FIFTY YEARS—CIRCA 1953-2003

Acknowledgments

I am grateful to all the physicians and their families who generously gave of their time and materials to bring this book to fruition. Robin B. Sloane and Nicole King of the Tarrant County Medical Society gave encouragement and support. Thanks to all.

Special thanks also must go to Ken Hopkins and his staff at the Fort Worth Public Library Genealogy and Local History Department, and to Sally Gross and her staff at the University of Texas at Arlington Special Collections Department for helping with research data on the pioneer doctors. Craig Elam and the staff at the Gibson D. Lewis Health Science Library, University of North Texas Health Science Center, provided valuable data on the fledgling Texas College of Osteopathic Medicine.

Photographs supplied by families and the libraries give the reader a glimpse of a bygone era and bring life to history. Bill Maize of Duo Design Group did a masterful job of putting it all together. And my colleagues at the Freelance Writers Network offered valuable editorial assistance.

I offer my heartfelt thanks to all.

Foreword

The history of medicine in Fort Worth is as rich and colorful as the story of Tarrant County itself. It is a record of selfless devotion to the sick, but it is also more than that. It is a history of pioneers with courage, vision, and a great sense of civic duty. Not only did the first physicians in Fort Worth put in long and hazardous hours, often without compensation, but they were active in the establishment of businesses, schools, mail service, and even the public water supply. This involvement in local affairs continues today.

Doctors with foresight have developed medical schools to train local physicians. They have been instrumental in the establishment of local hospitals, churches and other charitable organizations to serve the citizens of Fort Worth & Tarrant County. Most of these institutions continue in operation today.

Tarrant County physicians presently are experiencing many changes in the way health care is delivered. It behooves us to know our history, as well as to be active participants in determining our future.

JAMES L. NORMAN, MD
MARCH 2001

PART ONE

THE FIRST
FIFTY YEARS—
CIRCA 1853-1903

Introduction

"Doctor, lawyer, merchant, chief. . . ." All were important players in the saga that transformed a rude fort into a bustling city. The first doctor, J. M. Standifer, traveled to army camps from Waco to Fort Worth during the years 1849 to 1853.

Carroll Marion Peak is recognized as the first resident physician. He left indelible footprints on the city's historical map. William Paxton Burts, the second doctor to practice here, became the city's first mayor. He is remembered as the founder of the Board of Health.

Dr. Isaac L. Van Zandt, whose family made many contributions to the nascent outpost on the Trinity, was the first president of the Tarrant County Medical Society. Ever at the forefront of scientific advancement, he brought the first microscope to the city.

By 1870 the first hospital had been established by Elias James Beall. A quarter of a century later, he—with colleagues Bacon Saunders, W. A. Duringer, Julian T. Feild (also spelled Field) and others—organized the Fort Worth Medical College as a part of the Fort Worth University.

In the early days malaria was the most common summer illness, and winter brought the scourge of pneumonia. These diseases were conquered, only to be replaced by influenza, polio, and now AIDS. Courageous men and women fought enemies too small to be seen with the naked eye, as well as superstitions that hung on long after science had refuted their validity.

History is much more than dates and battles won and lost. History is the story of the men and women whose lives shaped our own. Hospitals and clinics were the battlegrounds. The pioneer doctors, and the many others who followed them, as much as the highly publicized cattle barons, contributed to the development of what has been called the "Texasmost City." This is their story.

CHAPTER ONE

THE TRAILBLAZERS: HOUSECALLS ON HORSEBACK

Horseback was the most common way to travel in early Tarrant County. Pioneer doctor Isaac L. Van Zandt told *Fort Worth Star-Telegram* reporter Mae Benson of days when he rode miles to see one patient, only to return to his office and find somebody waiting, wanting him to see a patient who lived within a few miles of where he had just been. "Frequently I would leave word the direction in which I was going and on the way back would meet a man who had come for me,"[1] he said.

When Julian Feild fell ill of a fever, his wife sent a rider to Dallas to prevail upon a doctor to treat him. The year was 1853, four years after Major Ripley Arnold and Major General William Jenkins Worth selected the bluff overlooking the Trinity River as the location of the newest frontier fort. Arnold commanded troops who protected the early settlers from marauding Indians until he and his men were ordered to move farther out onto the high plains. Feild, one of the first settlers at the fort, operated a general store in the abandoned army barracks.

Dr. Carroll M. Peak rode the thirty miles west to heal the stricken man. Villagers, pleased with Peak's medical skills, persuaded the Kentucky native to make his home with them. He moved his bride into a vacant barracks and became the first Fort Worth civilian physician in residence.

The young doctor, and those who followed him, worked under the most primitive conditions. Well educated medical men from whom they could learn and draw inspiration were hundreds of miles away. There were no laboratories in the modern sense; no hospitals, no trained nursing support staffs. And yet they held life and death in their hands.

Peak was born in Gallatin County, Kentucky on November 13, 1828 to a once prosperous family. The Panic of 1837 changed their status. After eight years of schooling in Warsaw the youth, knowing he must make his own way, resolved to become a doctor. He studied with Dr. A. B. Chambers, then attended the University of Louisville for a year, and graduated in 1851 from their school of medicine.

Like many others seeking to establish themselves, he headed west. Peak began his practice in Dallas, a village of 300 people. One year later he went back to Kentucky, married Florence Chalfant and brought his bride to Texas.

After deciding to cast his lot with the small band of settlers in Fort Worth, he closed his Dallas practice and made the move. In 1879 Mrs. Peak wrote to her son, Howard, describing the long ago trek to Fort Worth. She told of riding in a hack for hours and hours "going slowly across 'hog wallows' on the prairie without an intervening object of interest. . . ." They spent the night at Johnson Station, a stage coach stopover, now part of the city of Arlington. The second day of the trip she noted, "We, next morning, as Dickens says, 'were moving over an untraveled country,' reaching the Fort at 2 o'clock, hungry and tired."[2]

Their first home was a dog-trot double log cabin that formerly housed Arnold's officers. In 1856 Peak built a house on what is now Throckmorton Street. His wife planted trees and flowers, attempting to make their new home like what they had known in Kentucky. The First Christian Church of Fort Worth was organized in their parlor.

One biographer described Peak as stout, five-feet-nine inches tall and weighing one hundred and eighty pounds. He had light brown hair, "greyish blue eyes," and a high, wide and prominent forehead.

For a radius of thirty miles, Peak traveled by horseback to treat the six families in the hamlet and the slightly larger number of settlers outside the immediate area.

As the first full time physician, surgeon and dentist in the area, he identified his practice as "bounded on the west by the setting sun." In frigid winter weather or on summer days when the temperature topped one hundred degrees, sporting a six shooter and clothing appropriate for the season, Peak made his rounds. He rode his horse "Gray Eagle" to answer the calls of "Hurry, Doctor!" when an injured cattleman or a woman in labor needed him. In the days before newspapers he shared the results of his visits, joyfully announcing the birth of a healthy baby or sadly advising townspeople of the death of a neighbor.

In his saddlebags he carried an amputating knife, forceps, saw, and other "surgical" instruments. Nurse Cassie Watson Cook, in a 1977 essay, eloquently described those early surgeries. "The kitchen table was moved to the best and quietest bedroom. Everything was scrubbed with strong lye soap and rinsed well. Freshly boiled and ironed sheets were tacked over the table....The floor was then scrubbed. The freshly bathed patient was placed on the draped table during surgery. After the operation, the patient was returned to the bed and the kitchen table was put back in its proper place."[3]

Carroll Peak, equipped with the latest "pharmaceuticals" of quinine, blue mass, ipecac and rhubarb, performed needed surgery and ministered to the sick and dying.

Carroll M. Peak, Fort Worth's first civilian doctor. (from a photograph of a painting) Courtesy Fort Worth Jack White Photograph Collection; Special Collections Division, The University of Texas at Arlington Libraries

Dr. Peak devoted one room of the house on Throckmorton Street to his "drug store." There he prepared medicines from basic chemicals and pungent herbal substances. From records the doctor left of his remedies, one finds he prescribed a pain killer composed of alcohol, pepper, mustard, sassafras root, ammonia, and camphor gum. He mixed honey, diluted sulfuric acid and tincture of opium to make a cough syrup. This preparation he also used to combat "night sweats."

In summer young patients swallowed a sugary concoction containing mercury, and in winter they wore a lump of asafetida (a foul-smelling herb of the carrot family) in a sack around their necks to ward off diseases. Lard and turpentine were staples in medical use at that time as well.

Peak's fees ranged from $1.00 per tooth extraction to $2.00 for medical procedures. Often in the early years patients paid in flour, fresh produce or salt cured meat.

Despite their distance from eastern centers of commerce and government, Peak and other "Fort Towners" kept up with national events. He is remembered for his civic activities as much as for his medical practice. He organized the first mail service and hired a courier to twice weekly deliver mail to and from Dallas. He funded the service by charging ten cents per letter. This arrangement lasted until President Franklin Pierce appointed Julian Feild, Peak's first patient, to open a post office and serve as its first postmaster.

The Civil War disrupted lives throughout the nation, and Fort Worth citizens answered the call to arms. Peak organized the Mounted Tarrant Rifles which became Company K. In what must have been a colossal embarrassment, the doctor could not join his men when they recaptured Galveston. While drilling on the town square, he was injured in a fall from his horse. After his recovery, Peak saw military action in Louisiana.

Following the war, Peak led in an attempt to reestablish a school system. The ill-fated 1856 Male and Female Schools had closed after a few years. He and fellow citizens K. M. Van Zandt, Milt Robinson and W. H. Milwee raised $75.00 seed money to refurbish the dilapidated Masonic Hall to use as a school. After much struggle an election was held in 1877, and by a vote of eighty-five to five, citizens approved a tax base. The losers challenged the vote as not representing two-thirds of the property owners, and another election, in 1881, again was in the affirmative. Peak was a member of the school board that hired Miss Sue Huffman as the first superintendent of schools. In recognition of his unwavering support of education, an elementary school now bears his name.

In addition to his interest in education, Dr. Peak represented the city at the National Railway Convention in 1875, was a member of the city council from 1877-78, and a member of the Texas delegation to the Democratic National Convention in Cincinnati, Ohio in June 1880.

Carroll M. Peak died February 28, 1885. He is buried in Fort Worth's historic Pioneer Rest Cemetery.

★ ★ ★

W. P. Burts came to Fort Worth in 1858 after studying medicine at Geneva Medical College in New York. From his office on the northeast corner of Second and Rusk (now Commerce) Streets, between the White Elephant Saloon and a gambling hall, he entered into a friendly competition with Dr. Peak for patients. The rapid growth of the settlement ensured enough for both physicians.

Burts was known to mix superstition with medical knowledge. "When riding to an important case," historian Julia Kathryn Garrett noted, "if a jackrabbit leaped before his horse, miles did not matter. He reined his horse, turned him around and rode home; then took a fresh start."[4]

He supported the Confederacy and was conscript surgeon for Tarrant County. During the Reconstruction Period, he branched out into more lucrative enterprises.

In 1869 the physician participated in the post-Civil War cattle drives. "Dr. Burts gathered a herd on the Grand Prairie and hit the trail for Kansas,"[5] Garrett wrote. The drive was successful and he gave up his medical practice. A couple of years later he and two partners opened a general store. After two previous successful cattle drives, the 1873 venture proved disastrous. Dr. Burts resumed his medical practice and became the senior partner of the oldest medical firm in the city, Burts, Beall, Feild & Duringer.

In addition to professional activities, the physician's record in Fort Worth was one of civic participation. Burts crusaded for a reliable water supply. By the end of the early 1860s several deep cisterns were dug— some in the middle of Main, Houston and Throckmorton Streets. The purposes were threefold: to provide drinking water for the horses, catch rain runoff, and have a ready supply of water for the bucket brigade in case of fire.

Elected mayor in 1873, he was reelected in 1874. In one of his first official acts, Burts signed an ordinance establishing a Board of Health. While leader of the town, he marveled at the new technology of the day, especially a telegraph operated by Max Elser. Oliver Knight, in *Outpost on the Trinity*, recorded one such event. "Mayor Burts, whose strong face was accented by mustache and beard, was standing at Elser's elbow."[6] Max Elser fingered the strange contraption. A delighted grin spread over Burts' face. He had just communicated via telegraph with the mayor of Dallas. No longer would Fort Worth be an isolated cattle trail hamlet. While Burts took care of mayoral duties, his medical partner, E. J. (Elias James) Beall, took on more and more the care of patients.

At the time of his death in 1895 Burts was vice president of the Fort Worth University School of Medicine. The obituary in the *Fort Worth Gazette* read, "His health has been failing for some time past, with the advancement of age, and the cause of death was one of the infirmities of age, senile softening of the brain."[7] He was sixty-eight years old.

★ ★ ★

E. J. Beall came to Fort Worth in 1870 and spent the remainder of his life here. He began the study of medicine with his father, Dr. Jeremiah Beall in Shreveport, Louisiana in 1853. He earned a medical degree in 1856 and later took postgraduate courses at several medical centers in New York. Beall was one of the few American physicians at that time to have the opportunity to study in London, Paris and Berlin.

Beall practiced medicine in Marshall, Texas. During the Civil War he served as regional surgeon of the 15th Texas Calvary, then became chief surgeon of the First Army Corps. He took part in the battles of Vicksburg and Jenkins Ferry.

In 1870 he and his wife, Fanny Van Zandt, visited her brothers in Fort Worth. They stayed, and Beall worked with Dr. W. P. Burts. Dr. Beall became the third Fort Worth physician to join the Texas Medical Association and was a delegate to the International Medical Congress in Berlin.

According to unofficial Tarrant County Medical Society historian, Dr. Sam Jagoda, Jr., Beall ". . . was an early researcher in antiseptic surgery, modified radical mastectomy and also gastric surgery."[8] His scholarly papers appeared in state and national medical journals as early as the 1880s.

Beall established the first private hospital in Fort Worth. He named it Florence Sanitarium, in honor of Mrs. Carroll M. Peak. Just as he followed his father into the healing arts, two of Beall's sons, Heberdeen (Heb) and Frank, became physicians. He was in active practice until 1908.

As the number of patients grew, Burts and Beall expanded their medical team to include Feild, Duringer and Capps. The Feild member was Dr. Theodore, son of Julian Feild.

★ ★ ★

Julian Theodore Feild had been a student at John Peter Smith's school in Fort Worth. With the outbreak of war, the seventeen-year-old youth joined the 15th Texas Cavalry, where he attained the rank of lieutenant. Seeing young men die on the battlefield for lack of medical attention, prompted him to become a doctor.

Julian Feild wrote to Dr. Carroll M. Peak on behalf of the young veteran.

> "As my son, Theodore expressed a desire to read medicine and to give him the advantages of that profession is in all probability all that I will be able to do for him. I desire to place him under your tutorage if you are willing to accept him as a student. . . . I will spare no necessary means to give him a finished education."[9]

Theodore started his apprenticeship with Peak and after two years, Feild entered Louisville Medical School.

He graduated with the class of 1869, and upon his return to Texas married Sarah Ferguson, whose father was a druggist. They set up housekeeping in Mansfield where Feild practiced a short time before taking postgraduate work in New York. Again back in Texas, he joined Drs. Burts and Beall.

In the 1870s the building of the railroads not only increased employment, but increased the number of occupational accidents. Dr. Feild, an expert surgeon, made history when forced to amputate both legs and one arm of a man critically injured in a railroad accident. The patient recovered and lived out his natural life span.

Like other pioneer doctors, Feild's practice took him out of the city. His daughters recalled their father relating some of the dangers he faced when making horseback housecalls. They quoted him when talking to *Fort Worth Press* reporter C. L. Douglas. "I've ridden through wooded places west of the city, half dozing in the saddle, and be suddenly startled by a blood-curdling scream from the trees."[10]

This was a time when panthers still roamed the area.

Feild was the second Fort Worth doctor to join the Texas Medical Association and he remained active in professional organizations until his death on Christmas Day, 1932.

★ ★ ★

Feild's colleague, Dr. Bacon Saunders, the son of a Confederate surgeon, was born in 1855 in Kentucky. His father, Dr. John Smith Saunders, moved the family to Dallas in 1857. After the Civil War they established themselves in Bonham. Bacon graduated from Bonham's Carlton College when he was eighteen-years-old. "He then taught school and worked as a medical apprentice in his father's office for a period of two or three years,"[11] historian Bennett Smith noted.

The young man returned to the state of his birth and took his medical training at the University of Louisville Medical College. Saunders graduated as the top man in a class of 190. In 1877 he joined his father's practice in Bonham. "Early in Dr. Saunders professional career he was called out some twenty miles from Bonham to see a very acutely ill patient."[12] All symptoms led the young doctor to suspect appendicitis. He recalled reading in a medical journal of a similar case in Europe. Saunders returned to his office and reread the article. Although he had never seen a case of appendicitis, much less the operation, he realized only prompt surgery could save the man's life. "On a kitchen table in a farm house, with boiling water as the disinfectant, with his father as the anesthetist, Dr. Bacon Saunders performed a successful removal of an infected appendix. The patient recovered and lived many years."[13]

The doctor loved fine horses and realized his dependence on them for transportation, especially in emergencies. Mrs. Saunders told of, one might say, a burning incident on horseback. Her husband owned a saddle horse that traveled at a singlefoot gait, which is faster than a trot. "One day as the doctor was riding in from a country call his horse kept swinging along faster and faster and showing excitement. The doctor heard a roaring noise. He wore a long-tailed coat divided at the back. Glancing over his shoulder he saw his coat tails flying out like a banner and one of them afire! The noise he heard was the roaring flames lighted by a spark from his cigar."[14] By the time he got the horse stopped and tore off the coat, the garment was burned beyond repair.

Saunders moved to Fort Worth in 1894 and entered into a partnership with Dr. W. A. Adams and Dr. F. D. Thompson. By 1907 they had outgrown their original building and Saunders made a bold move. He built the city's first skyscraper, the seven story Flatiron Building at Ninth and Houston, reserving the top floor for his office. The physician hired Marshall Sanguinet and Carl Staats, Fort Worth's leading architects, to plan the structure, which was fashioned after one Saunders had seen in New York. Mack Williams' story in the News-Tribune included misgivings about the venture. "Work began . . . on Saunders' Triangle Building, as it was first known, and before long . . . neighboring merchants were protesting. A seven-story building, they complained, would cast a shadow over Fort Worth's entire downtown!"[15]

At that time it was supposedly the tallest building in North Texas and other citizens voiced concerns. Some feared it would topple the first time a West Texas norther blew in. Others just thought it was too high off the ground for prudent people to use it.

Townspeople hardly had time to acclimate themselves to the building before Dr. Saunders again stunned the populace. He bought the first electric car, a Studebaker.

In addition to helping establish the Fort Worth Medical College in 1894, he was instrumental in organizing the North Texas Medical

Association and was founder and second president of the Texas Surgical Association.

Like most physicians in the last half of the nineteenth century, he started as a general practitioner. Soon after his move to Fort Worth, the demands on his time became so heavy he decided to limit his practice entirely to surgery. "His fame as a surgeon spread and he became chief of staff at St. Joseph Hospital where he was chief surgeon for twenty years."[16] It was in this capacity he did more than anything else to promote the growth of St. Joseph Hospital and make it a central hospital for railroads. Yet he did not counsel the use of surgery as a cure-all. He is quoted in *History of Surgery* as arguing against the hurried judgment to operate. "There are times and, perhaps always will be, circumstances, when the best interests of the patient demand that the treatment of the case be conducted wholly on medical lines."[17] Before poor health forced his retirement, he amassed a long list of distinctions and honors. *The Medicine Man in Texas* noted he was President of the Texas Medical Association in 1897, taught in the Medical Department of Texas Christian University, and was a Fellow and one of the founders of the American College of Surgeons.

At the unveiling of the historical marker at the Flatiron Building on February 13, 1971, Bennett Smith summed up the pioneer surgeons life, saying, "As physician, surgeon, educator, church layman, civic worker and business man, Dr. Bacon Saunders achieved distinction during a professional career of forty-eight years out of a lifetime of seventy years. His work spanned the last quarter of the nineteenth century and the first quarter of the twentieth century."[18]

Dr. Saunders died July 15, 1925 in Colorado Springs. He is buried in Fort Worth.

★ ★ ★

Isaac Lycurgus Van Zandt, another who spanned the nineteenth and twentieth centuries, was born to Florence (Cook) and Isaac Van Zandt in a log cabin in the northeast corner of the young Republic of Texas on January 5, 1840. The boy grew up in what is now Marshall and attended school there. He graduated from Franklin College in Nashville, Tennessee before his eighteenth birthday.

After college he returned to Marshall and clerked in a drug store. One of the town's doctors, E. J. Beall, who later became his brother-in-law, encouraged him to study medicine. When the hostilities between the states began, Van Zandt was half way through Tulane University's medical school.

He entered the army and served both as a medical corpsman and soldier. Captured at Fort Donelson, Tennessee, the young medic spent seven months at a federal prison in Chicago. From there he was exchanged for Northern prisoners. Back in the South, he held the post of acting assistant surgeon at the Battle of Missionary Ridge. After recovering from minor wounds, he learned he was being transferred to division headquarters at Marshall. Eager to get home, he walked most of the way from Louisiana.

When the war ended, Van Zandt returned to Tulane and graduated in 1866. He first practiced in Dallas, but his older brother, Maj. K.M. Van Zandt, lured the physician to Fort Worth in 1868.

Van Zandt's interest in medicine was whetted when as a boy he listened to tales of home cures and "state of the art" folk remedies. Bess Stephenson interviewed him on the occasion of his ninety-third birthday. Referring back to his childhood, he told her of overhearing his elders tell of a man who had "gravel removed from his gall bladder." Soon thereafter young Isaac saw a man lying down, drinking from a stream. "Thinks I, that man will have gravel in the gall bladder."[19]

Dr. Van Zandt was an innovator in many ways. While on a trip to New York, so taken with the new aids in the practice of medicine, he brought one home with him. It was the first microscope in Tarrant County. He caught a frog and mounted its foot on the newfangled instrument. "For most of a day doctors and laymen took turns in peering through the glass at the webbing of the frog's foot and its network of veins."[20]

Van Zandt is credited with being the first Fort Worth physician to use forceps in handling surgical needles. Another first, he promoted the beneficial effects of creosote in treating pneumonia.

An avid reader of the scientific literature, Van Zandt also wrote numerous articles. One, considered a classic, traced the march of pellegra into Central Europe and then to America. The treatise appeared in the *Texas State Journal of Medicine* August, 1916 and was reprinted in national and international professional journals.

The Tarrant County Medical Society honored the revered doctor with a dinner at the First Christian Church. Dr. Holman Taylor told of the honoree's many medical achievements. In addition to the use of creosote mentioned above, Dr. Van Zandt used saw palmetto in the treatment of bladder and prostate problems, a remedy that has re-surfaced in herbal medicine today. Dr. Taylor noted, "It is impossible at this time to catalogue the numerous contributions made by Dr. Van Zandt to medical literature,"[21] but he read a long list of them dating from 1891 to 1921.

Dr. Isaac Van Zandt came from one of the most prominent families in Texas. His father, Isaac Van Zandt, helped negotiate the treaty between the Republic of Texas and the United States that led to the annexation of Texas. In 1842 Republic President Sam Houston had appointed Van Zandt ambassador to Washington. Many years later Dr. Van Zandt recalled his earliest memories in that city. He remembered seeing a tall, dark-haired neighbor to the Van Zandts, whom he learned later was distinguished statesman John C. Calhoun.

Interviewed in 1932 on the occasion of his ninety-second birthday, Van Zandt told of another Washington incident. As a four-year-old, he gathered wild flowers and managed to get "normal boy dirt" on his clothes. When his mother went calling on Mrs. Tyler, the First Lady, Mrs. Van Zandt was ". . . so humiliated at the sight of his soiled clothing that she had him climb quickly in the old-fashioned carriage and hide under the lap robe."[22]

Dr. Van Zandt preached good nutrition as a way to a long, healthy life. His mantra was "shorten the belt line, lengthen the life line." Interviewed at the age of ninety-five, he humorously ascribed his longevity to the selection of long-lived ancestors. The Van Zandt family seemed to have made a wise selection. His mother lived to be ninety-three, and the youngest of her five children was a mere seventy-eight at the time of the interview.

The pioneer physician died shortly after the interview cited, but at ninety-five he was the oldest doctor in Fort Worth. He retired at age eighty, but continued to consult with and prescribe for old friends and patients. He is buried at Oakwood Cemetery.

CHAPTER TWO

THE EARLIEST HOSPITALS: NO MORE KITCHEN TABLE SURGERY

Six of the earliest medical facilities contained the word "Sanitarium" in their names. Five were built by physicians, and one, the Howard Sanitarium, was built by the widow of Dr. W. R. Howard. As stated earlier, Dr. E. J. Beall established the Florence Sanitarium, on West Broadway. He and his staff operated the hospital for some years.

The Protestant Sanitarium was the next. Dr. L. H. Reeves wrote, "It was a fifty-bed hospital opened by Dr. A. C. Walker in 1900 and was located at the corner of Rio Grand and South Main Streets."[1] Fire destroyed it in 1907.

Dr. F. D. Thompson called his hospital simply "The Sanitarium." It was in the center of downtown at Lamar and 6th Street. Thompson, a surgeon, formed a partnership with W. A. Adams and Bacon Saunders in 1899. Prior to building the hospital he was surgeon for the T. & P. and the H. & T. C. Railroads. The Sanitarium had a maximum capacity of thirty beds. He retired and sold it. The new owners remaned it the Southwestern Hospital and operated it for a number of years.

Dr. J. S. Turner built the Arlington Heights Sanitarium ". . . for the care of mental and nervous diseases in 1907,"[2] Reeves wrote. He sold it to Dr. Wilbur Allison, who ran the facility for years. "It was later under the management of Drs. Bruce Allison, J. D. Bozeman and R. H. Needham.[3] It closed in 1935, a victim of the Great Depression.

The Bazwell Sanitarium, established by Dr. R. O. Bazwell and associates in 1921, served the community until Bazwell's death in 1932.

Dr. William R. Howard came to Fort Worth in 1886. He was in general practice, but was noted for his expertise in pathology and bacteriology. He maintained a laboratory just back of his home on Cannon Street.

In the young century, when other physicians were experimenting with those newfangled horseless carriages, Howard, in 1912, still used a buggy and his mare, "Dixie." Returning from a house call on Hemphill Street, Howard died in the buggy. Reeves noted, "Dixie, . . . was stopped (by a pedestrian) . . . at Pennsylvania and Henderson Streets as she was patiently bringing the doctor home."[4] As a memoriam, Mrs. Howard built a small, private hospital at Cannon and College Streets. In 1950 it was still in operation.

Yet another sanitarium, the Tarrant County Tubercular Colony, was established in 1915. Dr. J. M. Trimble was its first medical director. Dr. H. V. Helbing succeeded him and served for many years. The facility originally had only eight cottages, but by 1925 it had grown to twenty-six. In 1932 the name was changed to Elmwood. At mid-century, the hospital had ". . . a capacity of sixty-seven beds for white patients and nine beds for negro patients,"[5] according to Reeves.

★ ★ ★

St. Joseph Hospital, the biggest of the early day facilities, also lasted the longest. It met a need.

Railroading was a dangerous business. While building roads, gandy dancers fell from trestles, were crushed by rock slides, received broken bones and mangled limbs as they forged steel ribbons across the continent. In the cars, steam boiler explosions and multiple injuries from a variety of mishaps were common. Foremen calculated on-the-job experience of brakemen by the number of fingers they had lost.

Fort Worth based Missouri-Pacific Railroad recognized the need to provide aid for these accident victims. In 1883 the company opened a twenty-four bed infirmary in a two-story frame structure on the south end of Main Street. That was the beginning of what would become St. Joseph Hospital.

The Sisters of Charity of the Incarnate Word came to Texas and in 1885 answered a call from the railroad to operate the Fort Worth infirmary. Before the nuns accepted the call, Mother St. Pierre voiced reservations about the order's taking on new responsibilities. The reverend mother, knowing the railroad employed immigrants from strongly Catholic countries, reasoned the nuns could minister to both the spirit and body, and reluctantly she consented.

Eleven sisters journeyed from San Antonio. They found a small wooden building and few conveniences for effective nursing. It was so remote from central Fort Worth that a horse-powered trolley car was used for the long commute. Optimisticaly, one sister commented, "However, it does afford ample facilities for fresh air and light."[6]

Mother St. Pierre noted the opportunity to do good, but, " . . . the future will tell how things work out. It is certain (to) have its cross and contradictions; it would not be God's work if it did not meet with opposition or suffering from some source. . . ."[7]

Indeed it had its cross; the infirmary burned to the ground that same year. Patients were evacuated unharmed and the nuns continued their work in a nearby temporary building.

The Order purchased fifteen acres from the railroad and a three-story brick building replaced the pile of ashes. They named it St. Joseph's Infirmary after the patron saint of the working man. The designation "hospital" did not come into use until 1930. Even then, some people refused to go, calling them "places of death."

The new infirmary admitted its first patient, a charity case, April 26, 1889. Those with the means paid ninety cents a day, or one dollar if they required an ambulance. This service at times proved less than optimal. "The ambulance was telephoned for but on account of both horses being lame we had to call for an express wagon to accommodate the patient,"[8] according to old records. One patient paid three dollars a day, but insisted on getting his money's worth. He demanded the constant attention of a nurse. They were glad to see him go despite the loss of much needed revenue.

Those records provide a sense of what it was like in the early days. Word of typhoid epidemics appeared frequently in the old accounts. One

St. Joseph Infirmary, 1896. Courtesy Fort Worth Star-Telegram Photograph Collection; Special Collections Division, The University of Texas at Arlington Libraries

entry noted "No one attended mass this morning in consequence of its being wash day."[9]

St. Joseph's was open to other railroads, and employees of the Denver & Colorado, International and Great Northern, and Santa Fe took advantage of their inclusion. The first year the sixty bed facility served 456 patients.

For years, Dr. William Duringer and his nephew, Dr. Will Duringer, physicians for the M K & T and Frisco Railroads, saw their patients there. In *A Pioneer Doctor's Story*, Will Duringer wrote of some their experiences. It was not uncommon for an injured man to have a ten or twenty dollar bill sewed inside his clothing, so if he had too much to drink or got hurt on the job, he would have some money. Hygiene was primitive for most at that time and for railroad workers even more so. Dr. Will recalled seeing patients whose louse infested clothing had to be burned. Screw worms in the nose were treated with a derivative of carbolic acid, the same ointment used on farm animals with screw worm infections.

Because of the infirmary's remote location on the outskirts of town, some patients observed habit-clad nuns picking up stray rocks from their paths as they said their daily prayers. Others, due to the nearness to the railroad tracks, would be awakened by trains rumbling in the night.

The rudimentary institution was largely self-contained, with the Sisters maintaining a kitchen garden and orchard for seasonal food. They raised chickens for eggs, and cows for milk and butter. Two horses were kept to pull an ambulance, and the nuns did all of the hospital's laundry by hand.

Typhoid ravaged the area in 1890 and the city asked the hospital to take patients regardless of their ability to pay. The city's coffers were also bare and they paid for the indigent with script. So in addition to railroad employees, St. Joseph's became the city's charity hospital. Sixty years later the Order was still helping the needy. A physician recalled, "I don't know how many sandwiches the Sisters gave to the poor every day, but it was a great many."[10]

The Sisters helped the community in other ways. During the World War I influenza epidemic, soldiers stationed at Camp Bowie overran the base hospital, St. Joseph's opened its doors. Of the 300 men treated there, only two died.

In 1968 Assistant Administrator David DeBacker put figures to the never-ending problem. Even with John Peter Smith the designated charity hospital, St. Joseph continued to see non-paying patients. DeBacker told *Fort Worth Press* reporter Seth Kantor, "In the first half of the present fiscal year, St. Joseph spent more than a quarter of its entire working budget on charity and discount patients. That means the hospital is 'forgetting about' $223,050 in bad debts for the past six months."[11]

Business Manager W. C. Donohoo put a name and face to the problem. "(Last year) Larry Wade Gunsolus, a gangland victim with a bullet in his head and his throat knifed open, ran up a bill of $2133 . . . . You don't expect hoodlums to pay the bill. You're a hospital and your job is to save their lives. You do this, knowing they aren't going to worry about a bad credit rating when they don't pay the bill."[12]

Five brick and mortar additions were made to St. Joseph's before it closed in 1995. The 1889 facility soon became inadequate, and in 1904 an addition, larger than the original building, was begun. The school of nursing met in the original structure, known as the East Building, after the 1906 addition was finished.

By 1927 the hospital again desperately needed more room. A new five-story, $500,000 building, with its 200 bed capacity, was completed in 1929. Touted as the finest, most modern medical institution in the Fort Worth-Dallas area, the addition included a pediatric wing, a first in the area. Only twenty years later the hospital need more space. The Sisters added a 100 bed wing to the structure. This wing was air-conditioned and sound-proof. A *Star Telegram* reporter noted that hospital administrators learned from their earlier experience. "St. Joseph's is the first hospital in Fort Worth and one of the first in the state to inaugurate the new, soft shade of green for use in the operating room."[13] Doctors praised the innovation, citing less glare from operating lights and thus less eye fatigue and strain.

Patient rooms were painted a restful shade of blue. Soft pastel walls with contrasting drapes made the rooms seem more like hotel rooms than sterile hospital rooms. A new feature, "silent nurse," enabled a patient to raise or lower portions of the bed by pushing a button. A bed light could easily be adjusted for reading, or dimmed for sleeping.

St. Joseph's boosted the number of operating rooms to seven, and the maternity ward added two recovery rooms. Interns and residents' quarters, on the fifth floor, included a conference room and library. The common living area also sported a modern touch, a black and white television.

An average of more than 500 people received treatment in the emergency room each month by 1947. The remodeled area, which once served as the first operating room, contained two private rooms for severely injured patients. In the post-World War II era, the Cold War caused many planners to consider emergency room preparation. St. Joseph was one of only two of Fort Worth's major hospitals that stood ready to give instant care at any moment to those whose lives hung in the balance. Fortunately, relations between the USSR and the United States improved and the emergency room use was confined to victims of natural disasters.

Another important event occurred about mid-century. The hospital received full accreditation. The Sisters were justifiably proud of the designation. Not resting on their laurels, the administrators dealt with the accelerating need for more space and services. A *Star-Telegram* reporter noted, "According to American Psychiatric Association records, Fort Worth remains the largest area in the nation without psychiatric beds for the public."[14]

In 1957 plans were drawn up and the hospital began yet another five-story building, just north of the main structure. The new T-shaped addition was designed to enable nurses to be closer to patients. It also addressed two of the biggest problems for hospitals—transportation and communication. "The vertical transportation of supplies from Central Supply Department to the operating and obstetrical areas is accomplished by dumb waiters giving direct delivery,"[15] a *Press* reporter explained. Two dumb waiters and an elevator expedited the delivery of supplies, and a pneumatic tube delivered bills, correspondence and messages from floor to floor. The communication set-up included an interhouse dial telephone system, a televoice system for dictating medical records, and a two-way nurse call system between patients' rooms and nurses' stations. All of this was a marvel of technology at that time.

A wing to house psychiatric patients was included in the plans. For a time, cost over-runs threatened to doom the project. But the Governing Board of the Sisters of Charity of the Incarnate Word approved a $4,000,000 expansion program. The new addition added 102,000 square feet at a cost of $3,700,000. St. Joseph's administrative, emergency, obstetrics and radiology departments were up-graded and the psychiatric wing was built.

With the 1959 opening of the 127-bed addition, and its sixteen beds in the psychiatric wing, Fort Worth had a long-needed facility to treat the mentally ill. Previously some patients had been sent to Dallas or Galveston for treatment. Others were housed among the general or surgical population of St. Joseph's, which was often inappropriate and sometimes dangerous.

Yet another round of building was needed. "On May 28, 1965, at 2:00 P.M., The Sisters of Charity of the Incarnate Word held the Groundbreaking Ceremony for the 4½-million-dollar expansion program soon to be underway at St. Joseph Hospital,"[16] readers of the *St. Joseph*

Newsartery learned. The front page article included a photograph of Bishop Thomas K. Gorman, Mayor Willard Barr, and other local dignitaries. Sister Mary James, administrator of the hospital, in her lilting Irish brogue, welcomed those assembled. Rev. R. W. Jablonowski, pastor of St. Stephen Presbyterian Church gave the invocation and Rabbi Robert J. Schur of the Beth El Congregation offered the benediction.

Throughout the summer, workers demolished portions of the old building and constructed new ones. "Noise notwithstanding, our patients are the first to agree that it's good to see Fort Worth's First Hospital expanding again to meet the health needs of our . . . community,"[17] Billy Glen Marsh wrote in the employee newsletter.

The hospital continued to expand its services. In its centennial year, 1989, Dr. W. S. Lorimer, Jr. looked back at the progress in medicine and medical care. "In the 20th century alone," he said, "many formerly hopeless infections are now readily susceptible to antibiotics, surgical procedures have explored the cranium, chest cavity, heart, and blood vessels, and irreversible diseased organs have been replaced with new ones."[18]

But the future did not bode well for the venerable institution. For decades costs were kept low because many key positions were filled by nuns who gave their services without pay. At one time, twenty-nine nuns filled positions at the hospital. But as a nationwide shortage of women entering religious service cut into this ready supply of workers, the hospital was forced to hire lay people. It employed 530 people in 1953, with an annual payroll of $858,587. The average cost to a patient was $9.10 per day, $17.82 for surgical patients. With increased costs, the hospital had two unsatisfactory options—jack up the fees of paying patients, or increase the patient load. "One is an unpopular idea," said administrator DeBacker, "the other is dangerous."[19]

The advent of Medicare and the Hill-Burton Act brought about the inflow of federal dollars; new hospitals sprang up, and established ones, such as St. Joseph applied for grants. With the $1,500,000 grant awarded in 1963, the hospital added seven floors to the existing north and west wings. St. Joseph had expanded to the present twelve floors. "The new floors," Sister Alban said, "will contain 300 beds, raising the total to approximately 500. . . . the money will help pay for a new dietary department, new physical therapy section, a psychiatric floor with fifty beds, a medical intensive-care unit and new operating rooms with the latest equipment."[20]

Also in 1963 the city was galvanized by the impending visit of President John F. Kennedy. In an undated memo, public relations director Glen D. Bunn alerted Vice-President Lyndon B.Johnson to the hospital's special welcome. "As the President's plane approaches South Fort Worth, please point out to President and Mrs. Kennedy the large lighted sign on the roof of St. Joseph Hospital. The letters 'WELCOME JFK' will be in bright amber lights size 14'X30' each."[21] Sure enough, strung flat upon the roof, like Christmas lights, was the message.

In the 1960s and 1970s competing hospitals, All Saints and Harris Methodist, enlarged their facilities and built satellite facilities in fast-growing suburbs. Over-building resulted in fierce competition for patients to fill all the new beds. In a good news/bad news dilemma, miracle drugs and improved medical procedures cut the number of days patients needed to be hospitalized. It was good for the patient, but bad for the hospital's bottom line. The loss of revenue was in the millions of dollars.

Since 1976 St. Joseph had operated an Out-Patient Clinic. Located in the Convent Building, it offered chemotherapy, IV therapy, and day surgery. It served a need, but drained much needed revenue from the hospital proper.

To stem the flow of red ink, St. Joseph, the hospital's official name since 1959, attempted to change its mix of services. The Obstetric Department was closed and new departments opened.

A Cardiac Catheterization Laboratory began in 1987, partner to the Coronary Surgery Unit. The hospital boasted that "surgical teams could efficiently prepare an emergency coronary patient within fifteen minutes of arrival."[22]

Greater stress was placed on providing orthopedic surgery and rehabilitation. The hospital offered outpatient eye surgery, including cataract removal, lens implantation, and treatment of glaucoma. To meet the needs of a growing societal problem, a substance abuse program provided detoxification and therapy. Two weight loss programs were yet other attempts to serve the needs of the community. None helped the struggling hospital to survive.

After 102 years of serving the sick and wounded in Fort Worth, the Sisters of Charity of the Incarnate Word ceded ownership of St. Joseph to the Daughters of Charity National Health System. That system operated forty-five hospitals, including the St. Paul Medical Center in Dallas.

Efforts were made to contain costs without cutting the quality of care. Sister Nora Walsh, chairman of the board of Incarnate Word Health Services, viewed the change as one of sponsorship, with both organizations committed to a concern for patient health care. The Daughters of Charity saw their efforts as a mission, but managed-care plans—the major players—funneled their members to larger hospitals that offered lower costs. Quality of care, it seemed, became secondary. Moreover, those institutions advertised, thereby gaining the bulk of new patients. St. Joseph did not.

Newspaperman Jim Fuquay explained, . . . by 1991, it (St. Joseph) was simply one of more than a dozen Tarrant County hospitals. And despite investing tens of millions of dollars in the past decade, it was out-paced by competitors who adapted faster to a changing marketplace."[23]

The causes of the problems St. Joseph faced were multiple and complex. Michael Denis, Executive Director of the DFW Area Health Education Center, and veteran hospital administrator, believed the decline to be related to the closing of the obstetrical unit. "There is something magical about babies that promote good hospital care. It's a time of happiness and if the mothers had positive deliveries, they are inclined to continue using that hospital."[24]

The 1983 advent of Medicare going from cost-based to diagnostic pricing, hurt hospitals like St. Joseph. "The Sisters wanted to help sick folks, and they would take care of whoever walked in the door. The outcome was more elderly patients and less money,"[25] Denis said. The final blow came with the budgetary constraints of managed care.

The end of the 105-year-old non-profit status of the hospital came in April, 1994 when it was purchased by Columbia/HCA. Sister Magdalen Hession, a thirty-year veteran of the hospital, knew the end was coming, but grieved over it like the death of an old friend. For Sister Frances Evan, the greatest loss was when the religious symbols were removed. She told reporter Ginger Richardson, "To me, the cross is the symbol of the Lord's caring, and it's a symbol for healing."[26]

Columbia's restructuring failed, and in 1997 the building that stood sentinel at the south end of downtown Fort Worth was sold again. When the staff at St. Joseph saw its last patient, and closed its doors, an unknown writer left a heartfelt message on a bulletin board. "Alone I walked thru the vacant hall of the great building. Such a feeling of sadness overcame me. . . . Such history, such service, such love and dedication must have poured from these halls. Let us remember what St. Joseph's stood for and keep the memory fresh in our mind's eye, and thru this the mission of St. Joseph's will live forever."[27]

The second group of new owners in three years, Heritage Housing Development of Beverly Hills, California's plans for a facility to care for Alzheimer's patients also failed.

The lead in a *Star-Telegram* article by reporter Sarah Lunday revealed the extent of the problems. "Accusations of verbal abuse and errors in dispensing medication have prompted regulators to discontinue state payments to Heritage St. Joseph Gardens nursing home in Fort Worth."[28] Without such funding CEO Diane Colby predicted the company would be forced into bankruptcy. The facility closed April 16, 2000. A visit to the site by one who used the hospital in its glory days was sobering. Debris littered the almost empty three-story garage, where once parking space was at a premium. So sad.

CHAPTER THREE

THE PROFESSORS: MEDICAL AND NURSING SCHOOLS

"Early on, city fathers recognized the need for a center of higher learning."[1] Fort Worth University was chartered on June 6, 1881 and operated by the Methodist church. Initially, classes were held in rented downtown quarters. Mack Williams, in his compilation of the city's history, wrote, "In 1886 (it) moved to College Avenue, where a large brick and stone building had been erected by civic leaders. In 1889, Rev. Oscar L. Fisher, president, . . . saw the institution begin its greatest era."[2]

Five years later Dr. E. J. Beal and others chartered the medical school. It was the third medical college in Texas and the first in the South to provide a four-year course of study. Reeves, in his medical history, listed the founders as, "Drs. Beall, F. D. Thompson, Bacon Saunders, W. R. Thompson, J. W. Irion, W. A. Duringer, W. A. Adams, J. T. Feild, E. D. Capps, Frank Grey, Lyman A. Barber, W. R. Howard, W. Beverly West, I. C. Chase and James Anderson."[3]

W. R. Thompson's committee recommended a medical journal be published. Irion, in addition to his teaching and practice, served as medical director of a local life insurance company. Of the group of founders, only Duringer wrote of his medical experiences.

Grey came to Fort Worth from Kentucky. He maintained a low-key practice and left the politics to others. Adams was the second dean of the school. His scientific interest in the brain and nervous system led him to study in Vienna and other European centers. This advanced knowledge he shared with students. West taught at the school until 1918.

I. C. Chase literally gave his life to medicine. When he began to experiment with X-ray technology, its dangers were unknown. "In many of his experiments he used old German tubes, testing their efficiency,"[4] according to the *Star-Telegram*. Before his death doctors were forced to amputate a finger and an arm damaged from radiation. His condition grew worse and he died the day before the Exchange Club was to honor him by placing his name in its Book of Golden Deeds.

These professors moved with the medical school to a separate building at Seventh and Rusk (now Commerce) one year after the program began. From 1894 to 1911 a young man— there were few if any women medical students—could get a medical degree without leaving Fort Worth. Annual tuition, including matriculation fee, dissecting ticket, chemical and pathological laboratories was $75.00. Four years tuition, plus $25.00 graduation fee totaled $325.00. Should it be necessary for him to pay for a room, the cost was fifty cents a week. If meals were included the fee rose to $3.50.

An advertisement for the 1902-1903 session, with its abundant use of capital letters, stated, "The Medical Department was organized under the University Charter in July, 1894. The First Annual Session of 1894-95 was a Phenomenally Prosperous one. The Trustees, Faculty and Advisory Board are gratified and encouraged by the endorsement of the profession throughout the State; by the Ample Supply of Clinical Material; the Large Number of Capable Students, and the Prospect of a Largely Increased Attendance for the Coming Session. The Situation of Fort Worth has proved to be such as to Meet the Needs of a Growing Medical School. Its Large Number of Eminent Physicians and Surgeons from which the Faculty is drawn; its Private and Public Hospitals, Homes and Dispensaries, and the Immense Field Tributary to it, all combine in a peculiar degree to render it a Great Medical Center."[5]

The full page advertisement included the names of officers, faculty and advisory board. F. D. Thompson was president of the medical faculty; Frank Grey, vice-president; Ira Carleton Chase, secretary; and Bacon Saunders was dean. All were respected physicians. Also listed as officers were Dr. J. T. Feild and James Anderson. See Appendix A for a list of professors and their teaching specialties.

In 1905 the faculty moved into a new building at Fifth and Calhoun. According to Reeves' description, "It included larger and better teaching facilities and an outdor (sic) clinic was established. Also in this year a department of Pharmacy was established with Dr. R. H. Needham as its head."[6] The American Medical Association required an adjacent hospital and a twenty bed facility, complete with operating rooms, became part of the school.

Fort Worth University was never endowed adequately, requiring a constant search for funds. Also, Polytechnic College (now Texas Wesleyan University) on the eastern rim of the city, and Texas Christian University on the west, were formidable rivals for students. The student body, once more than 900, gradually shrank to an unsustainable low. In 1911 trustees voted to close the school and sell the assets to a Methodist school in Guthrie, Oklahoma. In 1912 the medical school merged with TCU as the Medical Department of that institution. This merger lasted until 1918, when as Williams noted, "The medical school moved to Dallas and became part of today's Southwestern Medical School."[7]

In its short life, the school produced many of the physicians who formed the medical community of the first half of the twentieth century. One such graduate, Dr. Isaac A. Withers, upon his 1898 graduation, entered the Medical Corps of the United States Army for service in the Spanish-American War. Withers returned to Fort Worth and taught gynecology in the medical school until it merged with Baylor University College of Medicine in Dallas.

Dr. Withers interrupted his practice to again serve during World War I. After the Armistice, he was assigned to Camp Bowie as chief of surgical services until he received his discharge. "Early in his career he served the city of Fort Worth as health officer. . . . he died December 1, 1940, at his home following an extended illness."[8]

Dr. Hubert F. Leach graduated a year after Withers. Leach practiced in Aledo and Weatherford as well as in Fort Worth. He was the first president of the Northwest Texas District Medical Society, which he helped to reorganize.

Classmate Dr. Edwin Petty Hall, Sr., practiced in Fort Worth from 1900 until 1948. During his long career, Hall taught physiology, hygiene, and anatomy at Polytechnic College, and from 1903 until his retirement, was the physician for the Fort Worth Masonic Home and School.

"The career of Dr. W. E. Chilton, who died . . . at the age of 78, bridged the wide gap from the days of horse-and-buggy medicine to the age of antibiotics,"[9] according to the October 29, 1955 *Star-Telegram* obituary. Chilton was a 1900 graduate of the Fort Worth Medical School.

Fort Worth native John Howell McLean was nineteen when he enrolled in the Fort Worth School of Medicine and obtained his M.D. degree, summa cum laude, in 1901. After further training in New York's Bellevue Hospital, McLean began his practice here. Although a surgeon of marked ability he, according to a profile in Reeves' *History*, "remained in the general practice of medicine because he liked the personal relation and close contact with his patients. . . ."[10]

McLean supported the work of the Panther Boys Club, an organization which offered after school sports and social activities for North Side boys. Reeves estimated between 25,000 and 30,000 Panther Boys knew "Dr. Jack" as their friend. McLean died in 1946.

Dr. Robert W. Moore, a 1906 honor graduate, studied at the University of Pennsylvania before enrolling at Fort Worth Medical School. Following his graduation, he specialized in treatment of the eye, ear, nose and throat. Dr. Moore was active in local and state medical societies and readily contributed papers at their meetings.

Dr. Frank G. Sheddan, a urologist, was a member of the Class of 1909. In addition to his forty-seven year practice, Sheddan engaged in part-time farming.

Classmate Dr. Arthur Brown grew up on a farm before entering Fort Worth Medical School. He graduated in 1910. In 1961 he was honored for his fifty years in medicine. In addition to his ophthalmological practice, he was at one time a member of the Fort Worth City Council.

Samuel A. Lundy taught school for five years before he decided to study medicine. A 1911 graduate, his was the last class before the old Fort Worth University moved to Oklahoma.

Another later alumnus, Dr. Young J. Mulkey, served an internship at St. Joseph Hospital after he graduated from Fort Worth University School of Medicine. He then became chief resident at Philadelphia Hospital for Contagious Diseases. Mulkey began his practice in 1916, and except for the time he was with the ambulance corps in World War II, he devoted forty-two years to the needs of Fort Worth patients.

Perhaps the most politically active doctor who never ran for office was Webb Walker. The Lufkin native came to Fort Worth in 1908 to attend medical school and remained after graduation. He officed in the Medical Arts Building from the time it opened until his death in 1962. The *Press* credited Walker with organizing the Citizens Committee ". . . a group of Fort Worth businessmen who began forming their own political tickets."[11] For many years their candidates controlled City Hall.

Walker held two offices—both appointive. He served as city health officer for seven years and board chairman of the old City-County Hospital. His medical speciality was eye, ear, nose and throat. Perhaps that helped him when he was held at knife point by three masked men at his home. He later identified one of the bandits by his crooked teeth.

These and other physicians mourned the demise of their medical school, but the damning evidence of the Flexnor report could not be ignored. Abraham Flexnor, in 1910 published *Medical Education in the United States and Canada:* A Report to the Carnegie Foundation for the Advancement of Teaching. The *Bulletin of the History of Medicine*, noted, "The Flexnor report of 1910 justifiably stands as a monument in the reform of American medical education."[12] The conditions cited in the well-documented report shocked the nation and led to the closing of a number of marginal schools.

Of the Fort Worth Medical School, he wrote, "Laboratory facilities: These comprise a dissecting room, ordinary laboratories for chemistry and bacteriology, and a single laboratory with a routine outfit for pathology and histology; recent provision on a small scale has been made for physiology. The classrooms are bare except for a reflectoscope and a defective skeleton. There is a small museum of unlabeled specimens and a small library.

"Clinical facilities: The basement of the school building makes a wretched hospital of 50 beds, 20 of them free. There is no clinical laboratory. One surgical clinic weekly is held at a private hospital two miles distant.

"For the dispensary a fair attendance is claimed, but no complete index is kept."[13]

There was no way the university could bring the facility up to standards demanded by the study. When it merged with Oklahoma University, the medical school became part of Texas Christian University for a short time. The Fort Worth Independent School District acquired the main building of the old Fort Worth University. Central High School opened in 1918 in what had been University Hall. The site at 1300 W. Cannon is now Green B. Trimble High School. The Fifth and Calhoun building which once housed medical classrooms and labs was torn down to make way for a parking lot.

Students seeking to become doctors were forced to travel to Galveston or other cities for their medical training.

★ ★ ★

About the time of the decline of Fort Worth University Medical School, another important training institution, the St. Joseph School of Nursing, came into being. In 1906 the Sisters of Charity of the Incarnate Word received a charter from the state to operate the new school.

It offered a three year course in theoretical and practical instruction. Young women were housed on the third floor. Like the hospital itself, the nursing program outgrew its quarters and in 1927 when a new hospital building was opened, the nursing program gained more space.

Advancement in the educational process was slow and uneven. The school did not seek accreditation until 1938. Deficits noted were lack of an adequate library and an affiliation with an umbrella school. That problem was solved in 1944 when the School of Nursing became part of Our Lady of Victory College. The advantage to a student was, in addition to her (ninety-nine per cent of students were female) Nursing Diploma, she would receive sixty-four semester hours of college credit toward a bachelor's degree.

The need for nurses skyrocketed during World War II. Again the nursing school outgrew its quarters. On May 6, 1954 Bishop Thomas K. Gorman dedicated a new wing—a residence for nursing students, completely fire-proof and air-conditioned. A mere fourteen months later yet another building opened. This one, next to and connected with the new residence hall, was an 18,350 square foot educational center. Classrooms, laboratory, library, conference room and a seven bed practice room were designed to give students the best nursing education in the area.

In addition to state accreditation the National League of Nursing Education put its stamp of approval by giving full accreditation in 1957. At the time of the accreditation, eighty students were enrolled in classes. Upon graduation they now would be able to work in any state in the union.

One graduate chose to stay, and for more than thirty years Clara Fisher helped alleviate pain and suffering at St. Joseph. "When asked

Dignitaries and nurses gather at groundbreaking ceremony for St. Joseph School of Nursing expansion. Courtesy Fort Worth Star-Telegram Photograph Collection; Special Collections Division, The University of Texas at Arlington Libraries

about the changes she has witnessed in nursing, her immediate reply was that when she first began nursing, few diagnostic tools existed. Equipment such as monitors, defibrillators. . . and scans that are so necessary in today's hospital, did not exist."[14] Fisher recalled the days when funeral-home operated ambulances were not staffed with medically trained personnel. Thus her assistance in the emergency room was the first a patient received. Another vivid memory was of nurses cleaning glass syringes by hand. Thermometers were also cleaned and shaken down by hand.

Fisher told of a major change that had nothing to do with equipment. In 1970, for the first time, nurses were allowed to wear pantsuit uniforms instead of the traditional, starched white dresses. St. Joseph Hospital issued a memo the week of September 14 giving nurses permission to adopt the new regulation uniform pantsuit—with the appropriate cap, white shoes and identifying pins and insignia. Mrs. Tommie Rodriquez, RN, a nurse in intensive care, applauded the change. She found, ". . . the pantsuits highly practical for women who transfer a patient from one bed to another, move furniture or even crawl about on floors to hook up equipment,"[15] she told newspaper reporter Katie Brown.

Fisher added, even as a student in nursing school, she was forbidden to enter or exit the building wearing slacks or jeans. "We used to wear pants with the legs rolled up under our skirts until we got outside. Then we'd take off our skirts and roll down our pants legs,"[16] she laughed.

A fellow graduate of the school, Sister Magdalen Hession, known as Sister Maggie, told of the many more conveniences than when she first began. Running water, available only in the supply rooms, required much trudging back and forth with water for baths. "You had to run a mile with a bedpan just to find a place to empty it,"[17] she remembered about the not-so-good "good-old days." Sister Maggie's habit also changed. No longer did the nuns wear the long robe and stiffly starched white wimple. She now wore a knee length skirt and softer headdress.

Like the hospital itself, nursing education was changing. Kay Fuhrman, Director of Educational Services, in a 1989 interview spoke of those changes. She noted the trend began in the mid-to-late 1950s, wherein students previously attending diploma schools, such as St. Joseph School of Nursing, moved toward university nursing programs. She cited the progress of technology and health care in general as the driving forces behind the changes.

Schools such as St. Joseph's usually offered three year programs that mainly concentrated on hands-on, task-oriented procedures. Although Fuhrman saw the need for practical, bedside nursing experience, she approved of the university programs' stress on a well-rounded curriculum. That curriculum included nursing leadership and management, something earlier programs did not teach.

As more students opted for university nursing degrees, rather than nursing diplomas, the enrollment at St. Joseph declined. Out of funds and students, the school closed in 1971.

PART TWO

THE NEXT FIFTY YEARS— CIRCA 1903-1953

CHAPTER FOUR

THE PIONEER DOCTORS: FROM HORSEBACK TO HORSELESS CARRIAGES

At the dawn of the twentieth century the American Medical Association acquired its first permanent headquarters in Chicago. It reorganized, created the House of Delegates, and accelerated its campaign to raise educational requirements for physicians. Fort Worth doctors approved the measures and added new techniques, such as X-rays, to their medical bag of tools.

In 1902 the first automobiles in Fort Worth were owned by bicycle dealer H. R. Cromer and minstrel man Billy Kasen. By 1910 the city licensed the dozen or so vehicles and allowed them to travel at speeds up to ten miles-per-hour.

Henry Ford had a plant at First and Commerce, and Chevrolets were built on West Seventh Street until the 1920s.

Physicians were quick to see the advantage of the horseless carriage in making house calls, which many times were actually far flung ranch calls.

Dr. John B. Cummins traded in his horse and buggy for a Model T. The December 11, 1956 *Look* featured a photograph of 98 year-old Cummins standing beside the coupe. The magazine identified the Fort Worth physician as America's oldest practicing doctor. Two years later reporter Tony Slaughter wrote a profile of Cummins for *Newsweek* magazine. The doctor was still practicing at age 100.

John, son of a self-taught Tennessee physician, was born in 1859. When the elder Dr. Cummins died, the family moved to Navarro

County, Texas. As a youth, Cummins read his father's medical textbooks cover to cover and taught school to obtain the money for medical college. A graduate of the University of Tennessee, the general practitioner held medical degrees from there and the University of the South.

He began his medical career in Oklahoma, then returned to Texas. In 1903 he set up a practice in Fort Worth. Dr. Cummins and his wife bought a house at 1126 Hemphill that year. Mrs. Cummins died in 1917 of Spanish influenza. The doctor continued living there for the rest of his life.

His residence was the scene of a "mystery" in the mid-1950s. Some boys, prowling around, found a skeleton under the house. They called the police, sure they had uncovered a murder victim. The "victim" was a demonstration skeleton the physician no longer used in his office.

At 100, Dr. Cummins was as spry as many a man half his age. He celebrated his birthday by attending the Southern Medical Association meeting in New Orleans, then flew (his first airplane ride) to Nashville to visit his birthplace.

Back in Fort Worth, he told Slaughter he only recently had to sell his Model T. "'I had to quit driving when the state wouldn't issue me a driver's license.'

"But his sight is good," Slaughter wrote. "He reads without glasses . . . hears well, his mind is alert and he has his original teeth with the exception of a two teeth front bridge. Only six weeks ago he performed a Caesarian at Fort Worth's St. Joseph's Hospital."[1]

Dr. Cummins put the figure at over 3,000 infants he ushered into the world, including one family for whom he delivered four generations of babies. In his sixty year practice many considered "Uncle Doc" part of their families.

He took naps on his surgical examination table. "One afternoon he rolled off the table," Slaughter reported, "with the steel table tumbling over on him." Others in nearby offices heard the crash, rushed in to find an embarrassed Dr. Cummins with a cut on his head. "He rose to his feet on his own power and doctored his head. Now he's quit taking naps."[2]

After he turned ninety, neighbors in his office building worried about his health. They shouldn't have, he opened the office at 8:00 every morning and worked until 5:00 or 6:00 in the evening. Saturdays and

John B. Cummins, MD, "Uncle
Doc." Courtesy Fort Worth Star-
Telegram Photograph Collection;
Special Collections Division, The
University of Texas at Arlington
Libraries

Sundays Dr. Cummins was available if needed. "People get sick on weekends too," he said.

The physician was a lifelong student. "You never get too old to
learn,"[3] the ninety-one-year old told a reporter at a meeting of the Texas
Academy of General Practice. At 92 Cummins signed up for a Dale
Carnegie course, "How to Win Friends and Influence People." The
Tarrant County Medical Society honored him by naming him General
Practitioner for 1950.   In 1957 the Southern Medical Association
presented Cummins with an honorary lifetime membership. He was 98.

Dr. Cummins scoffed at retirement and kept regular office hours until
to his death December 31, 1958.

★ ★ ★

Dr. Willis G. Cook, a contemporary of Cummins, began his practice
here in 1900. One of his medical professors had trained at Galveston and
often visited Fort Worth. He urged the intern to consider the city. A year
later Cook was in Fort Worth, where he specialized in internal medicine.

Cook is best remembered for his heroic work in 1913 when a meningitis epidemic ravaged the city. This often fatal disease struck both young and old, and the small clinic attached to the medical school quickly filled to overflowing. The city's four hospitals set up 300 cots. Through the medical society Cook heard of a new serum available in New York City. He arranged for a direct shipment of the one-ounce bottles from the Rockefeller Institute of Medicine. *Star-Telegram* reporter Blair Justice wrote, "And with that, Dr. W. G. Cook became the first man in Fort Worth to use an anti-meningitis serum that helped turn the tide against the epidemic."[4] The death rate dropped from 80% to 13%.

In 1958, when interviewed by Justice, Dr. Cook was the only living charter member of the Tarrant County Medical Society. He died in 1963 at the age of ninety-seven.

★ ★ ★

Another doctor, E. P. Hall, Sr. also began his practice in 1900. After graduating from Fort Worth University School of Medicine, Hall served as physician for the Masonic Home and School for forty-five years, and once said he willingly would give up the rest of his practice if he could "just keep on working with those kids." When his health failed, with great reluctance he turned the care of the children over to his son, Dr. E. P. Hall, Jr. The senior Hall died in 1949.

★ ★ ★

Dr. Harold L. Warwick graduated from the University of Georgia Medical School in 1900, but instead of coming directly to Fort Worth he did two years postgraduate study at clinics throughout Europe. The prominent eye, ear, nose and throat specialist, according to the *Texas State Journal of Medicine*, ". . . gained national distinction as an inventive genius. In his speciality he had been especially interested in otosclerosis. . . . He pioneered in the development of the audiometer. He also did original work in the ionization treatment of otitis media and hay fever."[5]

Warwick's inventions were mainly electrical and mechanical. One, a device for storing sound permanently on wire, led to talking books for the blind.

His work with X-ray equipment may have contributed to the cause of his death in 1941. "In his untimely death, this country lost one of its most brilliant inventive geniuses in the medical profession,"[6] the state journal noted.

★ ★ ★

Samuel Andrew Woodward practiced with his father for eight years before coming to Fort Worth in 1905. He served as dean and professor of clinical gynecology at Texas Christian University's medical school before it merged with Baylor Medical College. He was a member of the State Board of Medical Examiners and the State Board of Health. Active in civic activities until his death from a fall in 1937, he was survived by a son, Jack, a Fort Worth physician.

★ ★ ★

Dr. Alden Coffey was as well known for his love of golf as for fifty years of medical practice. Coffey attended the Fort Worth University Medical School, but finished his medical training at Vanderbilt in 1906. Dr. Coffey did post graduate study in Paris, France in 1925. That same year he established the Coffey Clinic at 306 W. Broadway.

His passion for golf led him to join Marvin Leonard in the successful effort to bring the National Open Golf Tournament to Colonial Country Club. Ironically, he died on the eve of the ninth annual tournament, May 26, 1954.

★ ★ ★

Dr. C. F. Hayes moved to Fort Worth in 1909. In 1926 Dr. Hayes became the first school physician for the Fort Worth Public Schools, a position he held until he retired in 1960, ending sixty-seven years in the medical profession.

★ ★ ★

Another doctor who began his practice in 1909 also made quite an impact on the school system—and had a school named for him to prove it. Dr. Hugh V. Helbing, practiced medicine in Fort Worth for fifty years,

H. V. Helbing, MD, long time
North Side physician. Courtesy
Fort Worth Star-Telegram
Photograph Collection; Special
Collections Division, The
University of Texas at Arlington
Libraries

using his Model T, the second automobile on the North Side. He delivered between 4,000 and 5,000 babies. *Star-Telegram* reporter Mabel Gouldy wrote, "For years Dr. Helbing averaged delivering 10 babies a month. At one time he and the late Dr. A. M. Cleveland delivered 60 per cent of the babies born north of the river."[7]

Helbing gained a seat on the Fort Worth school board in 1932, a position he held until 1947. Fighting for poor children and teacher pay raises caused him notoriety as one of the most revered and/or reviled physicians in the city's history. Helbing didn't consider himself a firebrand, but his tongue could be searing. Gouldy recounted a board meeting episode. "Battling for compulsory vaccination of students, Dr. Helbing read a newspaper while a long-winded objector orated at a board meeting. Suddenly the speaker asked the doctor a question.

"'I'm sorry I haven't heard a word you said.'

"'No, but when I get through you're going to introduce a motion for compulsory vaccination,' the opponent shot back.

"'Yes, I am, if you ever get through talking.'"[8]

One fight he won with pride involved starting a program to give free lunches to needy children. In 1948 Fostepco Heights was re-named H.V. Helbing Elementary.

In addition to his North Side practice, Dr. Helbing was medical director of Elmwood Sanatorium for forty-three years. Helbing died in 1968 at age eighty-one.

★ ★ ★

Another well known North Side physician, Dr. Abe Greines graduated from Fort Worth's North Side High School, Texas Christian University, and Baylor Medical College. From 1919 until 1953 he officed at 1549 N. Main Street.

Dr. Greines never sent a bill. A Fort Worth realtor remembered as a youth going to him with an infected leg. "He gave me a shot, and several years later I saw him and realized I hadn't paid. 'How much do I owe you?' Dr. Greines said, 'Five dollars.' He remembered me and the visit."[9]

Like Helbing, Greines served on the school board, but he is better remembered as a driving force behind the Fort Worth Boys' Club. Hazel Leigh, long time director of the club, told of Dr. Greines' involvement. In 1935 she happened upon a boy, shivering in the cold, but locked outside his house. He explained his mother worked late at the packing house. Leigh approached Greines with the idea of providing a place for boys to go for after school activities. The physician took the idea to the Kiwanis Club and it became a reality. Dr. Greines served as president of the Boys' Club for more than thirty years, raised money, and treated the youngsters when they fell ill. He helped establish the Little League of North Fort Worth. A baseball field and the Fort Worth School District athletic center bears his name.

In 1966 he was named "Jewish Man of the Year" by the B'nai B'rith. Two years later school superintendent Julius Truelson and Rabbi Isadore Garsek cited his contributions to medicine, education, social welfare and Texas Christian University, as the Women's Civic Club Council proclaimed him "Fort Worth's Outstanding Senior Citizen."

Dr. Greines died in 1978 at the age of eighty-one.

★ ★ ★

Dr. Charles W. Barrier taught histology at Tulane University School of Medicine and was on the staff or the Mayo Clinic in Rochester, MN before his 1924 arrival in the city. A heart specialist, he was the first Fort Worth physician to use an electrocardiograph.

★ ★ ★

Dr. Jack Ernest Daly, another 1924 arrival, specialized in surgery. He is believed to be the first doctor to use an oxygen tent in Fort Worth. " ... in 1928 he took the first lateral Xray of the spine to be reported to the Northwest Texas Medical Society,"[10] according to his 1967 obituary.

★ ★ ★

"Dr. Thomas J. Cross, one of U. S. aviation's first medical examiners, gave Wiley Post his first physical.

"'I flunked him,' Dr. Cross recalls. 'It was the only thing I could do. He had only one eye,'"[11] so reporter Horace Craig wrote in 1962.

The year was 1927 and new regulations required all pilots to pass physical examinations. Post, a veteran pilot, obtained a waiver and continued flying until his plane crashed in Point Barrow, Alaska in 1935. Both he and passenger Will Rogers died in the accident.

Dr. Cross earned his medical degree from the University of Tennessee and Randolph School of Aviation Medicine. He and Mrs. Cross, his secretary, travelled all over Texas in a Model T Ford giving physicals to pilots. At one stop, he recalled, he gave forty examinations and accepted checks for most of them. Craig quoted the doctor, "Twenty of the checks bounced. . .I never did try to collect them."[12]

According to Dr. Cross, commercial air transportation began about 1929, when Texas Air Transport, the forerunner of American Airlines, started to carry mail and a few passengers brave enough to try the new machines. Cross helped found the Texas Air Medics in 1949.

★ ★ ★

These are but a few examples of outstanding doctors who went to war, lost patients and loved ones in the 1918 influenza epidemic, treated patients during the Great Depression, and made lasting impacts on thousands of Fort Worth citizens. In transportation they went from horseback to horseless carriage, and in medicine they went from kitchen table surgeries to the miracles of anesthesia and antibiotics.

★ ★ ★

Along with the automobile, the telephone helped doctors better serve their patients. James A. McMillen, "Mr. Mac," established a physicians' exchange in one room of his South Side home in 1921. Using first two telephones, then expanding to three, he offered a twenty-four hour answering service. He and Mrs. McMillen screened calls for the degree of urgency, and contacted the appropriate doctors or whichever substitutes were taking calls. Mrs. Burgess Sealy said, "Every doctor in town knew Mr. Mac. We didn't make a move without telling him where we were."[13] If he really needed them and they weren't at home, he knew their favorite haunts, such as the golf course or a TCU game.

Jim McMillen, Mr. Mac's son, recalled his father charged doctors $3.00 a month for a service much appreciated. Today's telephone "menu" is considered better technology, but some would argue Mr. Mac's personal touch couldn't be beat.

CHAPTER FIVE

DOCTORS AS AUTHORS: THEY WROTE MORE THAN PRESCRIPTIONS

"What should a doctor do in his declining years?" asks Dr. Charles McCollum in the opening of his delightful little book *Pills and Proverbs*. "A few of my old doctor friends just faded away, some became grouchy and were miserable. . . . To occupy my extra time, I took to writing—a new, green field to me. At first I naturally thought of different medical subjects. These were eliminated, since most doctors have good medical libraries. I could write nothing new about Moses and Luke; the preachers beat me to them. . . . I finally decided to write about myself . . . during my professional career."[1]

Born May 17, 1874, Charles spent his early years on the family farm. The family moved to Texas in 1882. An uncle, a doctor, met the train and took them to their rented farm.

When Charles finished his meager education the prospect of going to medical school seemed impossible. Instead he found employment in a pharmacy. "At that time it was believed that the drug store was a good stepping stone for a doctor. I feel confident yet that a good druggist who becomes a doctor has many advantages,"[2] he wrote years later. His duties were sweeping floors and washing bottles. He left the pharmacy when he saved enough money to enroll in the Texas Medical School in Galveston. The United States' involvement in the Spanish-American War caused him to cut short his studies.

Grapevine Public Library
1201 Municipal Way
Grapevine, Texas 76051

McCollum served as a hospital steward. A typhoid fever epidemic raged, and "My job was nursing fifteen typhoid cases at night from 7 P.M. until 7 A. M.,"[3] he recalled. His most vivid memories concerning that time were of "sick folk, crippled people, death and swarming flies." Yet he valued it as an education on the complications of infectious diseases that he could never have experienced in medical school.

Following the war he attended Barnes Medical College in St. Louis and graduated in 1902. To celebrate, he bought himself a "brand spanking new" rubber-tired buggy to make the house calls he knew would be coming his way.

Dr. L. H. Reeves, in his *Medical History*, emphasized McCollum's continuing quest for knowledge. "He was a graduate also of the University of Vienna, Austria. During his professional career he had taken postgraduate work in St. Louis, and in clinics in London, Paris and Berlin."[4]

After his return from these European studies, McCollum settled in Fort Worth in 1914. He taught therapeutics and pharmacology at Texas Christian University's medical school, and was senior surgeon at St. Joseph's Hospital from 1918 until 1937. He died December 2, 1943.

★ ★ ★

Dr. William Commodore Duringer practiced medicine for more than forty years. He narrated his experiences in *A Pioneer Doctor's Story*. Mary Crutcher, of the *Fort Worth Press*, wrote it could easily have been called "A Love Story." In it Dr. Will, as he was affectionately known, reminisced about his childhood, schooling, family and practice.

Dr. Duringer was born November 12, 1882 on a farm in Johnson County. He attended the three-month session of the school on Grandfather Duringer's farm. Seeking a better education for their son, Will's parents sent him to school in Crowley. Following his 1903 high school graduation, he entered Fort Worth University's School of Medicine, where his uncle was a professor of surgery.

During the summer Will returned to his father's farm and helped with the harvest. It motivated him to finish school. "The heat would nearly kill me after being in the shade and school all year. (We) would work from sunup to sundown to get the harvest in before it rained,"[5] he recalled.

He was in his second year when his uncle called on him to assist in a surgery at St. Joseph Hospital. The two proceeded to the second floor operating area. The doctor instructed him to scrub. "I went over and took a brush and green soap and began to wash my hands. . . and then I quit," he recalled. His uncle ordered him to scrub ". . . 'until I tell you to quit.' So I went back and scrubbed and scrubbed until I thought I had pulled the skin off my arms and hands."[6] During the surgery blood squirted into his face. He jumped back, but stayed with the procedure. On the way home, his uncle indicated he had passed the test. "The blood didn't make you sick," he said, "and I think if you study hard, you might make a pretty good surgeon some day."[7]

Young Will graduated in 1907, *magna cum laude* and upon graduation he joined his uncle in family practice. Counting office visitors, and day and nighttime home calls, Dr. Will estimated the two sometimes saw as many as seventy patients in one day. ". . . a childbirth at 3 a.m., a hurried call just before breakfast (to a) scalded baby, an attempted suicide, an old lady with spasmodic asthma. . ."[8] were some of the cases he wrote about in his autobiography.

His first medical kit was a long bag with space to carry instruments, first aid equipment and medicines. Uneasy at first, he soon became accustomed to people making room for "the doc," on his way to see a man hurt in the workplace or later the victim of an automobile accident.

The Drs. Duringer were quick to use the latest medical equipment. They were among the leaders in the use of x-rays and electrocardiograms. X-ray machines at that time were crude and uninsulated. Dr. Will related the time his laboratory technician placed the wires too close to each other. The resulting shock knocked her to the floor. "She had metal stays in her corset and wherever one of those stays was, she had a streak that was burned by the X-ray."[9]

For a while the bachelor doctor lived in his office in the old T & P Building at Third and Main Streets. His waiting room couch became his bed at night. This enabled him to quickly answer emergency calls. Few nights passed in the rowdy town without a shooting or stabbing. "I would phone the livery stable . . . and I would be ready by the time that my horse and buggy were (brought around)."[10]

Dr. Will used St. Joseph Hospital for more serious procedures. In the days before air conditioning, he began surgery at 7:00 a.m. in the summer months. It was necessary to keep the operating room windows closed to prevent contamination. For the same reason, fans were not allowed. Duringer operated while a nurse cleared his brow of sweat in those bygone days. Once, he needed unusual assistance from the attending nun. "One day when I was operating, the pajamas I had on had a bandage through the top and I tied this to hold them on. When I reached over to do something, the string broke, and I had to finish the operation with one of the Sisters holding up my pajamas."[11]

Duringer had been in practice less than ten years when World War I began. As a Captain in the Medical Corps, he developed methods and tools to use in plastic surgery for them. Fifty years later although improved, those methods and tools were still being employed.

With the signing of the Armistice, he was primed to return to his wife and two daughters. Before he and thousands of other soldiers anxious to get back to their families could be mustered out, the flu epidemic put those plans on hold. Days and nights were spent doctoring the men in a seemingly endless procession. "One day . . . the Commanding Officer called me down to the office and said, 'Captain, how would you like to be transferred to Fort Worth?'"[12] The officer explained that Camp Bowie had medics who were from Des Moines and it made sense to him for them to switch assignments and let the Texans serve at Camp Bowie.

Dr. Will treated patients at the base hospital long after the flu epidemic was over. In addition to plastic surgery he did other reconstructive operations. He became so proficient at repairing hernias he could do the procedure in twenty minutes. When he finally received a discharge, he reestablished the civilian practice he left two years before.

In the years between the World Wars, Duringer practiced with his son-in-law, Hyal Brown. With the outbreak of hostilities in 1941 Dr. Will was again called upon to perform as he had in the First World War. He was a civilian, but tried to take on the patients of younger men who had been inducted into the service. The heavy caseload damaged his health, and in 1948 he suffered a massive heart attack. He survived, but was not able to continue to see patients. Dr. Brown took over the entire practice.

After his retirement, Dr. Will and his wife traveled, but Lillian Duringer was diagnosed with cancer. While at the Mayo Clinic with her husband and daughter, Dottie, their son-in-law Hyal suffered a coronary thrombosis. Dr. Brown remained in the hospital for five months. With neither Duringer nor Brown able to continue, their practice was sold and both lived in a near invalid state until their deaths.

Mrs. Duringer died in 1950. Her husand, Dr. Will, died March 12, 1966, seventeen years after his retirement.

★ ★ ★

Judge Lyle's workplace was a hospital, not a courtroom. His grandfather was a judge (lower case) and that's how Judge (upper case) got his name. Lyle was born February 9, 1896   ". . . in a little town known as Wheelerville, located about fifteen miles from Hattiesburg, Mississippi,"[13] he wrote in his autobiography. As a boy, Lyle noted, "I was never seriously sick except for a case or two of malaria (chills and fever) every summer. This was usually taken care of by many doses of Dr. Grove's tasteless Chill Tonic or Febraline. They both had quinine in them. I couldn't swallow a capsule of quinine so this served the purpose."[14]

At age ten Lyle abandoned his dream of becoming a street car conductor when he observed a country doctor easing his mother's discomfort when she suffered a gall bladder attack. He opted to go to University of Mississippi. The teen-aged premedical student found both the academic demands and the unfamiliar environment both daunting and stimulating. Lyle graduated in 1914, the same year that tragedy struck at home.

His father was a cotton farmer, and the 1914 boll weevil infestation completely destroyed his crop. Medical school for Judge went by the wayside.

A relative by marriage, Dr. G. A. Lindsey, invited the Lyles to visit Ralls, Texas. The hamlet, near Lubbock, was deemed ideal for cotton farming. Plus, the dry climate promised a reprieve from the all too frequent bouts of malaria Mrs. Lyle suffered. Judge's father liked what he saw in West Texas and bought two farms in the area.

Young Lyle landed a job in a Ralls bank and started saving money for medical school. Soon he became cashier, loan officer, teller, vice-president and janitor. He saved enough money for tuition, and enrolled at Tulane Medical School in New Orleans. His first year of medical school was all study and no play. The second year he and his fellow students were inducted into the army as medical corpsmen. He was required to drill as any other soldier during the day and go to school at night, but at least the government paid for his education.

The 1918 flu epidemic hit hard at Camp Martin, where Lyle was stationed. Many died in the infirmary. "We were all afraid of the hospital. Late one afternoon I had a severe headache and felt that I had a fever. . . That night I knew I had the flu."[15] Despite his condition, he carried out his duties without reporting his illness. Slowly he recovered, but it was more than a month before he felt completely well.

Just before being released from the army he was exposed to the mumps. Rather than endanger his colleagues, he checked into the only contagious ward in the city. Patients suffering from diphtheria, measles, smallpox and whooping cough were his ward mates. He survived and resumed his education.

Lyle had progressed far enough in his medical studies to put some of the learning into practice. In the summer of 1920 he did laboratory and x-ray work at the Lubbock Sanitarium. He also was allowed to work in the surgery unit. He returned to New Orleans, and the Hotel Dieu Hospital hired him as an extern on the night shift. Much as he had in Lubbock, he worked in the laboratory, but also gave anesthetics and helped in surgery. Classes during the day and hospital work at night left him very little time for studying, yet he persisted and graduated from Tulane June 6, 1921.

He applied and was admitted to Charity Hospital. As was the custom at that time, he and fellow interns received their room, board and laundry—no salary. "The only money we ever received was for filling out insurance blanks for the patients. For this we charged fifty cents."[16]

Lyle caught a glimpse of real life as a member of the ambulance crew. On one ambulance call he and another doctor arrived to find a man with a transverse incision across his abdomen. "He was on a dirty floor and his intestines were hanging out with trash sticking to them. A piece of the lower . . . liver had been cut off and was on the floor."[17] Lyle stuffed the organs back in place, did a bit of taping the wound, gathered up the piece of liver, and rushed the man to the emergency room. There surgeons threw the liver away, and repaired the intestinal damage. He left the hospital ten days later, hopefully wiser, or else the next time his wife caught him in bed with another woman he might not be so lucky.

Following his internship, Lyle settled in Fort Worth and went to work at Dr. Harold V. Johnson's Protestant Hospital. Johnson sold the hospital to the Southern Baptist Convention, and Lyle joined him in his private practice. He stayed with Johnson for a few years before striking out on his own.

A few years after the Baptists closed the hospital, he purchased it through Federal Bankruptcy and renamed it Pennsylvania Avenue Hospital. In exchange for taking charity patients the city agreed to tax the enterprise as a non-profit institution. Later it was advantageous for both, but at the beginning Lyle encountered one calamity after another.

During the three months between the time Lyle applied for and got federal approval, World War II broke out. The doctors he counted on to work in the hospital were drafted. Heavy rains left the basement swamped with two feet of muddy water. To make matters worse, the bathroom

Judge Lyle, MD, told of being one of the first surgical patients in his own hospital. Courtesy Mrs. Barbara Tatum, daughter of Dr. Lyle

plumbing stopped up. "To keep the rest of the hospital from being ruined, it was necessary to close the windows in the hot summer,"[18] he recounted in his autobiography. This caused steam to form and loosen the plaster on the walls. Lyle at this point wanted to forget the whole thing, but he was stuck with it. Taking another look at the situation, Lyle determined, like Job in the Scripture, he would overcome the problems that beset him.

Help came in the form of a benefactor who secured wartime priorities for materials. Workmen put the building in shape, and by the September 30 opening, the need for beds to care for the burgeoning defense work force was critical.

But like Job, his problems weren't over. Within a week of the opening, Lyle was stricken with acute appendicitis. First he telephoned Mrs. Lyle. "I'm going to have an appendectomy."[19] She responded casually that she would see him later and took their daughters out to eat.

Next he called a doctor to come over from Harris Hospital and bring an anesthetist. When Mrs. Lyle had not reached the hospital by the time of the operation, the surgeon called her. She thought her husband was doing an appendectomy, not having one done on him. With the clarification, she rushed to his side. Lyle was one of the first surgical patients in his own hospital.

He hired Alice Taylor, an experienced administrator to run the hospital. In Reeve's *Medical History* she described it as being "modern and well equipped with 68 beds for white patients and 10 beds for colored patients. Five (5) four bed wards two (2) bed wards and 10 bassinets and has modern, up to date laboratory equipment."[20] With Taylor in place, Lyle concentrated on practicing medicine at the hospital until he sold it in 1955. The new owners, International Bankers Life Insurance Company, asked Lyle and Taylor to stay on in the newly named Doctors General Hospital.

Like all physicians, some of Lyle's patients were more colorful than others. One he remembered, named Kelley, lived in the Morningside Addition, a middle class neighborhood of Fort Worth. The Kelleys were polite and seemed to be ordinary citizens. Mrs. Kelley called the doctor out to treat her father. Lyle diagnosed the man as suffering from a hernia and recommended surgery. "A few days later she sent him to Baptist Hospital and told me not to spare any expense because they would have plenty of money and would pay all bills when he left the hospital."[21] But before he could operate she pulled the man out and disappeared. Only later did the physician learn her husband's nickname. It was "Machine Gun."

Dr. Lyle also recalled an encounter with veterinary medicine. In his waiting room one morning he saw a woman holding a baby chimpanzee. She feared a veterinarian would be too rough and insisted the M.D. give the animal a penicillin shot. "I took a lot of razzing . . . about what kind of doctor I was."[22]

In his homespun manner, Dr. Judge Lyle gave glimpses into the practice of medicine in the middle decades of the last century. He died in 1983 at the age of eighty-seven.

★ ★ ★

In *Ramblings of a Country Doctor*, Zack Bobo, who actually practiced in the cities of Fort Worth and Arlington, told many an amusing anecdote of his life in medicine.

The 1922 graduate of Baylor Medical School interned at Charity Hospital, New Orleans, LA. Dr. Bobo recalled, ". . . I had a ward full of diabetics. We treated them by almost starving them, . . .the only way we knew to control the disease." His chief, Dr. J. Bernie Guthrie, visited Drs. Banting and Best. They had just developed insulin. "Dr. Guthrie brought back some insulin and gave it to me to use on the diabetic patients in my ward. . . .it worked like a charm. I had one patient, a Negro woman. . . . I was particularly interested in her, and had stationed nurses around the clock to see that nobody sneaked food to her. She later admitted that she chewed peachy plug tobacco which was full of sugar. . . . I considered her recovery remarkable."[23]

After Bobo finished the internship, he signed up for a year in the Merchant Marines as a doctor working on fruit ships routed to and from Central and South America. He was assigned to one ship, but replaced by another physician. The ship he had originally been assigned to ran into a hurricane and sank. He was then billeted to the *S.S. Cartago*. That ship also ran into a hurricane. The doctor and most of the others on board, as he said, "were so sick we didn't care what happened." Better weather brought better times and Dr. Bobo counted the adventures important learning experiences, especially as they related to treating tropical diseases.

Zack Bobo married Ruth Marrs in 1924 and they settled in Fort Worth. He officed in the Medical Arts Building. "I was very young, (he grew a mustache to make himself look older, but it didn't work) and in the 20s people didn't go for young doctors. I couldn't always pay my rent, but the manager, Clay Berry, was very lenient with me. . . .

"One night about midnight I was called to see a woman in labor who lived near the Trinity River back of Texas Christian University. While I was waiting for the baby to arrive, a cyclone came and rocked the one-room house which I thought was surely going to explode. It swayed and cringed and groaned. The lights went out and the husband struck matches, one after another, so that I could deliver the baby. I finally put a little male infant into the arms of the harassed father just before he ran out of matches. . . .I picked up my bag, stepped out, and fell, nearly breaking my neck. The cyclone had blown the porch away."[24]

In 1931 Bobo moved east to Arlington, a town of 2,100 population, including five doctors. Much of Bobo's book is about family, but Chapter VII gives an interesting interpretation of the practice of medicine from the turn of the century to the time he wrote it in 1977.

Dr. Bobo lived to be ninety years old. He died in 1987.

★ ★ ★

In the early 1950s Dr. L. H. Reeves and others wrote *The Medical History of Fort Worth and Tarrant County; 1853 to 1953*. This slim volume paid tribute to the memories of many pioneer doctors, told of the early hospitals, and listed past and (at that time) present members of the medical society.

R. G. Baker, in the Foreword, presented the author's credentials. "Dr. Reeves' long service in medicine, his devoted interest in all things concerning it, and his vast accumulation of knowledge of medicine's past and recent history, give him preeminent qualifications to record the history of medicine in Fort Worth."[25]

Reeves was for fifty years a family practitioner. According to Baker, "One would almost have to call the roll of officers and committees of the

Wise and Tarrant County Medical Societies . . . and the Texas Medical Association, to list the various offices held, and the honors bestowed on Dr. Reeves by his fellow members."[26]

In attempting to tell of the contributions of pioneer doctors, Reeves profiled more than twenty-five of the most important ones. These included such monuments to medicine as Drs. Peak, Saunders and Van Zandt. He wrote of the Fort Worth University School of Medicine and its historic faculty.

Reeves enlisted the help of other Fort Worth physicians to tell about the early hospitals and sanitariums. Dr. J. T. Tucker, Sr. wrote of St. Joseph's; Dr. R. G. Baker told the story of All Saints; Dr. Frank Sanders furnished the data for the old City-County Hospital. Administrator Ann Taylor aided Reeves in writing about Pennsylvania Hospital. Dr. Samuel Jagoda, Sr.'s material highlighted W. I. Cook Memorial.

An important part of the book dealt with professional organizations and included pictures of the seven Fort Worth physicians who had been president of the Texas Medical Association. Dr. A. P. Brown was the sixteenth president, in 1883. Seven years later Dr. W. P. Burts took the helm in 1890. Bacon Saunders was the thirty-first president. He presided in 1898. Dr. Frank Boyd was next, in 1914, the forty-ninth president. Dr. I. C. Chase was elected in 1920. Reeves himself was the seventy-fifth president, twenty years after Chase. The last cited was T. C. Terrell, eighty-seventh president of the state medical group, 1953.

Dr. C. C. Garrett wrote of the history of the Tarrant County Medical Society's journal, known as the *Bulletin*. Of the oldest copy, September 1908, he wrote, "This copy served as the official minutes of the August, 1908 meeting of the Society. . . . Registered in Tarrant County were 14 physic (sic) medicals 8 homeopaths 8 osteopaths and 21 eclectics."[27]

Dr. William M. Crawford, President of the Fort Worth Academy of Medicine, wrote an essay explaining the history and purposes of that organization.

Other professional associations' memberships included the American Academy of General Practice, The Fort Worth Medical Association, and the State Medical Association of Texas. Reeves listed all 1953-1954 members, as well as 130 deceased members of the Tarrant County Medical Society.

For those interested in the first century of Fort Worth's medical history Reeves' book is invaluable.

★ ★ ★

It would seem that Albert M. Goggans, M.D., is trying to put himself and other physicians out of business with books such as *Keep Well*. The Alabama native came to Fort Worth in 1951, where he was in private practice until 1988. Goggans served as medical director of the Community Hospice of St. Joseph from 1979 to 1980.

He was medical director of the Carter Rehabilitation & Fitness Center of All Saints Hospital from 1989 until July 1, 2000, and is now their Medical Director of Mind-Body Medicine. The cardiologist spends much of his time speaking to groups on the subject of healthy lifestyles as preventive medicine. In *Keep Well* he wrote, "Actually, I am speaking neither as a cardiologist nor as a psychiatrist, but as a physician who is expressing a philosophy of medicine in which the scientific, the psychological, and the religious are united in the celebration of both the science and the art of medicine."[28]

Dr. Goggans postulates that the physical, spiritual and emotional aspects of an individual's life all interact to determine one's level of health, a three-legged stool as it were. "A strong, positive spiritual core is central to the well-being of the body and the harmonious balance of the emotions. In turn, emotional states affect physical health, while the body's condition affects how one feels emotionally."[29]

Keep Well is a reader-friendly guide to enable one to develop or maintain good health habits. In the section on Guidelines for Health, Goggans advises specifics such as "Perform some type of aerobic exercise 25-30 minutes at least three or four times weekly. . . .Follow a diet low in fat and cholesterol. . . . Do not use tobacco in any form. . . ."[30]

These guidelines are not new, but according to Dr. Goggans they are essential and his crusade is to keep reminding people to follow them.

In the near future Dr. Goggans will have two new books out: *When I Have Fears That I May Cease to Be*, and *The Man with the Clear Head*. Both books deal with Mind–Body–Spirit medicine.

CHAPTER SIX

THE OSTEOPATHS: FROM HUMBLE BEGINNINGS TO THE TEXAS COLLEGE OF OSTEOPATHIC MEDICINE

*os-te-op-a-thy: n. [osteo- from Gr. osteon, a bone, and pathos suffering]
a theory and system of treating ailments based on the belief that they gen-
erally result from the pressure of displaced bones on nerves, etc., and are
cured by manipulation.*[1]

"The fundamental belief of osteopathy is that muscles and bones of the
body play a more significant role in most diseases than conventional medicine allows," Abigail Zuger wrote in the *New York Times*.[2] Osteopaths
contend that even problems with organs deep within the body, such as
the lungs, heart and brain, can be helped with hands-on techniques for
correcting muscle, tendon and joint abnormalities.

Former allopath Andrew Taylor Still is known as the father of
osteopathy. In 1882, in the small town of Kirksville, in northeastern
Missouri, he opened the American School of Osteopathy to teach his
new theory.

In 1900 the first Fort Worth osteopathic physician, Dr. Thomas L.
Ray, began his practice. Dr. Charlie Hook arrived in 1902 and doubled
the number of osteopathic practitioners. Dr. M. B. Harris began his
practice the following year. They opened the door for others, such as
Maude Russell, to enter.

One of the early adherents of Andrew Still's "new science of healing" was Maude (sometimes spelled Maud) Graham Russell. The Abbeyville, Mississippi native came to Texas in 1888. In keeping with the times and culture, her husband managed the family finances, and none too well. By the turn of the century all that was left of her inheritance was a house in Commerce. Inspired by an itinerant osteopathic physician, she made a bold decision.

Maude raised eyebrows in the small east Texas town when she left her husband and two small sons to enter medical school at Kirksville. After two years she returned to Commerce to her children, but not to her husband.

Son Phil recalled those early years. "Mother had a close friend who drove her on calls in his horse and buggy, and this is how she got around to see her patients. In 1907, this neighbor moved to a ranch in northwest Texas, and mother had no one to drive her."[3] At the insistence of a friend, she moved her sons and her practice to Fort Worth.

One of her first patients was Zetta Carter, wife of the publisher of the *Fort Worth Star-Telegram*. Amon Carter, described as nervous and high-strung, suffered from a series of ailments. He finally succumbed to his wife's urging to see Dr. Russell, but declared ". . . he'd never heard of a woman doctor that could do anything, but he'd give it a try."[4] He became a lifelong devotee of osteopathic medicine.

Maude Russell became a prominent physician in her adopted city and encouraged sons Phil and Roy to follow in her footsteps. A wing of the Fort Worth Osteopathic Hospital is named in her memory.

Phil R. Russell was born July 2, 1894 at Commerce. He attended Ft. Worth public schools, then continued his education at Carlisle Military Academy. At age nineteen he graduated from Bliss Electrical School in Washington, D.C., still undecided upon a career path. Realizing he preferred working with people more than with things, he applied to the Kirksville school. His brother was already a student there.

Phil and Dr. Maude called upon Andrew Taylor Still to gain admission. "I was excited and a little bit frightened, but his hands fell on my skull and he began to examine my head thoroughly. Then he told me to get up. 'I think he will do well. . . .'"[5] Phil was in the first graduating class after the college expanded the curriculum to a four-year program.

Prior to his 1917 graduation he married Ruby Davis of Kirksville. "To this union were born Philip Charles Russell in 1916 and Roy G. Russell in 1919."[6]

Russell first practiced in Terrell, then moved his young family to Cleburne. Residents of that farming community would see him riding a bicycle on his rounds. After he became more affluent, he bought a "hand-me-down" Ford from his mother for house calls. From 1920 to his semi-retirement in 1950, he practiced in Fort Worth with his brother, Dr. Roy G. Russell.

Following his mother's death, Phil became Amon Carter's friend and doctor. He told reporter Thayer Waldo, "You see, he (Carter) believed in osteopathy because my mother . . . saved his life back in 1909."[7] He carried a key to the publisher's home for twenty-five years. Carter rated Phil "a pretty good doctor" but not as good as his mother.

Another Fort Worthian who thought him a pretty good doctor was multimillionaire Sid Richardson. The oilman became a patient of the younger Russell when a broken leg healed improperly. The leg was so badly damaged, doctors (not Russell) wanted to amputate. Richardson refused, threatening to "kill the guy that cuts my leg off." Amputation was averted, but Richardson's injured leg lost slightly over an inch in length in the healing process. This imbalance led to a structural problem. Enter Dr. Russell, the osteopath.

Years later Russell was recovering from surgery when he accompanied Richardson to his private island. They landed in mid-afternoon and Russell strolled around the luxurious grounds while his host rested in the hideaway's penthouse.

The two had cocktails and dinner about 8:00 that evening. They made plans for the next day's activities and retired for the night. It was the last meal they would share.

When Dr. Russell went down to breakfast, Oscar, the house man, said, "I don't like Mr. Richardson's looks . . . I think maybe something's wrong."[8] Sid W. Richardson, oil field roughneck-to-bigger-than-life multimillionaire, had died peacefully in his sleep.

Russell, despite his own poor health, blamed himself. In hindsight he noted, ". . . if I'd been half myself at all when I saw a lot of things happen the day before, I'd have known he was in trouble."[9] Richardson died of a heart attack and Russell perhaps could have done nothing, but he lamented that he did not at least have closure with his old friend.

For more on Russell's medical career and his account of interesting well-known and not so well-known patients, the reader is directed to his autobiography, *The Quack Doctor.*

"Yes, I am a 'quack' doctor. My mother, Dr. Maude Russell, was a 'quack' doctor. . . . and my nephew is a 'quack' doctor."[10] So begins the delightful little book he co-authored with Judy Alter. Even a cursory glance at his achievements dispels the notion he was a "quack," and shows him to be an outstanding physician and leader in his field.

An ardent proponent of osteopathic medicine, Russell devoted many years to the development and improvement of public health. From 1921 until 1953 he was a member of the House of Delegates of the American Osteopathic Association. "During 15 of these years, he served as a member of the Board of Trustees of the American Osteopathic Association and served as President of the . . . (AOA) in 1941."[11]

The Philadelphia College of Osteopathy selected Russell to deliver the O. J. Snyder Memorial Address in 1958. He used that opportunity to criticize the medical community for paying too little personal attention to patients. Russell told the 300 doctors and guests, "Too many physicians are getting to be, not doctors, but traffic directors."[12] In addition to his plea for doctors to devote more time to personal diagnosis, he urged them to take an active role in the civic affairs of their communities.

All his efforts were not directed toward medicine. "One project was to bring the football team from the osteopathic college at Kirksville to Texas to challenge the Texas Christian University team."[13]

Russell was a builder, and his greatest achievement was his help in building the Fort Worth Osteopathic Hospital.

★ ★ ★

THE OSTEOPATHIC HOSPITALS

Drs. Roy B. Fisher and his brother Raymond D. Fisher were the first to establish a hospital open to DOs in Fort Worth. They opened a two-bed facility in the old Dr. Will Duringer home at 1402 Summit Avenue.

The stately three-story red brick building with white trim, supported a wide veranda on the east and south sides. The arched driveway on the north led to the entrance for patients, doctors and ambulances.

The operating room was on the sun porch; the nursery in an alcove. The delivery room was part of the surgical area and the basement housed laboratory and x-ray equipment. Roy's family lived upstairs, but as the patient load increased they moved to other quarters and the entire house became a ten-bed hospital. Within a short time, a dozen DOs were using the facility and the new hospital was bursting at the seams.

In its four-year history, the Summit Avenue hospital recorded 2,097 patients at the makeshift health care center. "The success of this early venture, not only created many new friends, but also gave rise to a public demand for expanded osteopathic hospital facilities."[14]

In June 1946, the Fishers, together with a small group of like-minded doctors, such as Phil and Roy Russell, formed the non-profit Fort Worth Osteopathic Hospital, Inc. Attorney A. M. (Abe) Herman served as legal council.

The twenty DOs contributed a total of $5,000, wrote a constitution and by-laws, and developed management guidelines. A reprint of the minutes of an early meeting which appeared in *By the Way* can be found in Appendix B.

On a blustery February 28, 1950, the second Fort Worth osteopathic hospital opened at 3705 Camp Bowie Blvd. "Up to the minute" the $100,000 completely air-conditioned building more than doubled the bed space to twenty-five. The nursery contained five bassinets. Built of Austin stone, it had all the latest hospital conveniences. Much of the credit, literally and figuratively, went to Amon G. Carter.

Phil Russell wrote of the back and forth effort. Carter wanted to create a magnificent structure, but didn't have the funds. The board, led by Russell, argued for a smaller, but doable project. Finally Carter said, "I'll tell you what I'll do. I'll take this property, (175 feet on Camp Bowie) and I'll deed them 95 ft. and give them a loan. Then I'll lend them as much money as they raise themselves."[15]

The board of directors agreed and work began. The money was raised by gifts from friends and $35,000 pledged by doctors. Carter and Sid

Richardson donated the money to furnish the hospital. Open House was held in April 1950. The *Star-Telegram* reporter covering the event estimated 1,000 visitors and well-wishers attended.

The hospital was open to all physicians "so long as he is in ethical and proper standing with his organization," according to Russell.[16] This was especially important to him because at one time DOs did not have hospital privileges and the exclusion galled. In his autobiography he recalled being able to treat only chronic cases. "I treated some acute cases at home, and I started to practice obstetrics. . . . (This proved to be impractical) . . . "So this pushed me into chronic office practice."[17] Bob Lanier, MD, taught immunology at TCOM in the 1980s, and had hospital privileges.

A unique feature of the hospital was the requirement that a physician donate fifty cents a day per patient, with a maximum of $2.50, into a charity fund to help cover the cost of indigent patients. For each baby he or she delivered, the doctor donated $5.00 to the fund.

By 1952 the hospital was crowded enough for the board to consider expansion. In 1955 they voted to build a new three story hospital on land (located on Montgomery and Mattison Streets) donated by the Amon G. Carter Foundation. Touted as the fulfillment of a thirty-year dream, it had seventy-five adult beds, five pediatric beds and fifteen bassinets. Recuperating patients could opt for one of the thirty-five private rooms, with their choice of full or half baths. All had telephones, piped-in oxygen and a call system activated by the spoken word. It was so sensitive it picked up sounds of breathing, allowing nurses to better monitor patients.

The newspaper account described it as being the latest in hospital design, equipment, and accommodations. A proud Phil Russell, Chairman of the Board of Trustees, greeted visitors and explained the unique design of the first floor. "This is the first defense hospital in this part of the country."[18] All major services—surgery, emergency room, delivery room, X-ray and laboratory—were located on the ground floor. With no windows, it was deemed safer in the event of an enemy attack. The uncertainty caused by the Cold War, dictated such measures. Later the design was useful in another way. Visitor, ambulatory patient and other nonessential traffic was kept separate from the area.

Like the two previous hospitals, this one proved to be too small. Unlike its two predecessors, the Montgomery Street hospital built up instead of seeking another location. It added additional floors as needed. The hospital expanded by eighty beds and established new ICU and CCU units in 1968. An $8 million, 60,000 square foot addition was completed in 1981. Emergency, surgery, labor and delivery facilities improved. Radiology and cardiology units were enlarged, and the renovation included updated lab blood equipment.

Throughout the eighties the hospital added new departments and more patient beds. That ever urgent need for parking space in an urban environment was alleviated with the building of a four-story parking garage. In 1994 the building of the V. L. Jennings Outpatient Pavilion demonstrated osteopathic medicine's emphasis on wellness and care for chronic health problems before they become critical ones.

Commenting on the growth of the hospital in the brochure celebrating its fiftieth year, Jennings, who served as the hospital board's first president, expressed astonishment at the phenomenal success. Dr. Roy

Osteopathic Medical Center of Texas, from a two bed facility to the largest osteopathic hospital in Texas. Courtesy Osteopathic Medical Center of Texas

Fisher agreed. "We never anticipated, never expected, the growth." Reviewing the expansion from two beds, he speculated, why not 265? "That takes a lot of effort from a whole lot of people. I mean if you did-n't have all these doctors and people who are influential in Fort Worth, besides all your nursing and administration and so on, you never could have done this. . . and we're still growing."[19]

The Osteopathic Medical Center of Texas is the largest osteopathic hospital in the state and among the largest 150 accredited by the American Osteopathic Association.

Not all the health care is dispensed from the main hospital. The Osteopathic Health System of Texas sponsors community centers scattered throughout the county. "These are fully staffed, extended-hour clinics pro-viding for family health care, screenings, immunizations, work-related injuries and industrial medicine, plus lab services."[20] That indeed is progress from the humble beginnings on Summit Avenue.

★ ★ ★

TEXAS COLLEGE OF OSTEOPATHIC MEDICINE;
A PART OF THE UNIVERSITY OF NORTH TEXAS
HEALTH SCIENCE CENTER

Prior to 1968, Fort Worth was the only major city in the state with-out a medical or professional school. That would change, thanks largely to the determination of George J. Luibel. Ask anyone who remembers the birth of the Texas College of Osteopathic Medicine who the father was, they will answer "George Luibel." Concerning the birth of what would become the foremost osteopathic medical center in the country, Dr. Luibel refutes one wag's comment that it was born in a bowling alley. This is because in the early shoestring days what was once the old Tavener's Bowling Alley building on Camp Bowie housed administrative offices. "The classes actually began on the fifth floor of the Osteopathic Hospital,"[21] he said in an interview.

George J. Luibel enrolled in Kirksville's American School of Osteopathy at the depth of the Great Depression, graduating in 1936. Seeking a warmer climate, he came to Texas. He recalled taking his Texas medical certification test in Austin. "It was 104^0 and no air conditioning."[22]

George J. Luibel, DO. Many credit him with the establishment of the Texas College of Osteopathic Medicine. Courtesy Gibson D. Lewis Library, University of North Texas Health Science Center

He noted that allopathic and osteopathic candidates took the same examination, and a board composed of medical doctors, osteopathic doctors, homeopaths, and doctors following the eclectic philosophy evaluated the applicants. Luibel passed, and after practicing in Ennis and Ferris, came to Fort Worth.

Colleague Elizabeth Harris described Luibel as an exceptional intellect, a rare and profound man, a visionary— yet Luibel's unassuming and unpretentious lifestyle was commonplace. He contended that people who accomplished great things were really ordinary. She characterized him as both an inspiring leader on some occasions and a helpful, caring physician at other times. Harris quoted patients as saying "The doc just fixed me up." Henry Hardt, the first Dean, speaking of Luibel's relationships with his patients said, "The man simply entering the room makes you feel better."[23]

For years Luibel and his wife Mary, Drs. Roy Fisher, Carl Everett, and Danny Beyer and their wives, dreamed of a school as they socialized at the Western Hills Hotel Coffee Shop. In 1965 Luibel became chairman of the committee to investigate the feasibility of establishing an osteopathic college in Texas. That committee, formed in 1961, met, agreed such a school was needed, deferred action until the next year, met, agreed such a school was needed, deferred action etc., until Luibel took the chair. Under his leadership the committee made six recommendations.

When the Texas Osteopathic Medical Association (TOMA) met, Luibel in a surprise move, urged action on the recommendations or dissolution of the committee. Tired of the back and forth discussions with no results, he concluded, "It was something everybody liked to talk about, but nobody really wanted to take the bull by the horns."[24]

At the spring, 1966 meeting of TOMA, rumors floated that the Des Moines College of Osteopathic Medicine and Surgery was looking for a new home. The committee invited the Iowans to visit and consider Fort Worth as their new site. In the end the school remained in Des Moines, but a new sense of urgency was applied to establishing a Texas school.

One of the problems the Iowa school encountered was the lack of a Texas charter. Attorney Abe Herman told the TOMA committee the cost of such a charter was not beyond their reach. Luibel renewed his efforts. "I was sitting and talking to my wife one night," the doctor recalled in an oral history told to Ray Stokes, "and I said, 'You know, I just wonder who I could get to go in with me on a deal like that?' . . . . And I called up two friends of mine and told them I wanted so much money from each of them and for what purpose and they said, 'Okay, I think you're crazy, but we'll do it.'"[25]

Luibel and friends Carl Everett and Danny Beyer contributed $600.00 and sent Herman to Austin to obtain a charter. Herman succeeded in getting a charter for an institution to grant D.O. and M.S. degrees in osteopathic medicine. Luibel met with an assistant to the Commissioner of Higher Education for directions. He was told ". . . I think if you are going to start a college, you ought to do it and then, if you want state support, come and try to get it afterwards."[26] The doctor followed his advice. Fort Worth was named as the site and he, Everett and Beyer were listed as the initial directors. Soon other DOs joined the Board of Trustees. They had a paper college, next they needed to turn it into a reality.

Luibel received a grant of $30,000 start-up money from AOA. Carl E. Everett, as treasurer, opened a campaign to raise capital. "We wrote to every member of the American Osteopathic Association and we got some very good results,"[27] Everett told Stokes. Solicitations of state osteopaths raised $200,000 in pledges.

At the 1970 TOMA meeting in Lubbock, one doctor expressed his skepticism. Luibel remembered the West Texan as pontificating a great deal and declared the whole thing   ". . . ridiculous—that we didn't know any more about running a college than we did about running a filling station . . ." and questioned why he should put money into something like that. "And I informed him that we really didn't know anything about a filling station either. If we bought a filling station, we'd hire a guy who knew how to run it. . . ."[28] First they hired C. Ray Stokes as Director of Development.

Stokes wore many hats in the early days. In addition to being development officer he was, ". . . business manager, student financial aid officer, purchasing agent, registrar and any other duties. . . ."[29] Board members and faculty attribute his greatest coup as wooing Henry B. Hardt, retired chairman of the TCU chemistry department, to accept the position of chief administrative officer.

Hardt insisted that "an absolute requirement in every good medical school instructor . . . is personal integrity, because without integrity, nothing else matters.[30] During 1970 he hired ten professors, recruited twenty volunteers from the medical community as adjunct professors and moved into the fifth floor of the Fort Worth Osteopathic Hospital. Hardt obtained the required pre-accreditaton from the AOA and welcomed the initial class—twenty students.

The board of trustees now turned its efforts toward securing a permanent site. They considered the Vandergriff property in south Arlington, but it had drawbacks. It was not accessible by public transportation. Furthermore, it was not near a hospital, a requirement for a medical school. Instead, "the college was to be located in Fort Worth due to the large concentration of osteopathic physicians there . . . ."[31] And—George Luibel wanted it in Fort Worth.

Trustees looked at several sites before leasing the bowling alley. Luibel noted, ". . . I think we finally ended up on the fifth floor of the Osteopathic Hospital, (because they) were the only people, in the final analysis, that welcomed us and were willing to underwrite us a little bit."[32]

Everett, Herman, Luibel and others lobbied Austin for support. Their logic swayed the legislature and the college first received state support when Senate Bill 160 was signed into law in May 1971. Alluding to osteopaths' historical roots as primary care doctors and the scarcity of them, especially in rural communities, the bill recognized, in particular, ". . . the lack of a public facility . . .for the education, instruction, training and preparation of undergraduate osteopathic medical students. . . ."[33]

Getting the use of the fifth floor of Fort Worth Osteopathic Hospital hinged on Dr. Phil Russell's approval, and the local icon of the profession was cool to the idea. Everett related to Stokes, "Dr. Phil Russell was Chairman of the Board. And Dr. Phil . . . was also a leader and a person with a lot of very strong ideas and he was very much opposed to using the fifth floor of the hospital."[34] He argued the Fort Worth Osteopathic Hospital should not become a teaching hospital. Dr. Everett was recruited to convince Russell.

The two discussed, argued and wrangled for hours one afternoon at Russell's home. Finally, he was persuaded. "Well, Carl, if that's what you want to do, we'll try it, but I just don't know whether it's smart or not, but I'll be for it," he told his visitor. "From then on, it was Dr. Phil's idea to put it on the fifth floor,"[35] Everett told Stokes.

Southwestern Medical School graduate and microbiology professor Elizabeth Harris, the first faculty member, described the physical set-up. "The hospital graciously allowed the College to remodel the unfinished floor of the hospital to our specifications. . . . There were three faculty offices—Dr. Tom Graham, physiologist; Dr. Charles Rudolph, biochemist; and I each had an office on the fifth floor. . . . The classroom and library were located across the hall from the offices and beyond the classroom, which was quite spacious for a class of twenty students. . . , we had a special prep room for the various laboratory courses and (individual labs). . . a fourth area that was kind of a super lounge where the students had a coffee pot and area where they could relax between classes."[36]

The college never advertised. The first class heard by word of mouth and got there almost before the ink on the syllabi dried.

The hospital assessed $40,000 rent, but it remained a paper commitment. As business manager, Everett paid $90.00 a month rent on a house on Mattison, across from the hospital. Hardt, Ray Stokes and his wife, Edna, who had joined the team officed there. "Mrs. Stokes thinks she is the only secretary who had to clean a bathtub. . . and the budget was so tight, she remembers, that she brought a coffeepot and a pencil sharpener from home—and she used to bring pencils too."[37]

TCOM also rented a small garage apartment across the street from the hospital for a dissection laboratory. Bodies were slipped in at night so as not to upset the neighbors. It barely had room for the twenty students to study them.

Elizabeth Harris recalled the early days. She told Stokes that Dr. Luibel gave them the first typewriter. Her husband, Joe, hauled donated tables and chairs in his truck. Faculty and students pitched in to help with whatever needed to be done. Dr. Charlie Rudolph, the first biochemist, used his carpentry skills. Dr. Harris said, "Charlie used to laugh and say that everyone thought he was a general contractor."[38] On a more serious note, she attributed the dedication of founders Luibel, Everett and Beyer, and the wise guidance of Hardt for the success of the college.

In almost reverential tones, Harris spoke of the exhilarating, yet humbling experience of being part of the historic undertaking. "It's one thing to build buildings on a campus, but to *found* a college is something very few people have the opportunity to do."[39]

From the beginning TCOM trustees realized the need to affiliate with a university. North Texas State University, (now the University of North Texas) with its own board of regents, seemed the school to approach. Meetings followed. Dr. Gwynn Silvey, distinguished professor and long-time head of the Biology Department at NTSU, suggested exploratory talks to NTSU President C. C. "Jitter" Nolen. They met with Dr. Henry Hardt and Harry Werst, who knew Nolen from his days at TCU. "We met over at Colonial Country Club for dinner, and incidentally, that was at my expense. I signed the darned checks for those things,"[40] Luibel reminisced.

Ray Stokes quoted Carl Everett, "It became apparent that we needed to be affiliated with one of the university systems in the state of Texas. And this just seemed natural. We already had worked with North Texas and they were interested and they were willing."[41] Elizabeth Harris credited President Marion E. Coy, Luibel, Hardt and Herman with planning and orchestrating the merger. TCOM board members, and Coy, Hardt and Harris, rode in a yellow school bus to Denton to inspect the campus, and NTSU regents learned about TCOM. Both governing bodies, after some-times heated discussions of the advantages and disadvantages, struck a deal.

Early in the next year, 1973-74 faculty members as well as the students, made the sixty mile round trip. "Harris remembers commuting to Denton and 'lots of headaches,'"[42] Stokes noted. Neither faculty nor students felt a part of the parent university and travel was just one of the problems. Laboratory and lecture rooms—inadequate or poorly designed—were stuck in the biology or chemistry buildings as space permitted. Things improved somewhat over time and by the mid-seventies all TCOM classes were meeting in the same location—the fourth floor of the biology building.

Dr. Ben Harris (no relation to Elizabeth), believing the statute of limitations had run out, told of thievery at the 1920s former dormitory, Terrell Hall. "(It was) an area with a 'paucity of air conditioners' (and) 'midnight requisitions' from other vacant rooms on the same floor made it possible to cool the faculty offices and student study rooms."[43]

With the passage of Senate Bill 216 in May 1975, Texas College of Osteopathic Medicine became a separate, state-supported medical school, but it remained under the umbrella of North Texas State University. Senator Betty Andujar, whose husband, John, was an MD pathologist, is credited with securing the passage. Representative Gibson "Gib" Lewis, Andujar's counterpart in the House, was rewarded for his efforts by later having the school's library named for him.

In 1978 the Texas College of Osteopathic Medicine Foundation was established to provide for things needed, but not included in state support. "To run a college and an institution such as we have, it is necessary to have money available that is not restricted."[44] Everett listed such things as recruiting, public relations, moving expenses, and hosting

Fort Worth skyline viewed from the Gibson Library. Courtesy Studio 44: Norman Morrow

campus visitors and speakers. "The Foundation is set up solely for the help of the College,"[45] he told Stokes.

In the 1970s, with $8,000,000 in state money and $4,000,800 from HEW, work began on Medical Education Building I. Medical Building II opened in 1982; in 1986 the Health Sciences Library moved into Medical Education Building III.

Building I housed administration offices, classrooms, and the clinical science departments. An outpatient clinic and student library were also located there.

From the start, the basic science departments needed more space for faculty research and programs. Historically, osteopathic medical schools have dedicated themselves mainly to teaching and clinical service, but TCOM realized that a strong biomedical research program was essential to the education of well-trained primary care physicians. Building II was planned to meet this need.

Building III, the most dramatic, is, "Built on a natural slope. . . features large expanses of bronze glass, with a spectacular view of Fort Worth's skyline, open balconies, and a two-story atrium,"[46] Stokes wrote. The Gibson D. Lewis Health Science Library is open to the public. It contains more than 90,000 volumes, a journal collection of more than 23,000 titles, and 3,500 audiovisual titles. "It is one of the most advanced information centers in the Southwest," according to Craig Elam, library administrator.[47]

The affiliation with then North Texas State University had been seen as beneficial for both. The passage of the 1975 bill was an early and major milestone. *Fort Worth Star-Telegram* writer Paul Bourgeous, in summarizing the first thirty years noted, "It became the UNT Health Sciences Center in 1993, with the Texas College of Osteopathic Medicine as just one of the components."[48] The others are the Graduate School of Biomedical Sciences and School of Public Health.

"By 1994 TCOM had graduated 1,519 osteopathic physicians."[49] Of those an estimated three-fourths are in family, general internal, or pediatric medicine. It is the only osteopathic medical institution in the nation to receive accreditation from the Joint Commission on Accreditation of Health Care Organizations. Dr. David M. Richards, UNT Health Science

Center president at the time of the interview, explained to reporter Lou Chapman, "The accreditation the Joint Commission carries the same significance and importance as does accreditation of education programs by the Southern Association of Colleges and Schools."[50]

Ronald Blanck, DO, succeeded Dr. David Richards as head of the institution. A former Surgeon General, and first osteopath to acheive that rank, Dr. Blanck is a strong believer of civic involvement. He told reporter Charlotte Huff, "We need to be a leader in change in working with all the other levels of the community."[51]

Officially inaugurated as president on April 7, 2001, the thirty-one year veteran of the U. S. Army stressed the need to make better use of innovative approaches in medical education. Concerning plans for new biotechnology and public health buildings, and opportunities to broaden research, President Blanck said, "It's a wonderful time to be here."[52]

In 2001, 453 students were enrolled in the Texas College of Osteopathic Medicine, an additional 38 in the Physician Assistant Program, 110 in Masters and Ph.D. Programs, and 140 in the School of Public Health.

How did TCOM get from discussions in a coffee shop to this? George Luibel would say it was because the founders didn't know any better than to try it. Others say Luibel, Everett, Byers and Hardt saw a need and acted—ordinary people accomplishing the extraordinary.

CHAPTER SEVEN

THE HOSPITALS: MODERN HALLS OF HEALING

By the turn of the twentieth century, St. Joseph Infirmary was an established institution. Other hospitals, privately owned and hardly more than clinics, opened, then closed. City-County, later named John Peter Smith, and the church related or non-profit hospitals survived and became important components in Fort Worth's medical history. One of them, All Saints, under the auspices of the Episcopal Church opened and flourished.

ALL SAINTS HOSPITAL

Dr. Sam Jagoda, Jr., wrote about All Saints Hospital in a 1977 *Tarrant County Medical Society Bulletin.* "On July 15, 1896, Mrs. George Beggs, Sr., Mrs. John Bevan, and 13 friends at Trinity Episcopal Church, decided to establish a hospital to provide medical care for the poor. . . . The hospital was to be called 'Maria Hospital' in honor of Mrs. Beggs.

"The group first attempted to rent a house for conversion into a small hospital, but the neighbors objected. It was then decided to purchase land and build a hospital. Property was purchased for $400 at the corner of Magnolia and Eighth Avenue, then called Cleburne Road. . . . On March 20, 1900 the Maria Hospital was deeded to its successor and named All Saints Hospital.

"The cornerstone was laid on November 1, 1900. In a few months the twenty-four bed hospital was completed and began serving the medical needs of Fort Worth.

"The School of Nursing was established the same year, but a separate . . . building was not built until 1918. . . .

"In August, 1921, the hospital was approved by the American College of Surgeons, and the maternity ward was added. By that time the hospital was serving over one thousand patients per year . . . .

"A large center section was added to the hospital in 1926. This . . . provided new surgery and delivery rooms, and added new elevators, a new kitchen and a new boiler room.

"The economic depression affected the hospital profoundly. Admissions . . . dropped from 2,000 per year in 1928 to 800 in 1932. The hospital was forced to close the School of Nursing and to default on its mortgage bonds.

"The Hospital Board, faced with the prospect of closing the hospital, (asked) Dr. T. C. Terrell to save the hospital.

"Dr. Terrell was assisted in the transitional period by Mr. Thomas Jones, Secretary of the Hospital Board.

"By 1939 the hospital was operating on a more firm financial base and could now afford to make additions. Thirty beds were added by conversion of the old Nursing building into hospital space. A dining room was added and, in 1945, a fourth floor was added, bringing the total beds to 110.

"By the late 1940s it was evident that a new hospital building was needed. . . . Many civic leaders recognized this need and a community hospital fund raising group was organized . . . . The Trustees agreed to construct a new 100 bed addition to the old hospital (on land to the west that had been the gift of a patient, Mrs. Dora Roberts).

"In 1953 application was made to the State Board of Health for a $1,830,000 Hill–Burton grant to build a completely new hospital. . . . The Hill–Burton grant was approved but was reduced to $1,300,000 and other necessary funding could not be obtained for a 300–bed hospital.

"In 1956 a $77,800 Ford Foundation grant was received enabling planning to proceed for the new hospital. Bids were opened in July, 1957. The lowest bid was found to exceed the available funds by $400,000.

"A committee was formed (to raise) the $400,000. . . . Individuals and companies donated gifts for specific hospital areas and construction began in 1957.

"The eight-story, 365-bed hospital was completed on All Saints Day, November 1, 1959 and, in 1973, a five story annex was constructed through the generosity of Mr. and Mrs. W. A. Moncrief. Completion of the annex brought the bed capacity to 533."[1] (Used by permission.)

As the population grew, so did the need for more patient facilities. Keeping with the trend, in 1993 the hospital began a $55,000,000 expansion designed to boost the hospital's outpatient services. Walking into the new building, one is struck by the airiness of the lobby rotunda, the

Twilight at All Saints Episcopal Hospital. Courtesy All Saints Episcopal Hospital

muted colors illuminated by 3,400 fiber optic lights, the potted foliage. Quay Lutrell, Director of Marketing, explained, "We wanted to make the entrance visually pleasing, we wanted to make patients more comfortable and at ease."[2]

Star-Telegram reporter Jim Fuquay noted, "All Saints . . . is being driven by demands for cost containment. . . . Outpatient care is one response to the demands because it avoids hospital long stays at expensive daily rates."[3] Lutrell concurred in his assessment. "All Saints is the only Fort Worth hospital where the main entry is to the outpatient part of the facility."[4]

The new construction included a birthing center. It is built around another new trend. Larger rooms allow for family members to remain with the woman during labor. In a LDRP (Labor/Delivery/Recovery/Postpartum) room the woman remains in the same location for all phases of childbirth. When birth is eminent, the bed is transformed into the "delivery table." Cabinets in the room contain all the needed equipment for mother and infant. After the birth, the delivery table again becomes a bed where the mother recovers in her room until time for dismissal.

In 2001, 802 physicians had hospital privileges. Of these 704 are MDs and seventy-eight are DOs. Seven podiatrists and thirteen dentists/oral and maxillofacial surgeons (DDS or DMD) are on staff. Nurses, technicians, and support staff bring the total number to 1500.

An early Fort Worth *City Guide*, listed All Saints Episcopal Hospital as "Location: Eighth Avenue and Magnolia Avenue. Reached by South Summit street car on Houston Street. Fare 10 cents."[5] Now bus fare costs more, automobiles park in one of the several lots. But All Saints' mission is the same—quality medical services to the citizens of Fort Worth. One way of providing services for cancer patients has been the long association with the Moncrief Cancer Center.

★ ★ ★

UT SOUTHWESTERN MONCRIEF CANCER CENTER

Dr. Tom Bond's story could fit in the chapter on "Family Practice" as his father and uncle were both physicians. His story could appropriately be placed with Gold-Headed Cane recipients—as he was awarded the Cane in 1955. But Tom Bond and the story of the Radiology Clinic, which became the UT Southwestern Moncrief Cancer Center, are inseparable.

Tom's father, Dr. George D. Bond, one of the first physicians in Texas to see the future in roentgenology, used X-ray in the diagnosis and treatment of illness, and specialized in this branch of medicine. He practiced in Hill County until he moved to Fort Worth in 1907. After relocating, he confined his practice to X-ray and electro-therapeutic work. He lectured on Roentgenology in the Fort Worth School of Medicine. George Bond died in 1924, ". . . but not before he had played a part in bringing Roentgen's discovery from a play thing to a recognized medical speciality with a section in the State Medical Society and in the AMA,"[6] according to the state medical journal.

Modest, well-liked Tom Bond studied electrical engineering. He designed and built, as well as maintained, much of his father's equipment. From those activities he developed an interest in radiology. Believing he

Tom B. Bond, MD, founder of the Texas Radiological Society. Courtesy W. D. Smith, Inc. Commercial Photography Collection, The University of Texas at Arlington Libraries

needed a better grounding in anatomy to design X-ray machines, he earned a degree from the former medical department of TCU.

In 1937 Bond created the Bond Radiological Group located in the Medical Arts Building, and the Department of Radiology at St. Joseph Hospital. Later Tom established the Radiology Department at John Peter Smith Hospital. Also with his father, Dr. Tom Bond founded the Texas Radiological Society.

In the 1950s, the recipient of the Gold-Headed Cane was not announced in advance. At the 1955 dinner, "The smiling, friendly Dr. Bond didn't know he was selected for this year's honor until the 1954 winner, Dr. R. G. Baker, walked up to his chair . . . and tapped him on the shoulder."[7] Bond said in acceptance, "I must confess a deep sense of humility and I must say a little feeling of guilt because, in my opinion, there are so many more deserving of this honor than I."[8]

Tom Bond died December 7, 1971. Dr. Bond, who devoted his life to fighting cancer, lost his fight to the disease, but left a sterling legacy— the Radiation Center.

One of Bond's friends and colleagues, Dr. John Alexander, was a part of Radiology Associates for thirty years. With a sense of reverence and respect, in an interview he related the history of radiology and the many contributions of Dr. Bond, Dr. Robert Moreton, and other pioneers in the field. Yet in a way, Alexander too pioneered in the changing technology of his chosen speciality.

When he joined the Bond group, radiologists did both therapy and diagnosis, but, he explained, as knowledge led to more and more complicated procedures, subspecialties emerged.

He recalled the time when physicians used radiation to treat benign conditions such as warts or inflammatory conditions of bone joints. However, as the side effects became known, radiation's use has been streamlined to treating cancer. For Dr. Alexander his greatest reward in all his years in medicine was finding an unsuspected tumor in the early, treatable stage.

★ ★ ★

In 1985 Nancy B. Kincheloe captured the history of the Radiation Center in *Twenty-Five Years of Service: One Day at a Time.* In the Foreward

Dr. Robert Moreton told of the beginning of the facility. "Radiation therapy has made a major contribution to the improved quality of care of the cancer patient, however, complex and expensive equipment is involved in the effective use of this modality. Centralization of radiation therapy is usually the most efficient way to minimize cost while providing high-quality patient care. Centralization not only achieves cost reduction, but ensures more efficient utilization of manpower.

"Realizing that no individual hospital could afford the type of facility needed for the patient to receive quality cancer care within a reasonable distance to his or her home, family, friends and livelihood, Doctor Bond set the goal of a community radiation therapy center, which is to make available the best in radiotherapy facilities and personnel to patients living in the Fort Worth area, without regard to race, creed, color or ability to pay."[9]

Tom Bond, Dr. Porter Brown, and Sister M. Claudine, mother superior at St. Joseph Hospital, began planning for such a facility shortly after World War II. They got city leaders interested in the possibility of a regional center. The Radiation and Medical Research Foundation of the Southwest sprang from their efforts. The board of All Saints welcomed the project, and Bond and Moreton decided to build on Enderly Place just south of the main hospital.

"The supervoltage equipment would be at one end with thick concrete walls for protection. The other end would contain examination rooms, office space for physicians, physicists, and allied personnel,"[10] Kincheloe wrote.

In 1956 the Donner Foundation of Philadelphia gave a $75,000 Van de Graaff supervoltage generator. Reporter Blair Justice noted, "It took a heated railway car to pamper its $5,000 X-ray tube in shipment here, it required concrete walls four feet thick to withstand its direct beam and it has taken five weeks to install."[11]

That same year the Leonard family donated a cobalt-60 unit with 2,500 curies. Kincheloe expained, ". . .the machine uses cobalt-60, a radioactive isotope material, placed in a lead container with a wheel or drawer. The wheel is rotated to an open port for treatment."[12] The unit lasted until 1970 when a new, larger 5,000 curie source machine was installed.

By the fifth year of operation the Center had gained experience in case management. Some techniques and dosages were modified, and more and more cancer patients sought treatment. Foundations, organizations and individuals gave generously to provide funds for the needy or uninsured. In 1967 W. A. (Monty) and Elizabeth Moncrief donated $500,000. That, with matching funds from Hill-Burton, allowed the foundation to expand for a tumor center.

Mrs. Moncrief, not satisfied with bleak, institution-like walls, took on the task of decorating. She was quoted in the *Dallas Morning News* as lamenting the cold, sterile atmosphere. Of the patients she said, "They're sick and apprehensive. . . what they need is a sunny, homelike atmosphere." She hung murals and paintings, installed Italian furniture and mirrors "She painted the Van de Graaff X-ray generator a soft pink. . . . flowers and carpeting appeared in the corridors and rooms."[13] Thirty years later, Jeffrey Bernard, Director of Therapy Services, pointed with pride to the fresh flowers throughout the facility, thanks to Mrs. Moncrief's eye for beauty.

The William A. and Elizabeth B. Moncrief Radiation Center became official January 11, 1980. The plaque reads, "In recognition of the active support given to the Radiation and Medical Research Foundation of the Southwest. . . this facility is named in their honor and so designated in perpetuity as testament to their continued support of the services rendered here by the physicians, therapists and staff in the treatment of cancer and allied diseases."[14]

In 1982, at the insistence of his family, Mr. Moncrief allowed John David Scott to write his biography. The Tarrant County Medical Society is the proud owner of a copy of the rare book. Scott related the Moncriefs' motivation in giving so generously to the Radiation Center. ". . . their interest in helping find a cure for cancer came about because of the death of their granddaughter, Monty Francine, who died of leukemia at the age of six in 1964."[15]

The Moncrief Radiation Center earned a reputation for giving of itself and turning away no one in need. In December 1994 the board voted to grant the facility to the M. D. Anderson Cancer Center. While well-meaning, this proved to be unsatisfactory owing to the distance between the

Houston and Fort Worth facilities. Five years later the Fort Worth-based center transferred its relationship to a partnership with the Southwestern Medical Center in Dallas. M. D. Anderson vice-president Dr. Martin Raber told reporter Charlotte Huff, "The shift made sense, given that insurers prefer to centralize cancer treatment in one region, such as the Metroplex."[16] It also made sense to Fort Worth patients—they would be nearer services offered by both the Dallas and Fort Worth locations.

Jeffrey Bernard pointed out that while not as big as M. D. Anderson in terms of research, the Moncrief Center offered the same quality of patient care as the Houston hospital. In an interview, he said, "It's important to hold true to the founding principles of this facility, because that will make us great for the future as well."[17]

Executive Director William H. Craig concurred, and added, "Part of our future is becoming more of a comprehensive cancer center, providing access and coordinated services for medical and surgical oncology in addition to radiation oncology."[18] Dr. Robert Moreton in 1985 wrote, "The citizens of the Fort Worth area are fortunate to have this fine facility and staff. . . . This center has set an unselfish example for many communities to follow. May the tradition continue for many years to come."[19] It has.

★ ★ ★

CITY-COUNTY/JOHN PETER SMITH HOSPITAL

William T. Harris, Jr., a teacher turned operating room technician, in 1967 wrote an account of the early history of John Peter Smith.

"In the beginning, the College Hospital, staffed by the faculty and students of Fort Worth Medical School, conducted treatment for those who could not afford medical care at a private hospital or clinic. . . . From 1904 until 1913, no formal hospital existed. Emergency surgery was provided in the basement of the medical school located at 301 East 5th. If a patient required a bed, it was provided in a makeshift hospital at 208½ East Weatherford. In 1913, a two-story, red, brick building with a basement was completed. Known as Emergency Hospital, it contained 25 beds.

"In 1913, a bond election was held and $20,000 was approved toward the purchase of the downtown site (and) county commissioners resolved

Emergency Hospital, the forerunner of John Peter Smith Hospital. Courtesy Fort Worth Star-Telegram Photograph Collection; Special Collections Division, The University of Texas at Arlington Libraries

the county would equally share with Fort Worth, the building and operating cost . . . .

"Much controversy arose over the exact location. In 1877 John Peter Smith had deeded a five-acre tract on South Main to the city and county. The stipulation was that it be used for a hospital. Some people objected to the tract because it was too far from town. Others objected to another choice on Jones Street between East Fourth and East Fifth Street because it was too close to town. Possibly, the fact that the Jones Street site was immediately behind the medical school helped that site be chosen for the construction of the City-County Hospital, which was completed in 1914. The faculty and students of the medical school comprised the medical staff.

"The hospital received much criticism. . . . Since both the city and the county governments joined for providing medical service for the poor and needy, the joint boards or broad members made the project a political football.

"To make matters worse, the medical school moved to Baylor University in 1918. Doctor Webb Walker, city health officer, and D. S. Rumph, M.D., county health officer, conducted much of the treatment and nearly all the administrative details. Their colleagues in the medical profession gave them some assistance, but this help proved to be inadequate.

"During the next few years, members of the Tarrant County Medical Society deplored the precarious management and started a movement to obtain a paid staff. This task was finally achieved by 1921. . . .

"In 1925, the city appropriated $18,000 for a needed expansion. There was no doubt as to the need for expansion. In operating rooms designed for one patient, there were often three surgery procedures going at the same time. Emergency treatment and first aid were often provided in the hall."[20]

For the next ten years citizens and doctors begged for more resources, but city and county officials played politics with their pleas. In 1936 WPA funds to build a hospital were channeled into barns for the Centennial stock show.

Harris wrote, "On August 19, 1937, D. D. Rumph, M.D., announced the gift of an "iron lung" to the city. It was one of three in Texas, the others being in Beaumont and Houston.

"In 1937, a new council was elected . . . . Through their efforts $137,000 in bonds were sold to construct a new hospital.

"After much controversy about where to locate the new City-County Hospital, the present site of John Peter Smith Hospital was chosen. Work began on . . . April 1, 1938.

"On June 9, 1938, the newly-appointed City-County Hospital board elected Webb Walker, M.D., as chairman, and approved payroll and other expense items totaling $10,271.81, leaving a cash balance to the hospital's account of $309.

"During the first six months of 1938, the expenditures averaged $11,565 a month.

"Although petty disagreements between the city and county retarded the progress of hospital construction, there was enough peace and harmony to move patients into the new City-County Hospital by July of

1939. . . . The cost of operating the new hospital was then estimated at $19,535 a month for the 186 beds. . . .

"By March 26, 1947, it was realized that facilities were needed for the treatment of polio. Some suggested the construction of a new 100-bed hospital for such treatment. By July 4, it was decided to remodel the second floor of the old City-County Hospital for such treatment. . . .

"On June 20, 1950, due to the crowded conditions in all hospitals with reference to polio treatment facilities, a difficult decision was drawn. The City-County Hospital would receive no polio patients east of Arlington nor west of Fort Worth. Seventy-six polio patients were treated during 1950.

"Sporadic construction marked the hospital's continued growth. . . . A new floor matured in 1950. When built the City-County Hospital remained overcrowded,"[21] Harris noted.

Throughout the years, several administrators guided the hospital from crisis to crisis as overcrowding and lack of funds plagued the institution. *Star-Telegram* reporter Blair Justice in 1955, using board minutes, listed some woes.

"1943—ambulance drivers were discovered bringing ineligible patients to the emergency room because other hospitals did not have interns.

"1943—104 resignations the previous six months because of low salaries.

"1946—one board member said the hospital would have to be closed if more money couldn't be obtained.

"1950—critical shortage of bed space reported to chamber of commerce (additional floors added 42 beds in 1951).

"1954—deficit of $32,823 reported in August even though hospital is operating $35,559 under proposed budget; tremendous personnel overturn."[22]

Blair quoted from some headlines of the same period.

"1940—City-County Hospital's Manager to Be Replaced (in effort to economize).

"1947—Story on charging patients 25-cent fees for clinic visits and $15 fees for childbirths.

"1950—City-County Having to Turn Away Surgery Cases; City Will Have to Boost Fund for hospital.

"1951—No Room for the Sick in City's Hospitals.

"1953—City-County Hospital Aid Below Other Cities; story on 'costly and poor' handling of certain items at the hospital; Commissioners Ask Hospital to Cut Expenses; County Hunts Cash for Hospital Share.

"1955—Voters Defeat Hospital District Plan, Jan.22."[23]

Dr. James A. Hallmark wrote in 1956, "As chief of staff of John Peter Smith Hospital during the current year, I have come to grips with the varied problems of its management and have come to the conclusion that there is only one major problem—not enough money."[24]

Again from Harris, in 1959, ". . . voters were urged to vote on a county-wide hospital district. There would be one tax levied to defray the cost of operating John Peter Smith Hospital and Elmwood Sanatorium. . . the proposal went over and the hospital had begun to grow. Expansion was on the way.

"After the hospital district was created in April of 1959, the staff and administration were removed from politics. . . .In 1959, federal funds, under provisions of the Hill-Burton Act, helped construct a mental health wing.

"In February, 1962, the hospital secured $250,000 in federal grants for a nurses' school, including training rooms and a library. The old school quarters were to be converted into an out-patient clinic, and would increase clinical space four and a half times."[25]

In 1985 a general obligation bond in the amount of $49.5 million passed and a major overhaul of the hospital resulted. The second floor was devoted to maternal and infant care, including an intensive neonatal care unit. In 1988 more than 6,000 babies were born at JPS.

The Family Practice Residency Program benefited from the expansion. An article in the *Tarrant County Physician* noted, "The addition of two floors on the district's Outpatient Clinic Building provided a 63 percent increase in space allocated to the Family Practice Program."[26] Described as a model for that type of residency, the program recorded more than 30,000 patient visits in 1988.

The new Emergency Services complex enjoyed a 308 percent increase in space for emergency and trauma care. The hospital's entire third floor was set aside for intensive care patient services, and the second floor was devoted to quarters for resident physicians and offices for physician support services. Within six years of the bond issue, the institution had a capacity of 600 beds.

Even with this enlargement and influx of funds, the hospital's patient load and expenses outstripped its resources. By the turn of the new millennium, crisis loomed again. *Star-Telegram* reporter Charlotte Huff interviewed more than a dozen employees about the situation. They spoke on condition of anonymity, but were in agreement that low staffing put patients at risk. Using data from a report, "Staffing & Productivity For JPS Hospital Emergency Services," Karpel Consulting Group, Long Beach, CA, Nov. 1, 2000, she found emergency room patients waited, on average, more than twice the median waiting time in 83 non-profit hospitals. In the comparison group, patients waited 30 minutes to see a doctor, at John Peter Smith Hospital the wait averaged 93 minutes.

Again, County Commissioners, board members and administrators were at loggerheads. Chief Executive Tony Alcini tendered his resignation, four board members were not reappointed, and as this book goes to press, the venerable hospital is bigger and better, but facing the same problems that have plagued it in the past.

★ ★ ★

Harris Methodist Fort Worth Hospital

It is impossible to separate Harris Hospital from the man so instrumental in its inception and growth—Charles Houston Harris. Yet the hospital's name is not to honor him, but his father.

Charles H. Harris was born in a one-room log cabin near the village of Alvarado, July 11, 1869. One of eight children, he grew up on a Johnson County farm, and the adage "You take take a boy out of the country. . . " applied to him. Despite his success as a physician, he remained a farmer at heart.

On Christmas day, 1887, Harris married Fannie Gardner of near-by Stubblefield community. Dr. Will Horn, in 1942, said, "For their honeymoon they killed hogs and picked geese."[27]

The Harrises moved to Anson, Texas. There, in addition to raising wheat, he operated a well and windmill supply business. In his spare time he began reading Gray's *Anatomy* and Barthlo's *Materia Medica.* Drought, plus the national business downturn, spurred him to take drastic measures.

Mrs. Harris and their two children went to live with her family in Moran, and Harris took what little money he received from liquidation and headed to Tennessee to study medicine. He also studied in St. Louis.

Returning to Texas in 1894, he was certified and began his practice in Moran. He was a popular doctor, but he became dissatisfied with his meager knowledge of medicine. In the fall of 1898, he returned to college. Harris graduated in April 1899 from St. Louis' College of Physicians and Surgeons, a Doctor of Medicine. At City Hospital, he experienced the challenge of surgery and later it became his speciality.

Now a degreed doctor of medicine, Harris returned to Moran. For several years he, according to Dr. Horn's biography, ". . . directed the

Charles H. Harris pioneered the use of Surgical Recovery Beds. Courtesy Fort Worth Star-Telegram Photograph Collection; Special Collections Division, The University of Texas at Arlington Libraries

control of epidemics of contagion, delivered babies and treated them when ill, removed tonsils and treated eyes. He pulled teeth and set broken bones, removed appendixes and did all the things that fell to the lot of a general practitioner in a small town."[28]

In 1909 he studied surgical techniques in Europe.

Dr. Harris is remembered for two important medical breakthroughs. "First, back in 1904 he had a patient with typhoid fever, and given up to die, . . . he gave the patient a subcutaneous salt solution. She revived and got well."[29] In 1906 he had another patient ". . .who was critically ill, and because of skin infection, he gave his first intravenous salt solution. . . . then considered radical treatment, for which he was severely criticized by his colleagues, has become today routine practice in hospitals all over the world."[30]

In the second area of pioneer work he established Surgical Recovery Beds. With the wartime shortage of nurses, Harris began putting several surgical patients in one room, under the watchful eye of one or two nurses, until the patients were well enough for less intensive care.

Harris had moved to Fort Worth in 1904 and on July 11, 1912, opened the Harris Clinic-Hospital at 5th Avenue and W. Rosedale Street.

Harris bought 405 acres west of the city and named it Harrisdale Farms. His prize-winning Hereford, "Prince Domino Return" proved to be Harris' best investment. Descendants of the bull were grand champions throughout the state. Periodically he added to the acreage until by 1935 Harrisdale Farms covered 3,700 acres.

Dr. Harris established the Harris School of Nursing in 1912. After Harrisdale Farms began to show profits, he donated as much as $150,000 a year in scholarships for young women to study nursing.

Harris was named to the Hall of Fame of the National Association of Methodist Hospitals. He outlived his wife and two sons and died January 20, 1958 in his seventh-floor apartment at Harris Hospital at the age of eighty-seven.

★ ★ ★

With its five building complex, Harris Methodist Fort Worth is the city's largest hospital. A visitor, after wandering down several corridors searching for an exit, stopped in an open-doored office. "What if I die of old age before I find a way out of here?" she asked. The witty office clerk replied, "We'll take you to our morgue, but I'll be happy to show you the nearest exit."[31]

Dr. Sam Jagoda, Jr. in a cogent history of the institution wrote, "Dr. Harris deeded his hospital to the (Methodist) Church in 1920. However, the hospital was returned to him when, in 1921, the Church purchased the property at 1300 West Cannon where the present hospital now stands. The property was purchased for $25,000.

"A fund raising campaign obtained pledges of 760,000 dollars and construction of The Methodist Hospital was begun in January, 1924. Opening was delayed until March 3, 1930 due to a series of financial difficulties. . . . The hospital continued to have financial problems reflecting the general economic conditions of the Great Depression.

"In 1933, Dr. Harris again offered to donate his hospital to the Church, move the Clinic, Nursing School, and his patients to the Methodist Hospital. He offered to operate the hospital. The Medical Staff rejected this proposal.

"By 1937, the debts mounted and no interest or principal payments had been made. On March 2, 1937, the hospital was sold on the Court House steps in a Sheriff's sale and was purchased by the Hospital's bonding company.

"Reverend H. A. Boaz, Bishop of the Central Texas Methodist Conference, approached Dr. Harris and urged him to save the hospital. Dr. Harris negotiated with the bonding company and regained the hospital for the Church. Dr. Harris donated $53,000 to the hospital and personally guaranteed the repayment of the $200,000 balance. Dr. Harris was given full authority as Director of the hospital and moved his hospital, School of Nursing, and clinic to the Methodist Hospital. His hospital was converted to a nurses' residence.

"In gratitude, the hospital's name was changed to Harris Memorial Methodist Hospital. This change in name occurred in 1939 and honored Dr. Harris' father. In 1941 the name was changed to Harris Hospital. . . .

"The hospital entered into an era of planning and growth from 1948 to the present. [1977] . . . .Land around the hospital was purchased for future expansion. Unfinished space in the hospital was gradually completed. . . . .

"The Jones and Children's Hospital Buildings were completed in 1961 and 1962. The Parking Garage was built in 1967 on the land east of the main building. A three story addition was made to the Jones Building in 1969 raising the bed total to 580. An auditorium, new intensive care area, and renal dialysis unit continued the modernization process begun in the 1950s. Computers were added to the hospital's equipment to aid in patient admission and data storage. An EMI Head Scanner brought computers to Radiology. The modernization plans continue and are now in Phase Five with $11 million in planned improvements."[32] (Used by permission)

By 1980 Harris under its new name, Harris Hospital-Methodist, reported a bed capacity of 628 and a host of new programs. The emergency room expansion included the Siemens Cardiac Monitoring System, a soft-tube landing system for transporting blood, and an X-ray treatment room. Careflite, a helicopter emergency care unit, began flights in 1979. According to *Scanner*, an in-house publication, "Traveling at 140 miles per hour, Careflite can be en route to hospitals, industrial sites and accident scenes within five minutes after receiving a call."[33]

Along with the increase in beds, at the time of the hospital's fiftieth anniversary it boasted a staff of 600 doctors, 2,200 employees, 200 volunteers, and 30,000 patients. Harris was the nation's eleventh largest obstetric hospital, where approximately 5,000 new Texans were welcomed each year. A May 1980 *Fort Worth Star-Telegram* supplement revealed other growth statistics. ". . . 1.3 million meals are served to patients, employees and visitors annually. More than 25,000 persons receive emergency treatment from highly trained professionals in this field. In radiology, 64,000 procedures are completed at Harris each year. More than 1,000 heart catheterizations are performed annually, and 1.5 million pathology procedures are made annually."[34]

Physical growth continued. In 1985 the hospital proudly announced the completion of the first step in the Harris Center construction, a 650-car parking garage. Step two, ". . . the professional building is 95% complete. Approximately 70 % of the office space is leased,"[35] according to a report in *Focus*, the hospital's quarterly magazine. A year later *Focus* reported, "The (Harris) Center includes an eight-story atrium, a physician's office building and Harris' Outpatient Radiology Center."[36] An elevated walkway connects the center to Harris' Intensive Care Units and the Sid W. Richardson Pavilion. The pavilion, finished in 1986, features a complete landscaped mall and garden areas.

Tarrant Business, in 1988 listed the largest metroplex hospitals— Harris ranked as the largest in Fort Worth, with a 628-bed capacity, 720 staff physicians, and 3,000 employees. In a 2001 interview, Barclay Berdan, chief administrator the past fifteen years, put the number of employees at 3,300.

As Laura Van Hoosier and Ashley Wesson of the public relations office combed through old records on the eve of Harris' seventieth anniversary, they ran across an interesting receipt. In 1933 a woman paid $3.00 for a three-night stay after the delivery of her baby. Three dollars won't buy much at today's prices, but modern medicine is far superior to what it was when Dr. Charles Harris began.

Harris Methodist Fort Worth Hospital is the largest in the city.
Courtesy Harris Methodist Fort Worth Hospital

Since 1930 Harris Methodist Fort Worth has earned a national reputation as being one of the nation's best run hospitals. Much of the credit goes to Barclay E. Berdan, President of Harris Methodist Fort Worth Hospital. The goal for the future, according to Berdan, is to interface technology and knowledge with hospital and physician services in order to remain a solid community asset in the next 100 years.

"We're still expanding," he said. "The new Critical Care Tower, with its Neuro ICU and Neuroscience Center, will open in March, 2001."[37] In the Jan/Feb house organ, *The Monitor*, the editor described the cutting-edge facility: "The Neuroscience Center will offer the following—an innovative stroke program, stereotactic procedures, epilepsy monitoring and treatment, neuro trauma, interventional radiology, neurosurgery, movement and spinal disorder services, and rehab services specific to neurological conditions."[38]

At least at Harris, medicine has come a long way since bleeding the patient was the accepted remedy for most ills.

★ ★ ★

Cook Children's Medical Center

A Writer's Project researcher wrapped the history of the Fort Worth Children's Hospital in compassionate terms. "The wan little face of a foundling in the arms of a helpless, distrated (sic) young physician, was the touchstone which engaged the sympathetic imagination of Mrs. Ida L. Turner, former Fort Worth Postmistress, and directed her dynamic energies toward the organization of hospital care for babies.

"A 17-year-old, destitute mother, no doubt praying in her heart for shelter and skilled care for her ailing baby left the infant in the office of a young Fort Worth physician. Having a brood of his own the doctor was in a dilemma, but as he trudged home, the child dangling from his arm, he met Mrs. Turner. Aghast at the condition of the child, blue with cold, suffering from malnutrition, with scarcely any clothes on its tiny body, and in the arms of a distracted appearing man, Mrs. Turner proffered aid.[39]

The Postmistress searched unsuccessfully for an agency to care for the child. Then she appealed to Rev. B. B. Ramage, pastor of St. Andrews

Episcopal Church. He arranged for the infant to be cared for at All Saints Hospital.

According to the Writers' Project, "The child was a beautiful blue-eyed, golden-red haired baby girl. Rev. Mr. Ramage christened the baby Virginia Scott Andrews. . . . Thus 'Virginia Scott' became the inspiration for the Fort Worth Children's Hospital."[40] A young couple adopted the baby when she was about nine months old.

Mrs. Turner continued to lobby for a place for sick children, but it was the population explosion caused by World War I and the Ranger oil discoveries that awakened others to the need. Mrs. Charles Scheuber and Mrs. J. H. Strayer joined Turner in her efforts. Strayer, chair of the Social Service Committee of the Fort Worth Federation of Women's Clubs, organized a fund raising committee.

The Writers' Project noted, "It was an appeal that touched all hearts. Contributions came pouring in from one to ten dollars. The whole community answered this prayer."[41]

Turner, Strayer and Scheuber convinced Ben L. Waggoman to donate unimproved property on Winton Terrace. Architects Sanguinett & Staats drew plans and supervised construction as their contribution. The building trades donated labor. Lumber yards, cement dealers and furniture stores supplied needed materials. The Free Baby Hospital's first patients were admitted March, 1918.

The Assembly Ball, on January 9, 1918 in the Metropolitan Hotel ballroom, became the traditional fund raiser for the hospital. Reporter Pauline Naylor recalled the gala events. "The famous Vernon Castle, then a captain in the Royal Air Force, stationed at the British Air Field at Benbrook, was the featured attraction at the ball and $800 was raised for the hospital."[42] From this, the Jewel Charity Ball was inaugurated as an annual benefit for the hospital.

Some twenty years later, Sioux Campbell, in the *Fort Worth City Guide* described the facility. "Beautiful landscaping decorates the approach, and the interior of the building has a pleasing effect with light cream and buff walls and white woodwork and furniture. . . .On the sloping banks of the river the hospital grounds has (sic) excellent drainage and a fine pasture of abundant grass for its six cows, ample space for chicken runs, and its apple, peach and plum orchard. The hospital supplies its own milk, eggs, and chickens, and in 1936 put up 250 cans from its orchard."[43]

Despite the best efforts of the Women's Club patrons, the hospital experienced financial shortfalls. The city began partial support in 1927 and two years later the Community Chest donated money to the hospital. From these two sources the hospital received $17,000 annually. The average cost to the city per day per patient was $1.25, and to the Community Chest $1.40. Children remained until well, and physicians saw approximately 450 patients each year.

During the Depression money from the city dried up. By 1940, as money became more available from bequests, such as the $500,000 from the Mrs. M. M. Barnes estate, and other sources, the hospital looked to expand its facilities.

Trustees bought a site at Sixth and Pruitt Avenues. A 70-bed facility was completed in 1954. Harris transferred its pediatric unit to Fort Worth Children's Hospital. Under the agreement between the two institutions, each would retain its board, but share some services. Doctors found the arrangement inconvenient. The hospital had no operating room, or X-ray facilities. Patients were taken through a tunnel to Harris for these services. It was in effect a "bedroom hospital."

As Fort Worth Children's Hospital was settling into its relationship with Harris, not too far away, on Lancaster, another children's hospital came into being. But it was part of a much older institution—W. I. Cook Memorial Hospital.

According to Dr. Sam Jagoda, Jr., "The W. I. Cook Memorial Hospital opened in 1929 as a thirty bed general hospital. Its story begins much earlier, in the 1870s, when Mr. and Mrs. W. I Cook purchased a 20,000 acre ranch in Shackleford County, Texas. The ranch adjoined the one of the Nails, Mrs. Cook's relatives. Nicknamed `Dude,' she worked along with the men in the care of the cattle and the routine ranch work such as riding the fences.

"The Cook's physicians were the Bealls of Fort Worth. Dr. K. H. Beall began practice in Fort Worth in 1909.

". . . the Cooks were grateful for Dr. Frank Beall's skill in attending Mrs. Cook's brother following a serious automobile accident, and for

Dr. K. H. Beall's care of Mr. Cook during his illnesses until his death in 1922. By 1923 Mrs. Cook had accumulated about $40,000 and wanted to build a small hospital in Fort Worth in memory of her husband and her daughter, Mrs. Jessie Cook Head. The Bealls convinced her this sum was insufficient to build a hospital."[44]

The problem was soon solved. Jagoda continued, "In the early 1920s, oil was discovered in Shackleford County. The Cook Ranch was leased for oil exploration by Continental Oil Co. . . . There were eventually 400 wells in the Cook Field. Mrs. Cook began plans for a new first class hospital in Fort Worth. . . . Nothing was spared in the construction to build the finest hospital possible for that time."[45]

Riley Nail, author of *Per Stripes: The John Nail Family in Texas 1839-1995*, wrote in detail about the facility. "The operating rooms, the clinics, and other departments were the first up-to-date ones in Texas. It is difficult (now) to realize a hospital that in 1929 which could boast private baths for each patient room as well as a signal call light system, an emergency bell, a telephone and a radio would be hailed as the most modern hospital in Texas. But it was."[46]

W. I. Cook Memorial Hospital was built with oil money from a grateful patient. (from a 1929 photo) Courtesy Fort Worth Star-Telegram Photograph Collection; Special Collections Division, The University of Texas at Arlington Libraries

Running ice water, built-in cabinets, shower baths, tubs, and bedpan washers in the bathrooms caused visitors' eyes to pop and jaws to drop. "Even the fact the faucets could be turned away from the basins, making it easy to fill pitchers and 'flower vases' was extolled in magazines and newspapers. . . . All the patients' rooms had ceiling fans and doors with two wooden transoms which allowed for circulation of air and privacy."[47]

The entrance courtyard featured bronze gates in a carved Italian Renaissance marble gateway. The foyer's ceiling incorporated heavy walnut beams against a gold background. Ornate furniture, some from Italian abbeys, adorned the library and offices.

Cook opened in 1929 with the Beall Clinic, now the Fort Worth Clinic, occupying the south wing on the first floor.

In 1978 Dr. Jagoda, Jr., wrote, "The Cook Trust has given over $3,000,000 . . .since 1926 and the hospital still shares in the oil and gas income. This income provides funds for charity care and offsets losses incurred by the hospital.

"A second benefactor to Cook Hospital was Mr. Tom B. Owens. At his death in 1948, he left $1,500,000 to the . . . hospitalization, rehabilitation, care, and cure of crippled children provided said institution was previously endowed with not less than $400,000 . . . .

"The Cook and Owen trustees formed a new entity, 'The W. I. Cook Memorial Hospital and Center for Children.' After remodeling, the new facility opened September 1, 1952. The $800,000 cost of remodeling and building new wings resulted in a bed capacity of 72."[48] (Used by permission)

The Tom B. Owens Institute for Crippled Children was part of the new facility. Cook marketed itself as being the best equipped children's hospital in the area.

The two children's hospitals paralleled each other in services and almost literally as they were less than one mile apart. For years civic leaders, and pediatricians, wanted to merge the two. Finally in 1984, the Star-Telegram noted, "The governing boards of the two hospitals concurred that state-of-the-art medical care for children could be accomplished by combining the two facilities and their services."[49]

In 1984 Cook Childrens' Medical Center moved to spacious new quarters at 801 Seventh St. "Everything . . . is kid specific,"[50] according to their web site. Patients and their parents enter a windowed six-story atrium. Glass elevators whisk passengers from floor to floor. Children observe fish tanks on every floor, and have access to a library and playrooms. Equipment is scaled to fit kids' bodies, and all Cook's doctors are specially trained to work with children.

Russell K. Tolman, President and CEO, states the hospital's purpose as improving the health of children. "We provide quality health care through an integrated system which oversees a continuum of services ranging from simple preventive checkups at pediatric offices to highly specialized hospital-based critical care."[51]

Known for having one of the best neonatal transport teams in the country, Dr. David Turbeville described his team. "(It) is made up of highly trained physicians, nurses and respiratory therapists . . . experts in newborn care and stabilization. Our team pioneered the use of jet ventilators for transport use. We can transport by ground ambulance, helicopter, and airplane as needed. We have the only jet plane in the country dedicated to transport of pediatric patients. (Thus) we are frequently able to get to a referring hospital in time to attend many high-risk deliveries.[52]

For these and other innovations Cooks Children's Medical Center is one of the leading hospitals for the care of children. Postmistress Mrs. Ida Turner would be proud.

CHAPTER EIGHT

"FAMILY" PRACTICE: SONS, DAUGHTERS AND SIBLINGS

It seems that medicine, more than any other profession, tends to run in families. Some of Fort Worth's most outstanding doctors are the sons and grandsons of doctors. Others who have made their mark in the medical community have seen their sons, and now their daughters, become physicians. This chapter spotlights some of these doctors who have made healing an "all in the family" practice.

THE TERRELL FAMILY

One of the most familiar names in Fort Worth medical circles is that of the Terrells. Charles J. Terrell practiced medicine in Kaufman County in the last half of the nineteenth century. His son, Dr. Charles E. Terrell was born in that county in 1863, but moved to Ranger in Eastland County.

C. E. Terrell opened Terrell's Drug Store on Ranger's Main Street in 1884. He taught himself medicine, passed the state boards and was certified to practice. He and his wife, Emma, were the parents of three sons. Two, Caleb and Truman, became medical doctors and the third, Sanford, was a dentist.

Ranger was a wild frontier town. As a child, grandson Ted Terrell heard of one incident that sounded like a western movie. "There was a gunfight out in the street. Grandfather went out and treated the wounded man. Not long after that somebody, believed to be the man's enemy, torched the drug store."[1] Dr. Terrell rebuilt the pharmacy.

Caleb Odhelius Terrell, Sr. took his premed studies in Austin, then transferred to the University of Texas Medical School in Galveston. Dr. Terrell graduated in 1910.

He practiced in Ranger before and after serving as medical officer at Kelly Field during World War I. He moved to Fort Worth in 1925. He and Edwin Schwarz were two of the first pediatricians to serve the community.

Caleb and Nona Garner had three sons before her untimely death in 1930. C. O., Jr. became a pediatrician; Charles was a surgeon and Robert, although not a physician, stayed within the field by working in a veteran's hospital.

C. O. Terrell met surgical supervisor Blanche Osborne when he brought a child to Harris Hospital. They later married and she left the hospital to become his office nurse. Blanche Terrell was the mother of two sons, Ted and Jack. The story of her medical career as a pediatrician is told elsewhere. Ted preferred teaching science to practicing it, but Jack followed in his parents' footsteps and is a specialist in adolescent medicine.

Ted recalled what it was like growing up in a family where both his mother and father were doctors, such as remembering exactly where he was when the bombing of Pearl Harbor was announced. He was at Harris Hospital, waiting in the car for his father.

He and Jack spent a lot of time at the Terrell's office in the Medical Arts Building. While their parents saw patients on Saturdays, the boys entertained themselves and visited with the concession stand owners. Other times they headed upstairs where the area's leading radio station was located. All the visiting celebrities came to the station for interviews. Ted remembered seeing W. Lee O'Daniel when he was the announcer for the "Light Crust Doughboys" before he became governor. Author and historian Boyce House used to regale the boys with interesting tales.

"My brother used to ride up and down with the elevator operators. He was the best psychiatrist there ever was—they told him all about their husbands and families. He would tell me and I would be speechless,"[2] Ted chuckled.

Hospitals were smaller then and the nurses and administrators knew the boys. When their father had an evening emergency their mother would sometimes dress them in pajamas, equip the car with pillows, and while he worked, she would read to her sons. If Dr. C.O.'s emergency was over in time, they would stop for ice cream on the way home. As they got older, the boys also helped around the office by pulling charts and getting examining rooms ready.

Ted told of making a home call with his father, when everything west of Texas Christian University was farm and ranch land. They went to one rural home and Dr. Terrell treated a sick child by the light of a kerosene lamp. The farmer paid with a "mess of poke greens." Dr. Terrell, raised on Southern cooking, gladly accepted the offering.

Ted remembered the fun he and his brother had in Galveston when Dr. Blanche was in medical school. "She had a classmate whose father was an oyster man. He had a place on Buffalo Bayou—we went out there. There were ducks and we could fish—it was a lot of fun."[3]

Dr. C.O. Terrell took a leading part the summer of 1943 in the fight waged against the polio epidemic. Ted said one could look in the windows of John Peter Smith Hospital and see row after row of patients in iron lungs.

C. O. Terrell's health failed and he died of Bright's disease in June 1951.

Tarrant County Medical Society President Larry E. Reaves, regarding the Gold-Headed Cane, wrote, ". . .in 1951, Dr. Porter Brown, gave a replica of a Gold-Headed Cane to the society to be awarded to outstanding doctors. Recollections indicate this was made because of his admiration and in recognition of the late Dr. C. O. Terrell, Sr. However, it was intended that all subsequent recipients to be living at the time of their selection."[4]

Dr. Truman Conner Terrell took a different medical path than did his older brother, but he too, left his mark on the Fort Worth medical community.

He went into private practice in Ranger in 1913, but a year later moved to Fort Worth, and in 1915 opened Terrell Laboratory in a small room at the old Medical School Building located at 5th and Jones. Dr. Terrell, writing in Reeves' medical history, told of the lab. "In 1916 we moved to the basement of All Saints Hospital. . . . Then, in 1917 we opened our offices in the Old Texas National Bank Building.

Brothers T. C. Terrell, left, and C. O. Terrell, Sr. right, are remembered for their service to the medical community. T. C. Terrell courtesy Fort Worth Star-Telegram Photograph Collection; Special Collections Division, The University of Texas at Arlington Libraries; C. O. Terrell, Sr. courtesy Ted Terrell

"In 1927 we moved to the Medical Arts Bldg., where we occupied a large part of the 6th floor, until 1933 we were occupying the entire 6th floor."[5] From a beginning of himself and one medical student, by 1953 Terrell Laboratory employed fifteen physicians and a total staff of 100.

When Dr. Terrell first came to Fort Worth, in addition to his pathology work, he taught clinical pathology and bacteriology at the old Fort Worth School of Medicine.

World War I interrupted these activities and he served a year in the Army Medical Corps. Before he reported for duty, he unknowingly was listed as AWOL. His papers were mistakenly routed to Camp Bowie. Had he followed his papers he would have been sent oversees. Instead he was stationed at Fort Sam Houston and Fort Bliss in charge of the laboratories.

Over the years, the laboratory expanded to include branches in other cities. Dr. Terrell encouraged research in these facilities as well as the usual pathology services. Scores of college students were introduced to medical science by working for him.

After the laboratory was well established, Terrell, in 1932 assumed charge of Methodist Hospital as director. Financial distress was all around and the hospital was in dire straits. Terrell held it together, but a dispute arose between him and the board of directors. In 1932 the hospital sued him, demanding an accounting of $129,000.

According to the *Star-Telegram*, "Return of indexes and records relating to the X-ray photographs and pathological specimens, of lists and records of notes and accounts due the hospital and of lists of names of subscribers to a hospitalization plan also was sought in the suit."[6] The gist of the problem stemmed from the hospital's belief that some supplies were paid for, but not delivered.

Terrell fought the allegations and counter-sued. He won. Rather than his mismanagement of funds, the court held he was owed $2,503 for inventory and and $3,000 in claims between the time of the filing of the suit and its determination.

This unpleasant episode did not keep him from immediately signing a contract with the Dallas Diocese of the Episcopal Church to manage All Saints Hospital. The *Star-Telegram* in July 1937 quoted Terrell, "An extensive program of improving both the physical and architectural properties of the hospital will be started next week."[7] Terrell Laboratory did the X-rays under the direction of Dr. Howard Walker. Dr. May Owen headed the pathology department. In addition to his work at All Saints, Terrell was in charge of the pathology lab at John Peter Smith Hospital.

In recognition of his almost fifty years of service to the medical community, Fort Worth doctors voted for Truman C. Terrell to receive the Gold-Headed Cane in 1962. The *Fort Worth Press* described the seventy-two-year-old physician as keeping a schedule that might tire a much younger man. "He arises at 6:15 a.m. and never goes to bed before midnight. He takes no afternoon nap. He reads technical information at least four hours daily. And for relaxation he walks the woods and streams to hunt and fish."[8]

Dr. Joseph McVeigh, in presenting the cane, noted Terrell's accomplishments filled four pages. "Beneath the abrupt exterior Dr. Terrell often shows the world, there is a sentimental heart—and a generous one,"[9] he said.

Dr. Truman C. Terrell died in 1971. He was preceded in death by a daughter who died at age three, and his only son was killed in World War II. But the Terrell name still lives in the children and grandchildren of his brother, C. O. Terrell. Dr. John S. (Jack) Terrell, son of two physicians, is a specialist in adolescent medicine. He is director of health services as Texas Christian University.

★ ★ ★

LEE S. ANDERSON

Like father, H. W. Anderson, son Lee S. Anderson attended Tulane University. H. W. Anderson served three years in the military. Lee S. Anderson served three years in the military. H. W. Anderson is a past president of the Tarrant County Medical Society. Lee S. Anderson is a past president of the Tarrant County Medical Society.

Soft-spoken Dr. H. W. Anderson came to Fort Worth in 1951 and soon became one of the city's busiest pediatricians. Lee remembers his father working long hours, then coming home to as many as twenty telephone calls to be returned. When asked what it was like growing up in the home of a doctor, Lee said with a laugh, "Well, for one thing you couldn't fake illness to get out of going to school."[10] He recalled several of his friends and kids in the neighborhood were from medical families and they tended to hang out together. They still do. Lee is married to the sister of Dr. Tom Kleuser.

In his first *Tarrant County Physician* president's letter, Dr. H. W. Anderson explained his concept of the physician's responsibility to the community as a "thinking machine." He told *Press* reporter Jean Wysatta, "With a trained 'thinking machine' and with his further daily experience in wrestling with diagnostic data in an effort to reach a reasonable answer, the doctor strikes me as being uniquely well-equipped to serve the community in areas not necessarily dealing with only problems medical."[11]

One aspect of community service led him to serve as a consultant for a most unusual patient—Mike, a rare baby gorilla. Said zoo director Lawrence Curtis, "We wanted Mike to have the best of care. If anything should go wrong . . . we'd consult with Dr. Anderson."[12]

The senior Anderson was a sickly child. His bouts with bronchial asthma meant much time spent with doctors as he was growing up. He developed an interest in medicine and graduated from Tulane University School of Medicine in 1945 and interned in that city's Charity Hospital. In 1946 he became an Air Force flight surgeon, stationed in San Antonio. Following his military work, Dr. Anderson returned to New Orleans to specialize in pediatrics. He and Mrs. Anderson liked Texas and chose Fort Worth to plant their roots.

Dr. Lee Anderson considered several professions before he settled on medicine. After medical school at Galveston, and an internship at Baylor Hospital, he did an ophthalmology residency in Oklahoma City. Anderson served in the Philippines during his military tour of duty. Back in civilian life, in 1982 he studied retinal diseases before beginning his practice here.

Dr. Anderson is a firm believer in physicians taking an active part in professional affairs and in today's environment that means being politically aware. The 1997 president of the medical society's objective was to speak frankly and candidly on issues of interest to patients and doctors. He peppered his *Tarrant County Physician* messages with this theme, urging his colleagues to support their professional organizations. Of the TCMS he said, "It takes many people's efforts to make this organization run. All participation is very important, and some is more public than others."[13] In a later message he declared, "I am for continuous quality improvement in health care. . . . for efficient and wise use of resources and funds. . . .for community cooperation. . . .for physician decision-making   . . . ."[14] His voice on these matters is still heard—in 2000 Governor George W. Bush appointed Dr. Anderson president of the State Board of Medical Examiners.

On a recent trip to Galveston to visit his son who is in medical school there, Dr. Anderson mused what the future holds for these upcoming doctors. "At this time," he wrote in a TCMS journal essay, "'I don't know,' but my plan is to be in there working in our community, in our state and in our country to shape the system as it evolves, so that these young physicians will have a 'place at the table' to apply their skills."[15] And perhaps one of those young physicians named Anderson will one day serve as president of the Tarrant County Medical Society, like father, like grandfather.

★ ★ ★

MARION J. BROOKS

Dr. Marion J. Brooks, with the wispy Salvador Dali mustache and silver white hair pulled back in a pony tail, remembers making a unique "house call"—to the White House. He was invited by President Lyndon B. Johnson to attend the 1965 White House Conference on Health.

The politically active physician was always encouraged by his mother, as well as his father, a postal worker. Marion obtained a B. S. Degree from Prairie View A. & M. and taught school for one year before enrolling in Howard University, one of only two medical schools for African Americans at that time. Brother Donald was already a student there. Dr. Donald Brooks became the first African-American to practice general

Marion "Jack" Brooks, MD. The politically active physician is one of six doctors in the extended family. Courtesy Dr. Jack Brooks

surgery in Fort Worth, and before the hospital closed, to serve as chief of surgery at St. Joseph.

In 1994 reporter Gracie Bonds Staples interviewed the Brooks family. She noted,". . . that when it comes to medical advice in Fort Worth, the Brooks name can yield a first, second, third, fourth, fifth and even a sixth doctor's opinion."[16] The six doctors in the family are: Marion and his son Clarence; Donald and sons Ralph and Michael, and Michael's wife Jennifer, plus two other medical doctors married to Brooks' siblings in other states, and two doctors of education. Dr. Marion and Dr. Clarence shared a family practice, Dr. Donald is a surgeon, Dr. Ralph is a dermatologist, Dr. Michael is a surgeon and Dr. Jennifer is an obstetrician-gynecologist.

The elder Brookses availed themselves of the GI Bill and worked part time to pay for their medical educations. When their children were of college age the two pooled their money to ensure the younger ones could get an education.

As a youth Marion Brooks saw a good education as the highway to a better life. There were not many choices for African-Americans in the first half of the twentieth century—teaching, preaching or medicine. In 1941 he taught school for $55.25 a month. The following year he joined the Army and commanded a chemical and engineering company. After military service, Brooks chose medicine and graduated from Howard in 1951 and interned at Friedman Hospital in Washington.

When Brooks returned to Fort Worth it was to the last vestiges of segregation. Only the old City-County Hospital allowed access to black doctors. Minor procedures were done in the office, major surgery was referred to white doctors. John Peter Smith accepted black doctors' patients and later St. Joseph set aside ten beds in the basement for them. But it would take legislation in the form of the Hill-Burton Act for all hospitals to accept African-American doctors.

Brooks later was on the staff of Harris and Children's Hospital. He counted this opening of all hospitals to all doctors as one of the most important events in his career.

In 1958 the brothers established a joint practice downtown on Ninth Street, then moved to larger quarters on Evans Avenue. It was at those clinics the younger Brookses spent most of their afternoons and summers working. Clarence told Staples, "As a kid, I cleaned up the office, and then I moved up from janitor to working behind the desk."[17]

"Marion, better known as 'Jack,' is the most widely known of the Brooks physicians, having established himself also as a community leader,"[18] Staples noted. In the early 1960s he was one of the first African-Americans appointed to city boards and commissions.

In 1963 Brooks led a civil-rights march to Austin that coincided with Martin Luther King's march to Washington. "Everybody couldn't go to Washington, and we felt we had plenty of messages we could deliver in Austin,"[19] he told reporter Hollace Weiner.

Beyond his civil-rights activities, Brooks was the founding president of the Sickle Cell Anemia Association of Texas. His many recognitions include the Prairie View A. & M. Distinguished Alumni Award, Fort Worth School District's First Century Distinguished Alumni Award, and the Howard Region V Alumni Award. Mayor Cliff Overcash proclaimed December 10, 1976 as "Dr. Marion 'Jack' Brooks Day."

In 1991 he and Dr. Edward Guinn were honored by the People's Salute as outstanding black role models.

Brooks is still active in community affairs, but he retired from health care in 1995. He'll leave that to the five still practicing medicine.

★ ★ ★

EMORY DAVENPORT

Dr. Emory Davenport's peers honored him for his years of devotion to the care of patients by awarding him the coveted Gold-Headed Cane October 29, 1971. Expressing surprise and delight, he admitted he did not grow up in a medical family. Nor did he have a close relationship with a doctor that led him to his chosen field. In an interview he told reporter Jon McConal, "Some time as a child, I just made up my mind that I was going to be a doctor. By the time I entered high school, I took all my courses with that in mind."[20]

The newspaper article simply states that Davenport served his internship at Detroit Receiving Hospital. Nothing was said about his work in treating casualties of the nation's worst race riot up to that time. It happened just days before he was due to be inducted into the army. Dr. Sam Jagoda, Jr., wrote about it.

"It was a hot Sunday afternoon in June, 1943. By 3:00 p.m. the temperature was in the 90s with high humidity. An estimated 100,000 people, the majority of them black, sought relief from the heat on Belle Isle, a 1,000 acre park in the middle of the Detroit River. A fist fight between a black and a white broke out on the bridge leading back to the city. False rumors, including one of a mother and baby being thrown off the bridge, sparked what became a full-fledged riot.

"Dr. Davenport was nearing the end of his internship year and, for $25 a month and room and board, had been seasoned by a year of ministering to Detroit's usual Saturday night ritual of bloodlettings. Still he and the rest of the staff were unprepared for the volume of humanity that surged through Detroit Receiving Hospital's emergency room that weekend.

"Dr. Davenport vividly recalls one instance during that first night of rioting when six seriously injured policemen, all needing immediate medical attention, lay in the emergency room beside the black citizens they had faced in the streets a few hours earlier.

"The hospital was strained to capacity. There was a rapid dismissal of any patient well enough to go home. Stacks of folding cots were assembled and sandwiched into the long unairconditioned wards now beginning to resemble a battlefield hospital.

"'Help was hard to come by,' Dr. Davenport said. "We called in the Wayne medical students and every available staff member.'

"Tension increased with each new report of violence. Police officers accompanied every ambulance load of victims. They stayed to pace the halls, a constant presence during the three-day nightmare.

"For three days Detroit Receiving Hospital's waiting rooms and halls were littered with bodies awaiting treatment. The hospital set up a clearing house to assess the degree of the injury.

"'It was like a battle that wouldn't end,' Dr. Davenport remembers. He and his colleagues labored day and night for those three days, snatching a snack from the hospital cafeteria or a few minutes of sleep when physical stamina challenged human limitations.

"At last the rioting ceased. Within a few weeks the hospital was cleared of the casualties. The city of Detroit would carry the scars longer.

"'I was involved in many battles in Europe, but nothing in as concentrated a dose as those three days in Detroit when an estimated 700 people were admitted to the hospital,' Davenport said."[21] (used by permission)

In 1946 he came back to his hometown and joined the Terrell Medical Group in the department of internal medicine. Another young doctor, Art Rutledge, became part of the group. They developed a deep and lasting friendship. They worked together for Terrell Medical Group twenty-two years before forming a partnership. That partnership is still strong and includes both Davenport's and Rutledge's sons.

Concerning his speciality, Davenport explained to the *Star-Telegram* reporter, "I think the internist has become what we thought of a GP being 25 years ago. He fills the gaps. He tells the person where he needs to go."[22] Even in these days of specialized medicine, Dr. Davenport feels it is important to develop a relationship with his patients. Of his own practice he noted in a recent interview, "Before the super-specialist, we did it all—heart, ulcer, kidney, colon. We were the neurologist, the psychologist, the pulmonologist, and the oncologist."[23]

Davenport has enjoyed a long and happy relationship with All Saints Hospital. In a 1998 video on the hospital he said, "It was our home away from home," declaring he sometimes spent more time there than with his family.[24] When All Saints was smaller, he knew all the staff as well as his patients—something he treasured.

The advent of antibiotics, immunization and organ transplants have been the most dramatic advances he has seen in his many years of practice. Recalling the days of crowded polio wards at John Peter Smith Hospital, he said, "The iron lungs were lined up like caskets. The emotional reaction from someone who had just been diagnosed as having polio was tremendous. They automatically felt doomed," he told McConal.[25]

Davenport maintained he did not encourage his son to go into medicine, rather Alan made the choice on his own. But the pride shows in his voice when he declared medicine is the greatest profession in the world. "There's nothing better you can do than to help a sick person,"[26] he said. Asked what the future holds for his son and others currently in practice, he thoughtfully replied, "I've been awed at the advancements. But I feel that by the time they reach my point in life, they will equally be awed."[27]

★ ★ ★

EDWARD W. GUINN

Many little boys play "doctor." Asked when he decided to become a doctor, Edward Guinn replied, "From childhood. My brother James and I always planned to be doctors. We even envisioned as children after we became doctors we would build and run our own hospital."[28] They did become doctors, but the hospital was never built. Instead Edward turned his attention to civic duties and his huge medical practice.

Civic-mindedness was a long family tradition. He attended James E. Guinn Elementary School, named after his grandfather, a well-known educator in racially segregated Fort Worth. After his 1941 graduation from I. M. Terrell High School, Guinn majored in biology and chemistry. He did not go immediately into medical school, rather he taught chemistry at Prairie View A&M.

Following military service Guinn graduated from medical school at Galveston in 1956. He was one of three Texans to do an internship at Philadelphia General Hospital.

Back in Fort Worth, Guinn began his practice where it was needed the most—the under-served Stop Six community. In 1992 *Dallas Morning News* reporter Jacquelynn Floyd wrote, "Most mornings, patients are already lined up outside the door by the time Dr. Edward Guinn arrives. Some of them have appointments, but many do not." She noted not all had the money to pay, but none were turned away. "There is no place for them to go."[29] Since that time other clinics have opened, but at one time Guinn was the only doctor for the roughly 15,000 residents of the southeast neighborhood.

He still treats patients, sometimes as many as sixty a day, in the modest brick building on E. Ramey Street. His no-frills waiting room houses a collection of mismatched chairs, filled with sick people waiting to see him. Floyd observed, "Despite the crowd, Dr. Guinn chatted with each patient, assuring a nervous mother that her son did not have mumps in one examining room, congratulating a middle-aged man on his effort to stop smoking in another."[30] A recent visitor found the same congenial doctor-patient relationship evident.

Family medicine has been described as from "gall stones to gun shots," and Guinn has had his share of both. He told of one young man, a security guard, who, practicing his fast draw, drew so fast he pulled the trigger before he got the gun out of its holster. He shot himself in the leg. The bullet traveled down the thigh and lodged in the space behind the kneecap. During the surgery, "I was right down to the bullet, [it was] resting against a large blood vessel, when the lights went out."[31] A nurse held a flashlight until the auxiliary system came on and all breathed a sigh of relief.

Guinn remembered another gun shot case, a much more serious one. One day he walked through the Emergency Room at St. Joseph Hospital and saw a police officer lying on a table. He recognized him—Lonnell Cooper, one of the first African-Americans hired by the Fort Worth Police Department. He had been shot twice, in both shoulders. "The mad man who shot him blew him down with the first shot and stood over him intending to kill him." Cooper rolled over and took a bullet in the other shoulder. Both shoulders received considerable tissue and bone damage. "Dr. Louis Levy and I operated on one side [of the injured man] and Dr. Donald Brooks and Dr. C. P. Davis operated on the other side, four of us at the same time,"[32] he recalled. Cooper recovered enough to return to the department, but with different duties.

In 1967 Guinn won a seat on the City Council in citywide elections. At age 42, he became Fort Worth's first black councilman. Of that experience he said, "Although my getting into the public arena and on the council was not a part of my being a physician, my being a physician made a difference."[33]

One important result of his concern for health issues was the change in the way jail prisoners were handled. At one time all those picked up for apparent drunkenness were jailed. But some were sick—their "drunken behavior" masked their illness. Guinn led to the establishment of an emergency review committee to insure proper care was given the ones who needed it. Not only did the committee prevent mistreatment of the ill, they also prevented victims or their families from suing the city over mistaken diagnoses.

Another concern of Guinn's was the lack of medically trained ambulance crews. When a person needed an ambulance, a funeral home vehicle was dispatched. The physician/councilman saw this as a conflict of interest. Moreover the drivers rarely had skills beyond the most meager of first aid. He worked with Tarrant County Junior College (now Tarrant County College) to overcome the problem. The Emergency Medical Technician Program that emerged was one of the first in Texas. It led to both personnel and vehicles being equipped to handle emergencies as we know them today.

After two terms on the council Guinn chose not to run again. Speaking of his council experience, Guinn told Hollace Weiner, "I'm not really fond of the idea of a person making politics a career".[34] Weiner was doing a story on the "People's Salute" award honoring local black role models.

The "People's Salute" was one of many honors Guinn has received in his forty-plus years of service to the community. The Fort Worth Press Club named Dr. Guinn "Newsmaker of the Year" in 1971 and in 1972 the National Conference of Christians and Jews honored him with the "Brotherhood Award."

For the generous giving of his time and his devotion to medicine, he was presented the "Minority Leaders & Citizens Council's Distinguished Service Award" by the U.S. Surgeon General in 1994. In his most recent honor, the Renaissance Cultural Committee designated him a "Living Legend" in 2000.

★ ★ ★

THOMAS M. KLEUSER

Tom Kleuser's father, despite a busy surgical schedule, always managed to attend the Kleuser kids' ball games and other important functions. When asked what was it like growing up in the home of a physician, Tom recalled, "Well, answering the phone [was different]. "If we answered we had to find out if he was on call. . . . . There were times when he would get a call early on a Saturday morning and be in surgery all day."[35]

Dr. Lawrence P. Kleuser, after residencies at Dallas' Veteran's Hospital and Scottish Rite Hospital, served as a medical officer in the Navy from 1947 to 1951. "As a captain in the Army, he was at Brooke Medical Center in San Antonio and at Ft. Riley, Kansas, as an orthopedic surgeon."[36]

Dr. Kleuser's career was cut short by his untimely death at the age of forty-seven. In 1971 he suffered an arterial venous malformation of the brain. He underwent surgery, but never regained consciousness.

His son, Tom, made his career choice public at an Eagle Scout banquet. In answer to the question put to most young people, the scouts were telling what they wanted to do "when they grew up." Thirteen-year-old Tom announced "Orthopedic surgeon." And he is one today.

At age fifteen he started helping his father in surgery. There was a lot of family history to spur him on—his grandfather was a physician. Both his late father and step-father were in medicine. "My dad was my hero and role model,"[37] he told an interviewer.

As an orthopedic surgeon he speaks to youth groups concerning safety. He notes the difference between car wreck victims who do and do not wear seat belts. "Those who don't wear seat belts we see in the emergency room. Those who do come into the office the next day." He's even more vivid when it comes to motorcycles; he calls them "donorcycles." Kleuser uses graphic slides to accentuate the mangled bodies he puts back together after an accident, and urges the students not to "become one of his slides."[38]

In an interview he told of receiving a 3:00 am call to the emergency room. The patient, Donnie, was driving with a friend when one of them stupidly jerked the steering wheel. The friend became a missile through the windshield two seconds before he became Donnie's dead best friend. The car rolled down an embankment. The driver survived, but among other injuries, both his ankles were smashed. Dr. Kleuser worked for five weeks to restore his ability to walk, but Donnie will never be the same.

He recalled another victim, a woman driving along Eagle Mountain Dam when a drunk driver plowed into her. "I took care of her, put her in a 'halo' [a brace that goes round the head] and fixed her broken neck. She was a sweet lady—never complained." Some years later Kleuser suffered a broken neck in a skiing accident. The woman heard of his misfortune. Concerned, she called and talked to Mrs. Kleuser, saying "... that should not happen to a doctor."[39]

Dr. Kleuser has seen the growth of out-patient orthopedic surgery as techniques and equipment have improved. Where once such procedures were done only in the hospital, now patients go home the same day. He still calls to check on them to make sure there are no complications. Whether out-patient or in-hospital, he is able to do much more than when he first began his practice. He cited the ability to replace joints and the use of orthoscopic surgery as examples. His father would be proud.

★ ★ ★

W. S. LORIMER, JR.

W. S. "Bill" Lorimer, Jr. fondly remembers his father making house calls. "First he went by horse and buggy, then he bought one of the first Model T Fords in the city, and later drove a Hupmobile. I went with him a lot,"[40]

Right after breakfast Dr. Lorimer, Sr. would make house calls, then hospital rounds, and then go to his office for the day. After dinner, he made more house calls, frequently with young Bill at his side. "He was so busy, this was an opportunity to be with him for a one-on-one conversation,"[41] he told an interviewer.

Bill recalled the scene at the Medical Arts Building where his father and many other doctors practiced. "It was so crowded people lined the halls all the way to the elevator."[42] Outside the building roped areas allowed patients to form a que, much like those at modern day amusement parks. To escape the crowding, the Lorimers found a building at Leuda and Alston Streets and there they established the Lorimer Clinic. He was familiar with the neighborhood—it was within a mile of where he was born and a block from his old high school.

As he was growing up, the local icons of early twentieth century medicine were frequent visitors to his home. Therefore, it seemed natural for Bill, following his graduation from Paschal High School, to study medicine.

Dr. Lorimer did both an internship and surgical residency at Cook County Hospital in Chicago. That was quite a learning experience with its 3300 patients and 100-plus beds to a ward. Chicago's weather made almost as great an impact on the Texan. While other young doctors counted the months and years left in their residency, Lorimer counted the number of winters he had yet to endure. Despite the icy winds blowing off Lake Michigan, he braved the weather for an additional year as an instructor on the Faculty of Surgery before returning to Fort Worth.

In January 1948, as a new doctor just starting out, he assisted Dr. Herbert Thomason on a daily basis at the Beall Clinic. With no automobiles available so soon after the war, he walked from the clinic to the Medical Arts Building where he shared an office with his father until the Lorimer Clinic was established in 1950.

As he perfected his medical techniques, Lorimer began to see his father in a different light. He told a group of colleagues, "The one man I wanted most to emulate in my practice. . . was my father. I learned from him the true meaning of the *art* of medicine. . . . I was soon to learn by his example that the art of medicine is as indispensable as the science of it. . . . the best physicians are those endowed not only with the latest knowledge and skills, but with compassion and human understanding."[43]

Because of his desire to stay current on the latest in surgery, Lorimer attended numerous professional meetings and participated in seminars and the exchange of research papers. In 1950, he helped found the Fort Worth Surgical Society.

One example of his never-ending quest for knowledge resulted in him becoming the Director of the Tarrant County Tumor Clinic. Asked by Dr. Porter Brown and Dr. May Owen to lead the weekly cancer forum, he did so for ten years. Explaining the purpose of the clinic, he said, "Doctors from all over the county brought their problem cancer cases for discussion. Besides many wonderful learning experiences, early contacts and professional friendships were made that were to last a lifetime."[44]

Two physicians who faithfully attended the weekly sessions were Dr. Joe White and Dr. Herbert Thomason. They sponsored his election into the Texas Surgical Society, an organization that promoted the presentation and discussion of advances in surgery. Of Dr. White, whom he described as "my surgical father" he said, "I revered him not only for his role as a surgeon and literary scholar, but also as a fine example to young surgeons."[45]

Lorimer became legendary for his innovative surgical skills. Making use of the latest technology, he often videotaped rare surgical procedures to use in teaching situations. Among firsts in Fort Worth, he performed the first liver resection, pioneered early vascular surgery and the first renal dialysis. On these and other topics Lorimer published some twenty papers in professional journals.

Awarded the Gold-Headed Cane in 1987, he harked back to his childhood in his acceptance speech. "'I am indeed grateful to have been selected for this honor. I am privileged to enjoy vivid memories of a boyhood filled with the presence of doctors like C. O. Terrell, L. O. Godley, R. G. Baker, and R. J. White, all colleagues and personal friends of my father, and Gold-Headed Cane recipients.'"[46] He credited these men and the Cane's donor, Dr. Porter Brown, with helping young doctors get started in very difficult times and establishing the tradition of a unified and friendly medical community.

"Today's young doctors must have a passion for the science of medicine,"[47] he said recently. This is a subject close to his heart, as sons W. S.,III and Douglas, follow in their father's and grandfather's footsteps, making three generations of physicians.

Dr. Lorimer, Sr., in his last days, lived with his son. After witnessing his father's death, Bill, who retired in December 1989, became interested in one's experience during death and dying. In 1990 he lent his talents to the Community Hospice as Medical Director. His philosophy is to enable the terminally ill to die without pain, but with dignity. Not surprising for a man who has devoted his life to the well being of his community.

★ ★ ★

JOHN D. PUMPHREY

The John D. Pumphrey family certainly qualifies as a multigenerational family of doctors. His paternal great grandfather began his practice in 1848 and his maternal grandfather also was a doctor. John's father began his Fort Worth practice in 1928. A. B. Pumphrey, Sr. was one of the first board certified OB/GYN physicians in the city.

John's brother, Andrew, followed in his father's speciality and John became a urologist. Their uncle, J. B. Cummins, practiced medicine until his death at age 100. John D.'s son, John A., is also a urologist.

John D., the future doctor, first viewed medicine from a different perspective—as a patient. Prior to the Sabin and Salk vaccines, young John was stricken with polio after joining friends at a swimming party. He suffered a light case with no lasting disability, but for three days his temperature spiked to 106^0 accompanied by hallucinations. Many years later on a cold, wintry day, the former patient handed out sugar cubes laced with the vaccine that would wipe out the dread disease.

John D. Pumphrey might have been a writer had he not been surrounded by stethoscopes. Indeed at any early age he was a published writer. A student of Julia Kathryn Garrett, the Arlington Heights Junior Historian penned an essay for *Down Historic Trails of Fort Worth and Tarrant County.* He researched a pioneer cemetery. "In this cemetery, marked with a white marble monument, are the graves of the Isbell family, Paul Isbell, his wife and his two sons. Paul Isbell was man of distinction in the early life of Fort Town, for he became a famous Indian fighter as well as a prosperous farmer and slave trader,"[48] he noted.

Instead of pursuing a literary career, John went to medical school at Galveston, interned at Charity Hospital in New Orleans and did his residency in Louisville, Kentucky. He recalled those days as long and arduous, but filled with educational opportunities. "I enjoyed it all— everybody I knew was doing the same thing so I didn't look at it as hard work,"[49] he said in a recent interview. He saw the necessity for long hours during that period as the only way hospitals such as Charity with its 1800 bed capacity could manage. Even before Medicare and Medicaid, Pumphrey said, "People were taken care of, no one was left in the gutter to die."[50]

Pumphrey reminisced about the not-so-good "good old days. "Before air conditioning, surgeons operated very early in the morning. Dr. Jack Daly performed four or five operations before it got hot."[51]

Another reason for early morning operations was to prevent an explosion in the OR. He remembered with a chuckle, the days when all OR personnel wore grounded shoes, and all metal tables had ground chains that dragged the tile floor— to avoid sparks.

"Most anesthetic agents were dangerous at high temperatures. When the thermometer reached 90^0 in Louisville, they canceled all but emergency surgeries."[52] At All Saints, a nurse was stationed by the open window, fly swatter in hand, to deal with uninvited guests. A St. Joseph Hospital surgeon operated sans shirt under his scrubs. This was better than the kitchen table surgeries of Bacon Saunders' day, but one willingly relegated to the past. Pumphrey began his Fort Worth practice in 1962. "Thankfully, air conditioning was commonplace,"[53] he recalled.

His patients ran the gamut of society. "One day in my office I had the chief of police and the head of the organized crime scene at the same time,"[54] he commented. They not only didn't have a shoot-out, they were in fact civil to each other. When pressed about the less upstanding member of society, Pumphrey said the man, in readying himself for examination, removed the gun from his belt, and the one from his sock, and placed them on the table with his clothes.

John D. Pumphrey is now happy in retirement and the only gangsters he sees are the ones on television.

★ ★ ★

John M. Richardson

"She saw the basket among the reeds and sent her maid to bring it. When she opened it, she saw the child. He was crying, and she took pity on him."[55]

John Richardson has cared for thousands of babies over the years, keeping some well and saving the lives of others. Thousands of babies state-wide will be saved because the South Side pediatrician became alarmed at the number of babies being abandoned and decided to do something about it. He shared his concerns with his niece, Judge Deborah Richardson. She agreed with her uncle there surely must be a better way, but warned it would involve changes in the Texas Family and Penal Codes.

Dr. Richardson, a member of St. Andrew Catholic Parish, sought the support of Bishop Joseph Delaney, Cook Children's Medical Center and the Children's Hospital Association of Texas. Austin attorney Bob Leonard, Jr. and Representative Toby Goodman, who chairs the Texas House Juvenile Justice and Family Issues Committee, became interested.

Representative Geanie Morrison, from Victoria, and Senator Jane Nelson of Flower Mound, carried the bill to provide a way for desperate mothers unable to care for their newborns to deliver them into the care of the state without endangering the babies' lives. Called the "Baby Moses law," it allows licensed emergency medical service providers, such as firemen or hospital staff, to take possession, without a court order, of an infant up to one month of age, when the parent voluntarily delivers the baby to the agency with no intent to return for him or her. The parent will not face legal action of abandonment and the child will be safe. A win-win situation according to the law's backers.

Governor George W. Bush signed the bill, the first in the nation, July 2, 1999. John Richardson was there to witness the result of one more way in which he serves the needs of children. "In a sense it is a throwback to the idea of a foundling home, where children could be left with the promise that a caring home would be provided,"[56] he told the *North Texas Catholic.*

Since then Richardson has spent time telling about the Baby Moses Project, including speaking at the April, 2000 meeting of the National Council for Adoption in Washington, D.C. He reported the message was well received nationally and even a television crew from Germany interviewed him about this effort to save babies. An article in *Our Sunday Visitor,* noted that Minnesota was considering an "abandoned baby" bill, and "Similar bills have been introduced in 22 other state legislatures."[57]

Richardson, the youngest of six children, is the son of Dr. James J. Richardson, an eye, ear, nose and throat specialist. In his family are two dentists and one medical technician. Being constantly around medicine, "I always thought I would be a doctor,"[58] he said. He spent the early 1950s in the Navy as a hospital corpsman stationed at Annapolis in the pediatric ward and out-patient clinic. There he made his life choice.

When Mrs. Richardson asked the most fun part of his medical training, "It was hands down pediatrics,"[59] her husband said.

Back in civilian life, he attended Texas Wesleyan College and then on to Southwestern Medical School in Dallas. Richardson took the first straight, rather than rotating internship at Dallas' Children's Medical Center. He began his Fort Worth practice in 1964. In addition to his private practice, he also served as pediatrician for the Edna Gladney Home, a position he held for twenty-nine years. He estimated he evaluated about 9,000 infants prior to their adoption.

Richardson is one of the few doctors who remains in a single physician practice, and one who takes Medicaid patients. His baby-friendly office on the near South Side sports white wicker furniture with floral covered pillows. His practice includes patients from both ends of the socioeconomic spectrum, and his impact on their lives is long lasting. "It's always rewarding when an adult comes up to me and says, 'Oh, you were my baby doctor.'"[60]

John M. Richardson, MD, goes beyond caring for babies to caring for the community. Courtesy Dr. John Richardson

The Fort Worth native throughout his career has sought ways to improve the welfare of children. He wondered why bright children were not doing well in school. His training included working with Dr. Lucius Waits of Dallas in evaluating learning problems of the young. This was in the early 1960s, before dyslexia was a household word. Richardson became the first physician in Fort Worth to evaluate these children in his office, exploring why they were having problems with reading. But more importantly he went beyond that. Gathering a group of eight to ten mothers, most of whom had degrees in elementary education, he formed a tutoring cadre. "First thing you know," he said, "Mary Ann Key organized them and that's how the Key School started."[61]

At first they met in Richardson's office, with Mrs. Richardson supplying the home-made cookies. He ordered books and arranged for the group to attend training sessions. Key recalled, "He would clear a path, with a phone call, or twenty if necessary."[62] He recognized the need for a school and Key opened one. The Key School's 100 children now have access to twenty language therapists. He serves on the board, and his advice is treasured because it's "from the heart as well as the mind,"[63] Ms. Key said.

Another caring effort brought about the WARM Place. "It's been a Godsend for so many. You just can't believe how we got that started,"[64] he recalled. A friend's daughter, Meghan, aged nine, was having a difficult time coming to terms with the death of her fourteen year old brother, Michael. Her parents appealed to Dr. Richardson for help. He advised them to find a support group. As a result of their search for grief support, they discovered there was no such program for children in the community.

The natural place to start such a program was at the American Cancer Society since cancer was the cause of Michael's death. Richardson called in some psychologists and social workers to "put together a twelve-week program to solve all a child's problems," he mused. A reporter from the local newspaper wrote a human interest article about the project and the next day Meghan's mother, Peggy Bohme, received about forty phone calls, only two or three being cancer related.

Realizing the extent of the need, Richardson and Mrs. Bohme approached the directors of Cook Children's Hospital and the Amon Carter Foundation. With the backing of these two institutions, they obtained the girlhood home of movie star Ginger Rogers on Cooper Street to house the program. After research and planning, the committee determined that an open-ended model for grief relief would be most effective.

Under the name of What About Remembering Me, Inc., they secured 501c3 non-profit status. Donations poured in. Thus the WARM Place came into being. Since its establishment in 1989 over 20,000 children and guardians have been helped through the grief process. Thanks to grants and financial support of donors, there is no charge to families.

Yet another effort that came to fruition was the establishment of the Ronald McDonald House. Realizing there were no hotels or motels near Cook Children's Hospital, and the inadvisability of parents trying to sleep sitting in their children's sick rooms, Richardson worked with others to meet this need. The Ronald McDonald House is a home/hotel for the families of children needing moderate to long-term care. Located in the Hospital District, the large facility provides as near a home-like atmosphere as possible at a reasonable cost. "It's so nice to be able to take a bath," said one parent of her small, but comfortable quarters.

For these and many unnamed deeds his peers honored him with the Gold-Headed Cane in 1994. With characteristic modesty, he commented to reporter Lou Chapman, "I'm just amazed. I have been around Fort Worth a long time, and I have taken care of a lot of doctors' children, and a lot of doctors' grandchildren. But I've not had a high profile in the county medical society. I'm really surprised."[65]

Dr. G. Douglas Tatum explained doctors have faith in Richardson, so they entrust their children to him. When asked how he manages to do so much community work and still take care of all those babies, he responded, "I don't play golf."[66]

Richardson helped in many ways to make Fort Worth a better place. But it is for the Baby Moses Law that citizens should be most grateful. Of that bill, he said, "It just shows that a small group can make a difference with the right support."[67] One might add, "And with the tenacity of a caring pediatrician such as John Richardson."

* * *

MAL RUMPH

Demetrious M. Rumph was born in 1883. A graduate of Stephenville High School, he took his premed education at the University of Texas. After graduating from the University of Tennessee in 1908, he returned to Erath County. Dr. Rumph came to Fort Worth in 1913. He became a leader in political circles, was president of the North Side Civic Association and a member of the Fort Worth City Council in 1937. Dr. Rumph chaired the City-County Hospital Board. Always one to speak his mind, he was described as "colorful" by both admirers and detractors. The doctor died in 1958.

His nephew, David Maltravers Rumph answered to "Mal." The son of a physician and nephew of five physicians, he was born in Mansfield, lived for a time in Fort Worth, moved west and graduated from Cisco High School. After an internship and residency in obstetrics and gynecology at Emory University's Grady Memorial Hospital, he settled in Fort Worth in 1934 and practiced medicine until 1985. In that almost half century he cared for as many as five generations of some families.

Members of the medical society recognized Rumph in 1983 by designating him the holder of the Gold-Headed Cane. In an interview, reporter Carolyn Poirot noted, "The recipient of the Tarrant County Medical Society's highest honor believes the most important aspect of his medical education was learning to empathize with his patients."[68]

Warren Moorman, in handing over the Cane, described Rumph as a doctor, ". . . who believes the heart of medicine is getting to know the patient, and that comes from a family deeply rooted in the tradition of medicine."[69]

Responding, Rumph revealed his philosophy, "I feel I have a good rapport, a true liking and a deep respect for all my patients, and this enables me to be a more effective physician."[70] Another honor came his way in 1983. *Private Practice*, named him "Physician of the Year."

Dr. Mal Rumph died in 1987 at the age of seventy-nine.

★ ★ ★

ART RUTLEDGE

Dr. Art Rutledge ran his hand through a shock of gray hair as he recalled his more than fifty years in medicine. The internist's grandfather and uncle were physicians and he credits them with arousing his interest in medicine. Asked when he got interested in medicine, he thought for a moment and replied he couldn't remember a time when he didn't want to be a doctor.

The 1944 University of Oklahoma graduate served an internship at the Bethesda Naval Hospital and later at Aieu Heights. This hospital, just above Pearl Harbor, had a capacity of 7,500 beds. The multiplicity of combat injuries from Iwo Jima and other war zones provided the young doctor with a wide range of experiences.

Out of the Navy, Rutledge visited Fort Worth, not expecting to stay. He did a residency at All Saints Hospital, where he met and was impressed by doctors affiliated with the Terrell Medical Group. He stayed.

The Oklahoman specialized in internal medicine and, except for teaching and helping the residents at John Peter Smith, made All Saints his home base. Concerning his early work, in a 1998 video of the history of All Saints, Rutledge recalled, "When I started the older doctors seemed to take it upon themselves to advise us,. . . on such things as how to act, how to dress, what not to do, in other words how to be doctors. This caring attitude made the young doctor feel a part of the All Saints 'family.'"[71]

Rutledge has seen tremendous progress in medicine. He cited antibiotics and vaccines as dramatic breakthroughs, but noted a less spectacular event has had equally or greater impact. "The public health system—clean drinking water for example—is terribly important."[72]

Of his many patients, one he remembered clearly. A well-known Fort Worth gangster one night asked Dr. Rutledge to go see his elderly, ailing mother. They left the office and the man offered, "We'll go in my car if you'll go around and get it." Dr. Rutledge realized the danger of a car bombing and replied, "If you don't mind, we'll go in my car."[73]

They went to a home just off Henderson Street near First, which at one time was a silk-stocking neighborhood. His patient, a woman about eighty-five-years-old, asked if he had read *Gone with the Wind*. He replied that he had, and also saw the movie. She said, "Well, I lived in those days." She went on to tell of riding paddle boats as they raced down the river and of being carried as a seventeen-year-old bride across the threshold of the house where she still lived. "A memorable lady," he recalled.[74]

Another memory involved the founder of a major oil company. This man was a good friend of Dr. T. C. Terrell. The year was 1949 and Mr. Mac, as he was affectionately called, still robust at age seventy-five, asked Rutledge how many boys his father had in the service. The young doctor answered, "Three of us, and a son-in-law makes four." Mr. Mac said that wasn't bad, but he had 160. He let Rutledge in on the joke. "He had become wealthy well before World War I and at the end of the war he established two orphanages in Enid, Oklahoma—one for boys and one for girls. The children's fathers had died in the war. Of that group all served in World War II. 'His boys'"[75]

It was after World War II that Rutledge and another veteran, Dr. Emory Davenport, joined the Terrell Medical Group. It was the beginning of a fifty-four-year relationship—without a fuss they hasten to add.

Not only were they partners, their sons are now partners. Dr. Brian C. Rutledge and Dr. N. Alan Davenport are both specialists in internal medicine. Like father, like son. And for that Fort Worth patients are grateful.

★ ★ ★

BURGESS SEALY

Young William Burgess Sealy's first responsibility was opening the gates so "Old Red" could pull the buggy up to the farm and ranch houses as Dr. T. Richard Sealy made his rounds. Burgess, as he was known, later literally helped build his father's hospital in the tiny Coleman County town of Santa Anna. "I carried the brick and hod for part of the building,"[76] he related in an interview. He worked at the hospital during vacations doing various tasks, including assisting his father in surgery. Seeing the good his father did, "There was never any doubt about me becoming a doctor."[77]

Sealy attended the University of Texas Medical School in Galveston. A member of the honorary medical society, Alpha Omega Alpha, he graduated in 1934, exactly thirty years after his father graduated from the same school.

Burgess was a fellow at Mayo Clinic when the elder Dr. Sealy died. The hospital was sold to the city for $10,000. The year was 1939—still hard times for farmers and ranchers. In keeping with his father's wishes Sealy and his brother forgave over $100,000 in debts owed to the beloved Santa Anna physician. But for nearly twelve years Mrs. Sealy occasionally received $10.00 and $20.00 checks in the mail.

Soon after the beginning of World War II, the Mayo Clinic organized a medical corps unit. Sealy served on the South Pacific island of New Guinea until the war's end in 1945. Out of uniform, he visited a medical school friend, Dr. Holland Jackson, in Fort Worth.

Dr. Charles Harris convinced the young man to make the visit permanent. He remembered Harris' words. "Son, there are several of us here who are going to retire pretty soon and if you are not here to get the business then somebody else will,"[78] Sealy said in a *Tarrant County Bulletin* interview. Charles Harris, Joe White, Herbert Thomason and a few other surgeons had been doing the bulk of operations back then.

Returning veterans, including Sealy, looked to Dr. White for guidance. "I'd never done a hypertrophic pyloric stenosis (a thickening of a muscle that obstructs the emptying of the stomach); I read up on it, and talked to Joe White—he'd done a lot of them. I asked him if he'd assist me on it. He said, 'Yes, on the *first* one, after that you're on your own,'"[79] Sealy recalled in a 1987 *Tarrant County Physician* interview.

When Sealy began his practice there were no doctors on staff in the emergency rooms. At Harris he spent one week-end a month in the emergency room. At other times if he got a call, he had to go treat a trauma patient. Mrs. Sealy remembered one such night. She and her husband had been out to dinner. This was before beepers and pagers. He called McMillen Answering Service and sure enough he was needed at the hospital. STAT! A well-known Fort Worth man had been shot. Mrs. Sealy dropped him off at the hospital. Dr. Sealy waded through a gaggle of reporters to get to the emergency room. It took him all night, but he saved the man's life.

There were times when his skilled hands were to no avail. Asked how he coped with the death of a patient, he said, "You must learn to accept it. You change the things you can change, the others you accept."[80] Sealy recalled one patient who was ready for death. He visited her, held her hand, and tried to ease her pain. "She kept asking, 'How much longer?'" He told her he not very much longer. She smiled and said, "Oh, goody, goody."[81] She died shortly thereafter.

During his forty years as a Fort Worth surgeon he witnessed many changes in medicine. Sealy and other physicians depended on the Tarrant County Medical Society to keep them up-to-date on medical advancements. We met once a month and everybody went. Someone gave a paper each time on a scientific subject."[82] This was especially helpful he explained, because right after World War II they had been without much scientific exposure, so they read, gave talks, and discussed medicine.

The advent of subspecialists and improved equipment led to more delicate techniques in medicine. These required additional training. For example, chest surgery was virtually unknown when Sealy was in medical school. Seeing the need to know the procedure he went to St. Louis for a week of observation and practice in thoracic surgery and anesthesia. He returned and performed the first lung operation in the city. This became a pattern for Sealy. He read the literature, attended meetings and learned from others the latest surgical skills, then used them to save lives.

Despite his busy surgical schedule, Sealy actively promoted nursing education. For many years he served as chairman of the board of TCU's Harris College of Nursing. In 1977 Mrs. Anne Burnett Tandy funded a cancer nursing section as part of the Learning Resources Center in his honor. He also served on the TCU Board of Trustees and that same year was awarded an honorary doctorate by the university.

Of the many honors Sealy has received, the Gold-Headed Cane was very special because it meant recognition by his peers. Paying tribute to his father, Sealy noted there were problems facing the medical profession, but "When I was watching my father, I didn't see the problems. All

I saw was him enjoying his practice, even though he did work all the time."[83] Problems and all, he still sees medicine as the best career choice a person can make. Speaking of the Cane, "This is the greatest thing that ever could happen to a man in my profession,"[84] he told colleagues and friends gathered at the Colonial Country Club dinner.

In 1999 the American Cancer Society honored Sealy, in his eighty-ninth year, for volunteer work and support. They named him Hometown Hero for his fifty-one years of dedication to the organization—a fitting tribute, but he was already a hero to his grandchildren.

Throughout his distinguished career Sealy made time to be with his wife, Beverly, their son and three daughters. Then in his well deserved retirement, he was the ultimate grandfather. Dr. Sealy died May 23, 2001 at the age of ninety-one.

★ ★ ★

John Trenton Tucker, Jr.

One father/son duo shared offices, names, and a combined ninety plus years of practice. John Trenton Tucker, Sr. was born in 1893. His father was affiliated with a wholesale drug company which later became Southwestern Drug Company. His decision to prescribe pills rather than manufacture them led the Central High School graduate to Baylor Medical School and additional study at the Mayo Clinic. He interned in New Orleans and at Fort Worth's St. Joseph Hospital.

In the early days of his practice he was associated with Drs. E. P. Hall and Bacon Saunders. Once, in 1924 while helping Dr. Saunders with a major operation, the pioneer physician collapsed and fell across the operating table. Tucker finished the surgery without further mishap, but Saunders never fully recovered his health.

Dr. Tucker, a designated surgeon for the Santa Fe and Rock Island Railroads, had many minority patients. It was a hallmark of his character that he always treated them with dignity and respect. They in turn held him in high regard.

He practiced at St. Joseph Hospital and wrote the history of that institution for *The Medical History of Fort Worth and Tarrant County*, edited by Dr. L. H. Reeves.

John Trenton Tucker, Jr. majored in pre-med at Texas Christian University and became a lifelong Horned Frog fan. He graduated in 1944 from Southwestern Medical School in Dallas. Affectionately known as "Tuck," he did an internship and residency at St. Joseph Hospital.

He was inducted into the Army and sent to Percy Jones Hospital in Battle Creek, Michigan. Six weeks later the Army transferred him to Camp Stone and he went overseas in 1946.

The young doctor was shipped to occupied Japan in the midst of a severe typhus epidemic in the Tokyo-Yokahoma area. He was in charge of a large district where he worked with Japanese doctors. After four months the epidemic subsided and Tucker, one of thirteen physicians, flew to Pusan, Korea to fight a cholera outbreak there. Back in the United States, Captain Tucker oversaw the Poly Clinic at Ft. Lewis, Washington until his discharge.

In 1948 he joined his father in the practice of family medicine. "They constructed a building on land they owned on West Third Street in downtown Fort Worth. The two officed there until 1975 when they moved to the new Professional Building on South Main across from St. Joseph Hospital,"[85] according to Mrs. Tucker. Their former offices were torn down to make room for the Fort Worth Central Library.

It was not uncommon for the children of Dr. Tucker, Sr.'s patients to become the patients of Dr. Tucker, Jr. The old-timers, however, stayed with the doctor they had known for so long. As Dr. Tucker, Sr. aged, he relinquished surgical and other duties to his son, but continued to counsel and prescribe for his loyal, older patients.

As was the custom, "Tuck" on the morning of January 8, 1976, stopped by his father's home to give him a ride to the office. A widower, Dr. Tucker, Sr. had died in his sleep. "He loved his work and worked until the day he died,"[86] his daughter-in-law said. He was eighty-two-years-old.

Dr. Tucker, Jr. practiced for thirty-nine years, including those years alone after the death of his father. With his kind, friendly personality, he developed a special rapport with his patients, just as his father had done.

Typical of his easy manner was the time a school teacher, his patient for more than twenty-five years, went to the office after being exposed to hepatitis. Her principal recommended she get a gamma globulin shot.

"You know I'm left handed and I don't want a sore left arm, so give it to me in my right arm."

"If you were exposed closely enough for a shot I'll give it to you in your cheek," he said.

Instinctively, her hand flew to her face.

"No, not that cheek."

"Oh, *that* cheek," she blushed.[87]

J. T. Tucker, Jr., was a member of the Tarrant County Medical Society, the Texas and American Medical Associations, and a fellow in the Academy of Family Practice. Both he and his father devoted their lives to their patients. However, Dr. Tucker, Jr's life was cut short at the age of sixty-seven. He died of cancer after a short illness in 1987.

★ ★ ★

JOHN WIGGINS

Brothers John and Kenneth Wiggins' grandfather was a physician in Munday, Texas at the turn of the century. Their father was a banker in the small Parker County town of Peaster, but they and several cousins followed in grandfather's footsteps. John became a respected pioneer in the treatment of lung and respiratory diseases, and Kenneth had a long and successful career as an internal medicine specialist. Both went to medical school in Galveston, but then their paths diverged. Kenneth did an internship at Wisconsin General Hospital in Madison, and John became a patient at the tuberculosis sanitarium in San Angelo.

John Wiggins planned to be a general practitioner. Following medical school he interned at Parkland Hospital. When he could no longer attribute his fatigue and shortness of breath to long hours at work, he had chest x-rays made. The results were frightening, because in 1937 tuberculosis was a leading cause of death. At age twenty-four he needed healing, and he put his plans to heal others on hold.

Interviewed at the time of his receiving the 1974 Gold-Headed Cane, he recalled the incident to *Press* reporter Jean Wysatta, "Bed rest was the prime treatment. Sometimes doctors collapsed the lung, putting air between the chest wall and the lung. Sometimes they took out ribs,"[88] For six months his regimen consisted of bed rest and a nourishing diet. His health improved, and he changed his mind about the future. He decided to specialize in diseases of the chest. For the next four years the Parker County man worked at the sanitarium. He divided his residency into half days working at the hospital and half days regaining his health.

Finally given a clean slate, Wiggins, nicknamed "Wig," came to Fort Worth in 1941. He was the city's first chest specialist, according to brother Dr. Kenneth Wiggins, also a Fort Worth physician.

Much of his work was bronchoscopic. Examples of foreign objects he removed, John told reporter Wysatta, were cedar bark, grass and tiny plastic wagon wheels. "There was one person I felt the sorriest for. It was the mother of a little boy. She kept telling him not to eat from a dish of peanuts.

"He kept on though and she slapped him. He aspirated a peanut and had to have surgery."[89]

Empathizing with patients was one of his trademark characteristics. "He was intellectually honest without arousing undue anxiety,"[90] Kenneth remembered about his brother.

When time permitted Wiggins could be found on the golf course at Colonial Country Club. It wasn't his swing or his score that caused heads to turn—Wig played golf left-handed. Friendly and outgoing, he loved to tell a good story, some of which never made it into his pastor's sermons.

The recovered TB patient saw many changes in the treatment of chest diseases during his practice. He told *Star-Telegram* reporter Jon McConal, "With the advent of drugs and the new tools we have to work with, it's an entirely new ball game."[91] Tuberculosis was no longer the deadly threat it had been, but new illnesses took its place.

Wiggins worked diligently to educate others about the nature of lung diseases. He never hesitated to express an opinion, and he was sounding the dangers of smoking long before scientific proof supported his contention. He believed chronic bronchitis and emphysema were eight to ten times more prevalent among those who smoked. "Cancer of the lung is 35 times more common among smokers than non-smokers," he told McConal. Noting the strength of nicotine addiction, he told of a man in an oxygen tent following surgery. "He tried to light a cigarette and set himself on fire."[92]

After thirty-three years of medical practice, including being medical director at Elmwood Sanitarium until it closed, Dr. John Wiggins in 1974 received the Gold-Headed Cane. Modestly he thanked those gathered at Colonial Country Club, and declared himself undeserving, but deeply honored.

Dr. Wiggins liked to distribute little leaflets that summed up his challenge to the youth of the 1960s. Friend and reporter Mack Williams shared some of them.

"—I would like you to look and see some of the most remarkable people who walk the earth.

—These, your parents and grandparents, are people who in just five decades have, by their work, increased your life expectancy approximately 50 percent, while cutting the work day by a third, have more than doubled per capita output.

—They are the people who have given you a healthier world than they found, and because of this you no longer have to fear epidemics of flu, diphtheria, smallpox, scarlet fever, measles or mumps they knew in their youth. Once-dreaded polio is no longer a factor, while tuberculosis was virtually stamped out. . . .

—And if your generation can make as much progress in as many areas as these two generations have, you should be able to solve a good many of the world's ills.

—But it won't be easy, and you won't do it by tearing down or belittling. You may and can do it by hard work, hope and humility, and faith in mankind.

—Don't knock it! Try it!"[93]

After a lengthy illness, John Wiggins died in June 1981. In eulogizing the physician, Rev. Albert Pennybacker told of another example in which Wiggins was held in high esteem.

". . . he was named to an honorary life membership on the board of directors of the American Lung Association of Texas, only the fifth person to be so honored." The minister summed up his life by saying, "But the essence of his work—his life—was not in associations and degrees and honors. His life has been in people. He was diligent, decisive, caring, wise in making them breathe with health. The respect afforded [by his peers] was a respect born of the years and the person, not demanded by his manner or position. . . . John Wiggins was a rare, precious, good man."[94]

CHAPTER NINE

MAY OWEN, MD: FIRST LADY OF FORT WORTH MEDICINE

"She liked to tell the story that her parents were expecting a boy, and didn't have a name in mind for her, so they just selected the name of the month when she was born May 3, 1891, on a farm in Falls County in central Texas,"[1] Dr. John H. Smith wrote. Near the end of her long life she reluctantly allowed Ted Stafford to record her story.

Her mother's health failed after the birth of her eighth child. Young May held the country doctor's visits with awe. "It wasn't the man as a person that fascinated me as much as his profession devoted to helping people and the education he had received to become a doctor,"[2] she told Stafford.

May entered the first grade in September 1897. In the small community schoolroom she experienced the greatest thrill of her young life—learning. An excellent student, she became an avid reader. The family Bible was the only book in the Owen household. The precocious child read the entire Bible several times. When someone loaned her a book, she would seek out a quiet spot and devour her treasure.

After the death of her mother, May's father grew even more remote and strict with his children, especially this strong-willed girl. He expected her to milk the cows and work along side her older brothers in the fields. When these duties were finished, he allowed May to do her schoolwork.

As she grew older, most of the care of the livestock fell on her small shoulders. She related to the animals. Stafford wrote, "Often when she walked across the pasture, the cows and horses would come to meet her and follow her to the house. There was a rapport there that no one else in the family had."[3] She became the family veterinarian. At times she stayed in the barn all night, nursing a sick animal. "Usually by morning the animal was on its feet, and May could get the milking done before getting ready for school."[4]

She became friends with the county veterinarian. When she confided a desire to be a vet, he hoped to lower the expectations of the eight-year-old. He would say, "Maybe by the time you grow up a school would accept females." He really had no such expectations, but he did give her a stack of old veterinary journals as a sop to his conscience.

On Saturday, May 3, 1900 the reed thin girl with soft brown eyes picked a time when she had her father's undivided attention. That time came after he admired a new calf she helped deliver. Stafford recreated the conversation.

"Dad, I have decided I would like to be a doctor." He scoffed and declared, "That is the most ridiculous idea I have ever heard." He ended the conversation by telling her to get that silly idea out of her head. A pain she endured all her life was the realization he never approved of her work, never acknowledged the accolades given her.

In the spring of 1904 May graduated from the little community school. For the next eight years she worked on the farm. Louis, an older brother, came to her rescue. He arranged for her to attend Texas Christian University. At that time the school offered high school courses in its academy as well as traditional college fare. She would have a work/scholarship to pay her tuition. The twenty-one-year-old farm girl was about to enter high school. In a rare moment of sentiment her father said, "We'll miss you, May. You have always been the best hand I have had in the cotton patch."[5]

May's job was to monitor the girls living in Jarvis Hall. Older and taller than her charges, they presented no resistance to her authority. And May discovered heaven on earth—a library filled with books. "I was determined to read every one of them,"[6] she told her biographer.

As if classwork and riding herd over a dormful of girls weren't enough, her father wrote of the difficulty of getting the cotton crop in. He enclosed train fare home. May returned home every Saturday. She picked cotton until dark, and again all day Sunday, and into the night if the moon provided enough light. Early Monday morning she boarded the train for a week of classes. She followed this routine until all the cotton was picked.

May's grades were the highest in the academy. The university granted her a work/scholarship for her degree. The college freshman graded chemistry papers, worked in the biology and chemistry labs, and occasionally taught a class. Throughout her college years, she refrained from social activities, believing they would not further her education.

Dr. Truman C. Terrell of Terrell's Laboratory, needed a student to do unappealing, mundane tasks. May took the job. The relationship grew from professional to personal and for the rest of her life the Terrells became the warm family she had been denied as a child.

She cared for the experimental animals and served as a courier between doctors and the lab. "I must have walked a thousand miles in that job, but I enjoyed it. When a doctor had a specimen to be examined, he would call, and I would be sent out to get whatever it was, then rush back to the technicians for examination."[7]

After obtaining her degree, and with the insistence of Dr. and Mrs. Terrell, May applied to several medical schools. No matter how the rejections were worded, they said the same thing. They did not admit women. Giving up on medical school, she applied to Massachusetts General Hospital in Boston to study nursing. Again she was rejected. She kept the letter. It said, ". . . . Your university grades are excellent. . . . but it is our opinion that you are not a well rounded person since you have no extracurricular activities. . . ."[8]

While pondering what to do about her future, a letter arrived that led to the next great event in her life. Louisville Medical School accepted her—the first woman accepted by the school and the only female in her class.

May was frugal. She saved eighty to ninety per cent of her laboratory salary, yet she did not have enough money to see her through medical school. When the Terrell's loaned her the needed money, she took out a life insurance policy on herself with her mentors as beneficiaries. This she did in case of her death prior to the loan repayment.

Before she left for Kentucky, May went home for a short visit. Things had changed little on the farm, and her father's low opinion of her desire to be a doctor was as strong as ever. She told him of being accepted in medical school. Stafford wrote, "His comment was, 'I still can't understand why you are doing it.'"[9] And he never did.

With the exception of a young black man from New York, all her classmates shunned her. For weeks they were visibly cool, but grudgingly realized she was no threat to them.

Medical school was even more challenging and thrilling than she dreamed possible. When topics were taught the men thought would be an embarrassment to the lone female, she was excused from class. They took notes for her. May, with her quick mind and experience as the family veterinarian, had no trouble passing tests on the "delicate" material.

Busy years passed quickly. The graduation ceremony for the class of 1921 began. Stafford noted, "When the dean called out, 'May Owen, Doctor of Medicine,' the entire class stood and applauded as she made her way to the stage."[10]

Now thirty, the long hours—and a sixteen hour day was not unusual—were attempts to make up for the lost years of her youth. Work became the center of her life. If any of her colleagues told a "May Owen" story, it almost always revolved around work. Dr. David Pillow remembered how very early every morning, Dr. May, carried her sack lunch, walked the short distance from her Hotel Texas home to Terrell Laoratory. Many days she worked through the dinner hour. The hotel kitchen staff would prepare a light meal, even after closing time.

Another told a work story of a winter day when the city was virtually shut down by an ice storm. At daybreak Dr. May was seen slipping and sliding from parking meter to parking meter on her walk to the lab.

Terrell Laboratory served doctors in both human and veterinary medicine. Two events elevated Dr. Owen in the eyes of area vets. Working in Terrell's North Texas Pasteur Institute lab, she and others developed a rabies vaccine. Moreover, she tested suspect animals locally rather than sending all animal heads to Austin, and expedited matters by telephoning results rather than relying on slower, less certain mail, as the Austin labs did.

In the fall of 1931, stockyard officials asked Owen to help diagnose a disease that caused the death or severe illness of sheep in the feed lots. The officials told her the animals had been fattened on molasses cake to improve the flavor of the mutton. She discovered the sheep suffered from diabetes and published her findings in veterinary journals. It changed the way sheep were fattened, and made her a celebrity. Sheep raisers as far away as New Zealand and Australia lauded her work.

Perhaps her greatest contribution to medical science was the discovery of the dangers of glove powder in the operating room. In 1935 Dr. Hodges McKnight consulted with Owen about a patient. He found an unidentified substance growing in her abdominal cavity. Medical records showed the woman had undergone surgery to remove a diseased appendix two years prior to her present problems. At first her recovery was satisfactory, but within a year she developed severe cramps and vomiting. By the time she sought Dr. McKnight's help, her abdomen was distended and she was in constant pain.

McKnight sent sample tissue to Owen for evaluation. Under the microscope she detected within the fibrous tissue a number of cells with cores of small, irregularly distributed, colorless-to-light-brown crystals. These would not stain like the rest of the tissue. Through the process of elimination, she ruled out any foreign bodies that might have been left from the appendectomy. This led her to examine the talc used in gloves during surgery. She used one hundred rabbits and talc taken from all local hospital operating rooms to reproduce the adhesions. Talc proved to be the culprit.

Owen presented her research, "Peritoneal Response to Glove Powder" at the 1936 State Medical Association meeting. The assembled doctors gave her a standing ovation. Later that day the Texas State Pathological Society awarded her a certificate of Meritorious Research. Her paper was published in the *Texas State Journal of Medicine* in November, 1936.

After World War II she hoped some of the returning servicemen would go into medicine. Four, who became the first of "May's boys," were Charles Rush and David Pillow, followed by Bruce Jacobson and Earl Brewer, Jr. In an interview Rush explained how they worked in the lab, doing blood counts, urine analyses, and other medical tests.

Rush worked from six p.m. until midnight, every other night, went to school year round, and graduated with a degree in chemistry in three years. Owen wanted him to go to medical school, and with her financial and moral support he did.

David Pillow's boyhood dream was to become a doctor, but the dream got side-tracked. In 1941 he joined the Navy as a hospital corpsman. Five years later, June of 1946, the veteran began working for Dr. Owen. "When I came back from the service . . . I needed to work." Married, father of one child and another on the way, he applied for a job at All Saints Hospital. "I had been trained in lab work in the Navy and Dr. Owen hired me to work at Terrell Laboratory."[11]

With a small family to support, the GI Bill funds helped, but were not sufficient. Dr. Owen loaned Pillow money. "It was never real formal, I never signed a note or anything. . . . When I needed money I would call her and she would write a check."[12] He kept his own records. Her only stipulation was the loan would be repaid when he could.

From this simple arrangement grew the May Owen Student Fund, which she created in 1986. In a rare moment of making public acknowledgement of her philanthropy, she wrote the following:

Why I Have Shared

"I have been committed to a medical career since I was nine years old. It seemed then—as it has always seemed and likewise seems now—that through medicine, I can best help people. Does it not follow then, that I would want to do everything possible to help people who aspire to follow medicine? Without help, financial and otherwise, I could never have attained my goals. As long as I live, there will always be an 'accounts payable' to which I am dedicated; that is, I shall always have a commitment to help aspiring medical students. . . .

Dr. Owen went on to describe how she set up the fund and concluded with these words:

"Sharing helps me maintain an optimistic view."[13]

And so a woman born in the nineteenth century, gained renown in the twentieth, is still helping students in the twenty-first century.

In 1974 she endowed a Chair in Pathology at Texas Tech University Health Science Center. A Fiscal Year 1999 Endowment Report shows a market value of $1,056,029.10.

May Owen, MD, a farm girl who became world famous for her research.
Courtesy Charles A. Rush, MD.

Dr. Owen also was interested in education closer to home. She attended a meeting at the Fort Worth Town Hall in 1964 and heard the need expressed for a junior college for the county. For the next year or two she worked behind the scenes to get one established. Bill Lace, writing of the origin of the college, related, "She was shocked when asked by a member of the Chamber of Commerce committee working on the project if she would be a candidate for the first Board of Trustees."[14] Assured by attorney Jenkins Garrett she would not have to campaign, she agreed. Dr. Owen was elected, and served as secretary from 1965 until her death in 1988.

By 1980 the administrative offices had outgrown their leased space. Plans were drawn up for larger quarters. Stafford offered the following account of how the new center got its name, "Mr. Chairman, [John Lamond said] I would propose that the new building be called the May C. Owen Tarrant County Junior College District Center."[15] Owen objected on two counts—one, she had no middle initial, and two, she didn't think it should be named after a person. The board out-voted her. The only change in the name was the elimination of the initial "C" which saved the college five dollars in sign expense.

"In addition to her involvement with TCJC, [now TCC] she helped establish a School of Medical Technology at All Saints Episcopal Hospital . . . ,"[16] according to Lace.

In *Momentum* he wrote, "Her long-term dream of a museum of health for Fort Worth took form through her work as chairman of the Health Fair Committee of the Tarrant County Medical Society in 1963."[17] It led to a medical wing at the Museum of Science and History, appropriately called the Dr. May Owen Hall of Medical Science.

Education was her emphasis as the 1960-61 president of the Texas Medical Society, its first woman president. She also was the first woman president of the Tarrant County Medical Society. Owen believed in supporting organized medicine. Not only did she join, she attended meetings. Dr. John Smith told of one. "Years ago she was due at a meeting in Galveston, but was stranded at the airport in Houston with no transportation. She stuck her thumb out and hitchhiked to Galveston, arriving with just minutes to spare."[18]

In 1986 she was elected to the Texas Women's Hall of Fame, one of only thirteen women so honored. The relatively new Gold-Headed Cane Award was presented to her in 1952. Stafford wrote, "She was so taken by surprise when her name was called . . . she could not believe she heard it."[19] Gathering her wits about her, she thanked them for the honor.

In 1963, sixty years after the farm girl cared for her father's livestock, the American Veterinary Medical Association made her an honorary member. Charles Rush believed this a fitting tribute to a woman who, of all the things she did, especially enjoyed working with animals.

The Texas Society of Pathologists named Dr. Owen the 1985 Caldwell Award recipient. This honor, the highest paid by the organization, also recognized her as one of very few women in the field.

Despite the heights reached in professional circles, and advancing age, Owen continued to do what she loved most—working in her lab. Even a broken hip failed to slow her down. She slipped on loose gravel at St. Joseph Hospital in 1985. With typical good humor, she quipped, "If it had to happen, I picked the right place."[20] Wanda Stowe, her secretary, went several times a week to take dictation while Dr. Owen recuperated. After her recovery, the pathologist resumed her full schedule.

In December 1986, she fell in the self-service elevator of the Hyatt Regency (formerly the Hotel Texas) and injured her spine. She spent Christmas that year in the hospital. On January 31, 1987, Emory Davenport, her personal physician, discovered a heart problem in the ninety-five-year-old woman. He ordered an extension of her hospital stay. Stafford related, "As she had done in the past, she complained that she should be at work instead of occupying a hospital bed, but she took Dr. Davenport's advice and stayed."[21]

Friend Catherine Terrell Smith converted two storage rooms at All Saints into an apartment. Happy to be back in a medical environment, Owen exclaimed, "It seems I have come full circle now since I began my career at All Saints when I went to work for Dr. Terrell in 1917, and now it is home."[22]

For the rest of her life she maintained her office and living quarters at the hospital. She "slowed down" to ten or twelve hour days, but continued to consult with hospitals in neighboring towns too small to have staff pathologists.

And she allowed Ted Stafford to spend hours with her as she reminisced about a near century of living.

"You know," she told her biographer, "the funny thing is that some of the people I have known through the years always felt sorry for me because I am a single woman, and they thought . . . I must be a lonely woman. But I have never been lonely in my life . . . . Who has time to be lonely or bored when work has been as fascinating as mine?"[23]

Work was important to her, but she enjoyed many friendships as well. She was a doting "aunt" to the Terrell youngsters. She liked children and the children of her associates, such as the Rushes, Pillows and Jacobsons, were the beneficiaries of her warmth. Wanda Stowe, her long time secretary, recalled Dr. Owen's fondness for her two daughters and that love was reciprocated by the girls.

Dr. Owen counted as friends some of the leading families of the city. Isabelle Newberry, a daughter of Dr. Porter Brown, said Dr. Owen was a regular visitor in their home. As often as she chose, she was a dinner guest in the home of the Amon Carters, the Staley McBrayers and others.

Dr. May Owen died April 12, 1988. In a poignant tribute Dr. John Smith wrote, ". . . and the day before she died she made her usual trip to Dublin as their consulting pathologist. We should all be so lucky—to work at something we love to do, until the day we die, at age 96."[24]

Star-Telegram columnist Jeff Guinn noted at the time of her death in 1988, "A list of Dr. Owen's professional honors could fill 10 of these columns . . . ."[25]

Honored by thousands, she never received the words she yearned to hear—her father's praise. Yet it may be only a slight exaggeration by Dr. David Pillow, one of "her boys" when he summed up her life. "She was the most fantastic woman who ever walked the face of the earth."[26] To which Dr. Charles Rush added, "Amen."

PART THREE

THE PAST
FIFTY YEARS—
CIRCA 1953-2003

CHAPTER TEN

WOMEN IN MEDICINE: THE REAL DR. "MOMS"

In 1864 Ann Preston, M.D., tried to fill requests from small towns and cities for "reliable lady physicians," but requests outnumbered the available doctors. Dean of the Women's Medical College of Pennsylvania, the first of its kind in the world, Preston attempted to enlist more women into the study of medicine. Dr. Susan Rudd Wynn, in writing on the history of women in medicine noted, "Society wanted and needed more doctors, but rarely considered women when it came to formalized medical training."[1]

Thus, twenty years later only a handful of schools admitted women students. Those that did, limited the number to a token four or fewer per class. Women physicians sought to counter this discrimination by establishing women's medical colleges, complete with dispensaries and hospitals to provide opportunities for clinical training. By 1900 women physicians numbered a mere four or five percent.

Maude Russell, DO, practiced in Fort Worth from the early 1900s until her death in 1921. Her career is chronicled in the chapter on osteopathic medicine.

Women made little progress in the first half of the century. After the women's movement of the 1960s things began to change. By 1970 the number of women who applied to medical schools quadrupled. Wynn wrote, "In the fall of 1989, women comprised over 39 percent of the students entering American medical schools, compared to only 9 percent exactly 20 years earlier."[2] The September 6, 2000 *JAMA* reported 45.2 percent of 1999–2000 applicants to U.S. medical schools were female, with 42.4 percent graduating.[3] Predictions are that men and women medical students will be in equal numbers by 2010.

This chapter profiles women who made and are making important contributions to the medical community.

★ ★ ★

Catherine Kenney Carlton, DO

Professionally Catherine Carlton, DO, made great strides, but geographically she didn't go far. Her clinic is at the exact location of her family home. The Kenney family moved from Laredo in 1920 when Dr. Charles Kenney realized his daughter spoke Tex-Mex, but not English. They settled on Lipscomb Street and in 1933, during the depths of the Depression, moved their family practice to their home. "'I grew up on this corner,' referring to the office where she had practiced for 55 years and where she and her husband had a new building constructed in 1953,"[4] Catherine was quoted in the *Kirksville Magazine*.

When Dr. Carlton began, she delivered babies at home. She spoke Spanish and many of her patients were Hispanics living in "the river bottoms." She told reporter Madeline Williams, "'One time after I had delivered a baby by lamp light in the barrios on the Northside, I returned to my car to find it stuck in the mud on an unpaved street.'

"Not a good place for a young woman in her 20s to be stranded."[5] Neighborhood men came to her rescue, got the car out of the mire and saw her to a paved street. However, none of her visits compared to one her mother made.

"When she (Dr. Helene Kenney) graduated she heard they needed doctors in Laredo," Carlton recounted her mother's story. The year was 1910 and Dr. Kenney offered her services to the border citizens. "One day, when Mother was on her way to see a patient, one of Pancho Villa's men grabbed the reins of her horse, demanding she give him the animal. She whacked him across the shoulders with her buggy whip and said, 'Get out of my way. I'm on my way to deliver a baby!' He backed off and she went on her way,"[6] Carlton recalled. Including her parents, she has nineteen relatives who are doctors.

In an interview Carlton recalled being one of five females in medical school. They studied together and made better grades. After graduation they remained in contact with each other for years. "We stuck together like a covey of quails."[7] As one of the few females in her dissection lab, frequently she found distinctly male parts in her lab coat pockets, put there by male students trying to embarrass her. When she refused to be alarmed the tricks subsided.

The twenty-three-year-old took her state boards in Austin, again one of five women. She remembered someone asking, "What are you doing here?. . . .We (the women) passed. We knew we had to pass,"[8] she told an interviewer.

World War II took many of the male physicians. Also, her father died during that time. She and her mother continued their practice. They saw sick people during the day, and nights and weekends as well. The hard work paid off in acceptance by the community. Now Dr. Carlton cares for some who have been her patients for forty years.

In 1997 the Texas Society of the American College of Osteopathic Family Physicians named Dr. Carlton outstanding practitioner of the year. Another honor, Kirksville Alumnus of the Year Award, came her way October 30, 2000.

Carlton welcomes the advances in pharmacological science, but maintains that good health is a "three legged stool." Good nutrition, good structure and a good state of mind are the three components by which she swears. In her more than sixty years in medicine she has seen many changes. When she began in 1938 the only two medicines that were used then and still used today are morphine and quinine. Because there were no antibiotics then, pneumonia and influenza were treated with packs on the chests, mentholatum and manipulation. Still sprightly, Dr. Carlton has no plans to retire as she embraces the present and remembers the past.

★ ★ ★

Nelda Cunniff-Isenberg, DO

Although Nelda Cunniff married young and raised a family, she didn't give up her interest in science and health as a career. She obtained a degree in nursing from John Peter Smith Hospital in 1963. Five years later she graduated from Texas Wesleyan College, cum laude, with a bachelor of science. Six years after that, she was in the first graduating class of the Texas College of Osteopathic Medicine. Because her children were older, one in junior high, one in high school and one in college, Cunniff didn't encounter the same problems as medical student moms of young children. Yet it was not easy for her. She did not have a high school education as a foundation, and had been out of school for several years before she continued her disrupted studies. Innate ability and acquired determination allowed her to succeed.

The petite physician began as a nurse in surgical recovery at the old Boulevard Hospital on Camp Bowie. She enjoyed nursing, but sought to advance in health care. If she went into administration, however, it would take her away from patient contact, which she considered important. From a lab technician she heard about the new Texas College of Osteopathic Medicine. She applied and was accepted into the first class—the only woman student.

When asked what it was like being the only female in her class, she responded, "For me, it was better than for some because I'm not confrontational with males. I was treated very well."[9] Older than most students, she was the "mother" figure and enjoyed a warm camaraderie with all. What she remembered most about her medical school experience was the dedication of the faculty and staff and their determination to make the college thrive.

Dr. Cunniff graduated in 1974 and did a rotating internship at Stephen-Park Hospital in Dallas.

For twenty-five years she has practiced in Burleson. Asked by reporter Angelique Siy what she liked best about her work, Cunniff answered, "As a D.O., I enjoy the hands-on manipulation. I enjoy interacting as a family physician with the patients and getting to know whole families,"[10]

Dr. Cunniff was elected president of the Texas Osteopathic Medical Association in 1998, the only woman president in more than fifty years. She was the first president to be a graduate of Texas College of Osteopathic Medicine, and only the second woman from Tarrant County to hold that office. "My goal as president was to bring osteopathic families in Texas closer together,"[11] she said in an interview. She saw her presidency as an avenue to help osteopaths maneuver in managed care and HMOs as limitations to good patient care conflicted with bottom line economics. While she welcomes the advances in medicine, she cautions, ". . . we're able to practice the best medicine in the world, but if we take out the heart and soul and spirit we're not treating the whole person and we will have lost a lot."[12]

Dr. Nelda Cunniff-Isenberg loves medicine and feels she is meant to do what she does now. "I tend to be a little proud of that,"[13] she told reporter Siy.

★ ★ ★

DOROTHY PATRAS, MD

To a trivia quiz question, "What Fort Worth doctor watched the Pentagon being built?" the answer is Dr. Dorothy Patras. "Riding the bus to Emergency Hospital in the fall of 1941, we detoured down various streets, depending on where the construction blocks were,"[14] she said in an interview.

Pennsylvania native Dorothy Patras obtained her medical education in four stages. The seventeen-year-old Franklin High School graduate took the business track, and in 1936 landed a job in a doctor's office. Her employer asked if she would be willing to take some courses to enable her to do lab work. It would mean more money, so she went to chemistry class at her high school, then to the office, and back to an afternoon class in biology. She found she liked the laboratory work. That was step one.

Patras learned that with one year of college and one year of hospital training she could take the examination to become a medical technician. With financial help from her father, a school grant, and a part time job, she enrolled in Grove City College in southwestern Pennsylvania.

From there she was accepted by Temple University's School of Medical Technology. After earning a Bachelor of Science degree in 1941, Patras took a job at the old Emergency Hospital in Washington. D. C. In 1944 she heard of a position at Harris Hospital in Fort Worth. Their affiliation with Texas Christian University sounded like her experiences at Temple and she applied.

Dr. John Andujar, impressed by her resume, hired her. For several years she worked with him at Harris and when he opened his pathology lab. But Patras wanted more education. The aspiring pathologist applied to Southwestern Medical School in Dallas.

Ten of the 100 applicants were women. When asked by the advisory committee about the possibility of marrying and dropping out, she countered with humor. "Gentlemen, I'm thirty-three-years-old. I'll stand on my record." They questioned her because of the lag in time since she had been in school. She informed them that in the interim she had done some teaching, "and you had to stay one page ahead of your students" so her study skills were intact. The committee, satisfied with Patras' desire to succeed, admitted her.

And so she began the third step of her educational odyssey in 1952. Patras graduated in 1956. After a two year residency at Bellevue Hospital in New York, she did another residency at Cincinnati General Hospital. From these extended residencies she qualified to become board certified in both anatomic and clinical pathology.

Patras returned to her job with Dr. Andujar at the Fort Worth Medical Laboratories on Pennsylvania Avenue. Much of their work involved serving as consultants to hospitals in Azle, Glen Rose, Graham, Jacksboro, Mineral Wells and Stephenville. Because she traveled so many miles every year and depended upon reliable transportation, her favorite automobiles were Cadillacs. "When I had to be in Mineral Wells at 7:00 a.m. I knew I would get there,"[15] she said in an interview. She is still loyal to Cadillacs.

Active in professional organizations, she served as a Tarrant County Delegate to the Texas Medical Association for twenty years. In 1974 she was president of the Texas Society of Pathologists and five years later that organization selected her to receive the coveted Caldwell Award.

One of her long time hobbies has been always having a camera at hand during conferences and meetings. Now retired, the silver-haired energetic Pennsylvanian-turned-Texan is busy organizing photographs to display at the forty-fifth Southwestern Medical School reunion.

Would she encourage a young person to go into medicine today?

"Yes, but let them know there will be some problems along the way." If they have the spunk of Dr. Patras they will handle them.

★ ★ ★

MARGIE B. PESCHEL, MD

Dr. Margie Peschel's delightful stories of her life in medicine could be a book unto itself. Asked at what age she decided to become a doctor, she told of a Christmas long ago. "I was five and Santa brought me a nurse's kit and my four-year-old brother a doctor's kit. My mother said I threw mine across the room, declaring 'I want to be the doctor.' Mother wisely said, 'Santa must have made a mistake,' and she gave me the doctor's kit. My brother got the nurse's kit."[16] She grew up to be a doctor, he became an engineer.

On a more serious level, when asked why she became a physician, she recalled a beloved, sickly grandmother who seemed to be better after the doctor visited. "It made me want to do something like that—to make people better."[17]

Margie B. Peschel, MD, famous for her collection of hats as well as her contributions to the medical community. Courtesy Tarrant County Medical Society archives

The Georgetown University premed student was accepted in medical school at Galveston. She recalled, as a twenty-year-old, her encounter with her first cadaver.

"I had been there two weeks, and with an anatomy professor who did not think women belonged in medical school. I started on the head and neck. I accidentally opened the jugular vein. I decided if I go out, I'm going out in style, so I got my little stool—I got out my blue embroidery thread and I sutured the vein.

"'What do you think you are doing?'

"Oh, Dr. (she couldn't remember his name), you see that cute little jugular vein? I think I opened it, but I'll close it. Let me tell you how I'm going to close it. This is a French knot. Do you know how to do a French knot? It's a very difficult stitch.' The whole class was watching. 'Let me show you how to do it—I'm closing it and it'll be just perfect.'

"He said, 'Get off that stool.'

"I thought, 'Oh God, I'm going to get thrown out.'

"He said, 'Were you a Girl Scout?'

"'Yes sir, I was a Girl Scout.'

"'I want you to get off that stool, get down on your knees, give me the Girl Scout sign and swear to me you'll never be a surgeon,' and I did. And now you know why I'm a pathologist."[18]

At Harris Hospital in a rotating internship, she found herself enthusiastic about every phase. "When I was in pediatrics I wanted to be a pediatrician—when I was in obstetrics I wanted to be an obstetrician," she reminisced. "One day," she said, "Drs. (T. H.) Thomason, (DeWitt) Neighbors and (Burgess) Sealy sat me down and suggested I try a year in pathology because of my curiosity about everything. I respected their interest in me —a lowly intern. I did a pathology residence and it was like a whole new world."[19] She had found her niche. Peschel readily gives credit to those who mentored and helped her along the way. She named Drs. O. J. Wollenman, W. S. Lorimer, Jr., Warren Moorman, and R. J. White as influencing her by their professional actions.

She worked as a pathologist at St. Joseph Hospital for about ten years. One of those years was the seventy-fifth anniversary of the Catholic institution. When hospital administrator Sister Mary James indicated they needed to do something special, Dr. Peschel suggested having a Mass at the new downtown Convention Center. The next thing she knew, non-Catholic Margie Peschel was planning an elaborate service in a non-church setting. "But I went out to Holy Family (church) and I measured behind the altar to see if we could get three bishops back of there, and the priest said, 'When was the last time you were at Mass?'

"I said I've never been to Mass."

The night before the celebration she and Sister Mary James took one last look at the arrangements. On the way back to the hospital, with a twinkle in her eye, the nun said, "You know, Dr. Peschel, if you and I hook a left turn right now we could be in Mexico before this takes place."

"But not being a Catholic, I forgot the Knights of Columbus. They showed up, and I said, 'I'm so glad you're here. We need ushers.' The TCU choir was there. It was a really wonderful experience,"[20] she recalled.

When asked about interesting patients, she related the following story from her days at the Carter Blood Bank.

"I got a call. . . . The patient had a severe infection and diarrhea. Specialists had been brought in, the patient's hemoglobin was dropping (and the caller) thought they were going to lose him. Would I help, he asked?"[21]

She discovered the "patient" was a horse and the doctor asking her assistance was a vet. The pathologist accepted the challenge and received some samples for cross matching. Peschel called Texas A & M, but they had never transfused a horse. The people pathologist was on her own. She knew how to transfuse a 150 pound human, but this "patient" weighed 1500 pounds. She worked out the ratio for the sterile coagulant needed for the compatible horse blood. The animal survived. Only later did she learn he was worth more than $225,000.

Dr. Peschel married and started a family before she began her practice. Her children never lacked for attention. Their father's work schedule allowed him to be with them when she was on call. "I also had the help of baby-sitters, who made more money than I did at times,"[22] she said with a grin.

Peschel balanced home and office with the same skill and meticulousness that was her trademark, all the time giving credit to others who helped make it possible. Her experiences led her to an appreciation of spouses—male or female—of doctors. As president of the county medical society, she placed spouses on committees, a first that is now routine.

A list of her other accomplishments and awards runs into multiple pages, but the high regard of her peers tells more about the kind of person she is. Her colleagues describe her as amiable, brilliant, charming, dedicated, and they could probably go through the rest of the alphabet with accolades.

In 1986 Dr. Peschel received the Gold-Headed Cane. As was her custom, in her remarks she paid tribute to others. "The words of Dr. Joe White. . . have guided me throughout my professional life. He said, 'If he is diligent and persistent in his efforts to improve and to realize his limitations and errors. . . if he is eager to help the younger men about him and pass on whatever ideas he may have'. . . ."[23] All who know her agree she exemplifies the best in her profession.

Peschel was a frequent contributor to the *Tarrant County Physician*. She wrote a column as Medical Director of the Carter Blood Center. She retired from that position in 1995 after nineteen years. In a touching farewell Dr. Peschel wrote, "Medicine. . .is. . .a life of study and discipline; but more than that, it is a life in which individual desires are secondary to the welfare of humanity. . . ."[24]

In retirement she will be able to spend more time with favorite hobbies—home-baked bread (she had bread in the oven as the author conducted this interview) and sewing. She makes most of her own, her daughters' and grandchildren's wardrobes. Decorated with French knots?

★ ★ ★

Blanche Terrell, MD

In 1923 Blanche Osborne told a lie. In front of her mother. The seventeen-year-old Utah girl with excellent high school grades was ready to begin her studies toward a nursing degree. But the Salt Lake City Presbyterian Hospital Nursing School required students to be eighteen years of age. Not wanting to waste a year of her life, Blanche said she was eighteen. She was admitted and years later characterized it as one of the best learning experiences of her medical career. "They (the supervisors) were so exacting; everything had to be done right, and that discipline I appreciated the rest of my life,"[25] she told an interviewer.

As early as high school her ambition was to be a doctor, but she spent several years as a registered nurse first. In 1929 she came to Fort Worth to be surgical supervisor at the new Harris Hospital. She ordered all the equipment for the eighth floor surgical suites and trained the nurses to staff them. The hospital administration created an apartment close to the surgery suite for the young woman so that if they needed her during the night she would be near by.

"It was over a blood transfusion that I met Dr. C. O. Terrell. . . ,"[26] she told Dr. Susan Blue in an interview for the *Tarrant County Physician*. He had a young patient who needed a transfusion but the girl's parents didn't have the money for the procedure to be done in the operating room. He asked Blanche to set it up elsewhere in the hospital. She did, but the room was too small for all the needed equipment and personnel to fit in comfortably. She asked when the child would need the next one, and said she would set it up in the operating room even if she had to pay for it herself.

From that encounter a mutual respect and admiration grew. She and Caleb O. Terrell, a widower, married in 1931. Their son Truman O. "Ted" was born in 1933 and his brother Jack was born in 1935. Blanche worked in her husband's office. She gave him credit for teaching her more than any formal medical education, and with his encouragement, she obtained a bachelor's degree from Texas Christian University.

In 1941 she entered the University of Texas Medical School in Galveston. Blanche worked nights as an anesthetist to help defray the cost of full time domestic help to look after the boys. In the summer Jack and Ted stayed with her in an apartment near the beach. She hired a young man to serve as their life guard while she was in class. After a grueling four years the determined wife/mother/nurse graduated.

Asked by Dr. Blue if she encountered any hostility in her efforts to become a doctor, she told of a dean informing her that he was ". . . opposed to women in medical school, to married women, and especially to married women with children."[27] She sent him an invitation to her graduation.

Dr. Terrell was the first woman to intern at Harris Hospital. After completing her residency in pediatrics she joined her husband in his practice. It was always a balancing act between her time with patients and time with her sons. After the death of her husband, the boys— now in their teens—went with her on emergency calls. If they hadn't had dinner, they got to choose where they would eat after she had seen the patient. This happened so often, ". . . the waitresses got to know and pamper them,"[28] she recalled.

Blanche Terrell loves children, including a lad who refused to take his medications. "He would knock the pills out of the nurses' hands. I told him if he took his medicine I would give him a puppy,"[29] she said in an interview. (Her poodle had just had a litter.) He didn't believe her, so late one night she sneaked a puppy into his room. Seeing was believing, he swallowed the pills, and when he left the hospital, she presented him with his reward.

Part of Dr. Terrell's work involved late night home calls or hospital emergencies. One or both of her sons usually went with her. Once—she didn't recall the reason—she answered a call to Cook Children's Hospital alone. About a mile from the hospital her car quit. It was 3:30 in the morning. Moments later a policeman tapped on her window. To the surprise of both, they knew each other. He was the father of one of her patients. "I guess God told me to come here because I don't know why I came this route." He took her to the hospital in his squad car, and when the emergency was over, she discovered her car in the hospital drive. The policeman had gotten it started and left it for her.

Dr. Terrell left her private practice for a while to serve the students of the Fort Worth Independent School District. Finding she missed the close relationship with patients, she returned to private practice after five years as Administrator of Health Services. Still later she joined her son, Dr. Jack Terrell, at the TCU Health Center.

For her work there, the university recognized the alumna by conferring on her an honorary doctorate of humanitarian service. The May 1982 citation reads, "Everyday she brings fresh flowers from her greenhouse to the Health Center; every day she *is* a fresh flower."[30] That is one of many honors she received for her untiring devotion to children. Citations and certificates would cover a wall if she choose to hang them.

Dr. Terrell retired in 1983 after almost sixty years in medicine. Dr. Blue, writing in 1984, observed, "She is a mature lady who commands respect just by her appearance."[31] At the turn of the twenty-first century she still does.

★ ★ ★

SUSAN RUDD WYNN, MD

When most thirteen-year-old girls were reading Nancy Drew mysteries or movie magazines, Susan Rudd devoured the "Home Medical Guide" cover to cover. She did not have a family legacy of doctors, but allergies and asthma as a child kept her in close touch with physicians. "They practically raised me," she joked. "I was always fascinated with life sciences, medicine, and would read every lay medical book I could get my hands on,"[32] she told an interviewer. By the end of high school Susan knew she wanted to be an allergist.

Susan R. Wynn, MD, the first woman to be accepted by the Texas A & M Medical School. Courtesy Tarrant County Medical Society archives

Texas A & M was just starting a medical program and she headed for College Station. The perky coed followed many interests—drama, music, and student government. A biochemistry major, she entered the medical program after three years as an undergraduate, but not without some hassle. The advisory committee criticized her for participating in extra-curricular activities rather than solely concentrating on academics. This infuriated her. "I have always felt and still do that the experience I got in student government and drama have made me a better doctor. Today the activities I have in the county medical society, TMA and AMA . . . make me a better doctor and help me better care for my patients,"[33] she declared. Just as she believed education was more than class work, the allergist–immunologist believes there is a lot more to medicine than what happens in the examining room.

Susan was the first woman accepted by the A & M Medical School, and one of seven women in the 1977 charter class of thirty-two. Recalling those days, she noted the men were totally accepting of their female colleagues. Being the first in a brand new school, all experienced a close relationship. The soon-to-be doctors took their clinical training at Scott and White Hospital in Temple.

After graduation Dr. Rudd interned at the Mayo Clinic. In addition to the pediatric internship she spent three more years there in an allergy residency and research program.

She was on the teaching staff there before she returned to Texas. Her job now, as she sees it, is to help patients live as normal a life as possible by controlling the attacks.

Wynn recalled a patient, a little girl, whose mother realized the child's asthma got worse when she played outside. The well-meaning mother's solution was to forbid the girl to go outside. Dr. Wynn's solution was medication, therapy and "a lot of encouragement for the mother" to allow the patient to play soccer with other children her age.

Dr. Rudd married a radiologist while in residency and is the mother two sons. Like other career women, she juggled her schedule to be with the boys as much as possible. As president of the Tarrant County Medical Society, Susan Rudd Wynn observed that one of the most interesting and challenging parts of being in a leadership position wasn't meetings or organizational duties. "It's combining the role of mom, chauffeur, chef, wardrobe mistress and social chairman along with. . .(the president's duties). . . and keeping your practice afloat at the same time."[34]

Her two sons are her top priority, and she oversees their homework, drives them to school every morning, and attends their ball games and other activities. But the boys' upbringing necessarily is somewhat different. She recalled in a *Tarrant County Physician* President's Paragraph essay, "I remember bringing my youngest son with me to a TMA Session when he was 5 years old. I had him join me on the floor of the House. . . . The Speaker . . . Dr. Bernard Palmer, gave us the eye at one point during the proceedings, and I braced myself for a scolding . . .about how inappropriate it was to have a mere child on the floor of the House. . . .(Instead, later Dr. Palmer remarked) '. . . Stephen's attention span was much better than some of the delegates out there.'"[35]

It's too soon to know if they will follow in their parents' footsteps, but Dr. Wynn said, "Whatever they decide to be when they grow up, I hope that they've learned how important their family is, and how rewarding it is to be involved in their profession and in their community."[36]

After twenty years in medicine Wynn is still as enthusiastic as when she was a first year student at Texas A & M. Asked if she would encourage a young person, male or female, to go into medicine her answer was an unequivocal "yes." She agrees that medicine is changing rapidly, but she sees exciting new things on the horizon. "Tomorrow's physicians should go into medicine with their eyes wide open to enjoy the many *wonderful* things about being a doctor."

With a smile, she elaborated. "I think that being a physician is the most rewarding, intellectually challenging, and meaningful career a person could have outside the ministry."[37]

CHAPTER ELEVEN

THE
GOLD-HEADED CANE:
DOCTORS' DOCTORS

When Dr. Porter Brown presented the gold headed cane to the Tarrant County Medical Society, the year was 1951 and some people thought physicians did not appreciate and support each other. Fort Worth medical historian Dr. William Crawford wrote, "Dr. Brown gave the cane so that we could have a banquet to show our solidarity, and at the same time show our respect for one of our members that we admired."[1]

The Greek god Asculapius believed illness was caused by evil spirits. To drive off those spirits, a healer needed to carry a staff. When he encountered a snake, he put the end of the staff on the ground for the snake to entwine itself around it. Then the healer hurled the snake as far away as possible, and with it the evil spirit.

Centuries later in England, doctors carried canes rather than staffs, as symbols of their standing in the community. Crawford noted ". . . during the eighteenth century a cane was part of his professional equipment and no good doctor would be seen in public or visit a patient without one."[2] The head of the cane was gold, silver or ivory and contained a cavity in which the doctors placed aromatic substances. Before entering homes of patients, they put a bit of the rosemary, or camphor in their nostrils, believing this would ward off contagion and lessen the impact of offensive odors.

Dr. Margie Peschel, in an essay on the history of the cane stated, "One such cane is a very famous Gold-Headed Cane, which, from 1689 to 1823, was continuously carried by the most outstanding London practitioners of the times."[3] The men who held the cane were: John Radcliffe (1689-1714), Richard Mead (1714-1754), Anthony Askew (1754-1774), William Pitcairn (1774-1791), and Matthew Baillie (1791-1823). Mrs. Baillie, following her husband's death, gave the cane to the Royal College of Physicians in London.

Dr. William MacMichael, who at the time was register at the college, wrote a famous book about the cane. Using first person point of view, as if the cane itself were telling the story, he told of the adventures of the doctors who had owned it. By doing so, he also told the history of medicine during the years 1689-1823. The book has become a medical classic. There have been twelve editions, including the 1912 edition with a preface by the famous surgeon Sir William Osler.

The cane given annually by the Tarrant County Medical Society was fashioned by the Haltom Jewelry Company. It is a resplendent work of art, whose beauty can not be captured by photographs. Each recipient's name is added to a gold band when it is passed to the next honoree. Dr. John Freese set forth his regard for the cane and those named to receive it. "To me the award honors someone who considers his work more important than his self; it honors a willing submission to the requirements and disciplines of the job; answering questions patiently and accepting responsibility for doing what can be done, even where the satisfaction of a successful outcome is unlikely." He went on to say, "The occasion of the Cane Award also affirms the fellowship of medicine. We all aspire to be accepted by our peers as being 'real doctors.' Physicians who have the satisfaction of that acceptance belong to what must be the greatest of all brotherhoods. The Cane Award brings out the best in our profession and helps us to identify what is real and what is important in medicine."[4]

It is impossible to think of the Gold-Headed Cane without paying homage to Dr. Porter Brown, a son and grandson of physicians. As a child Porter experienced suffering—he was a victim of polio, and while other boys in the small town of McGregor, Texas, ran, played and climbed trees, he coped with leg braces. Much of his time he spent riding in the family buggy as he and his father made house calls. From this association came his interest in medicine.

Once, while fishing by himself, he fell into the water. The heavy braces pulled him under and he almost drowned. When finally he crawled to safety, the boy removed the braces. With great effort he learned to walk,

Porter Brown, MD, initiated the tradition of the Gold-Headed Cane in Fort Worth. Courtesy Mrs. Isabelle Newberry, daughter of Dr. Brown

first with canes, then without aid. The only lasting effect of the polio was one leg shorter than the other, but his limp was hardly noticeable.

He began practicing in Fort Worth in 1924. Daughter Isabelle Brown Newberry recalled her father telling of the early days. He and Caleb Terrell officed in the downtown Medical Arts Building. One day they were in the barber shop there. "Caleb said, 'Porter, have you had any patients today?'" Brown replied, "'No, and we never will if you say things like that in public.'"[5] He joined Tom Bond and Terrell in establishing the Radiation Clinic. Ironically, all three died of cancer.

Brown's speciality was skin cancer. His practice grew to the point where he kept office hours on Saturday, and sometimes Sunday, to accommodate farmers and ranchers from West Texas. These men, and other outdoor, fair-skinned workers, seemed especially prone to develop the disease.

Fort Worth policemen were also patients. Due to their daily exposure they too were candidates for skin cancer. These men knew it was difficult for Brown to walk long distances on hard surfaces, so they "always managing to find" a close-in parking space for him at public events.

Brown was the only physician in town to have radium. Used in the treatment of cancer, he had two pellets which he kept in a lead container. One day he discovered one of the radio-active pellets was missing. Brown alerted the newspapers to let citizens know of the danger. Panic-stricken, he sent to Chicago for help. A man with a Geiger counter was sent down and for three days they searched unsuccessfully for the metallic element.

They gave up hope of finding the radium. Brown was driving the man to Meacham Field for a flight back to Chicago when the Geiger counter began to react. They found the pellet near the county court house. It seemed a patient accidentally rubbed against the pellet and it adhered to his sleeve. As he walked by the court house it fell off. A relieved Brown found it on the steps. The doctor typically shied away from publicity, but this event made *Time* magazine.

Brown was a scholar and knew of MacMichael's account of the gold headed cane. He presented a golden replica to the Tarrant County Medical Society and began a tradition that is still treasured fifty years later. Dr. Larry E. Reaves, 1999 society president, noted, "Recollections indicate this was made because of his admiration and in recognition of Dr. C. O. Terrell, Sr. Thus, the first recipient was deceased. However, it was intended for all subsequent recipients to be living at the time of their election."[6]

Members of the medical society annually received a voting list of eligible doctors. Brown requested there be no campaigning, and only the committee would see the votes. Another of Brown's stipulations was that he should never receive the award.

Dr. Blanche Terrell, widow of the first recipient, found a way around Brown's reluctance to be honored. She gave a dinner for him at the Fort Worth Club in 1958. Present were previous holders of the Gold-Headed Cane and their wives. Dr. Terrell presented him with a silver ice bucket, which now Newberry proudly displays in her home.

Porter Brown was a family man. He told his daughters, Isabelle and Edna, "I may leave you little else, but will hope to give you the best education I can offer." Indeed, both hold master's degrees. He told them something else, applicable beyond his family. "People are either leaners or lifters. Never be a leaner."[7]

Dr. Porter Brown died in March 1965 of cancer, a disease he fought all his medical career.

CHAPTER TWELVE

THE GOLD-HEADED CANE HONOREES: 1950-1980

THE DECADE OF THE 1950S

Dr. Margie Peschel penned an article for the *Tarrant County Physician* to commemorate the 1999 Fort Worth Sesquicentennial, about doctors and the medical society. Drawing heavily from her essay, of the 50s she stated:

"It was a decade of progress, everyone was better fed and better housed than ever before. Yet fear of the (atomic) bomb hung over the country like a black cloud.

"The society's membership in 1951 was 367. Carter Blood Center, brought about by the (medical) society and Carter Foundation, formally opened on Dec. 6, 1959.

"Additions to hospital facilities leaned heavily toward air-conditioned private rooms (at $12 a day).

"In September, 1953, the Fort Worth Academy of Medicine building was dedicated, providing the first home for medical activities in Tarrant County by the generous Amon Carter and the Carter Foundation. Polio was one of the most feared diseases. In April 1954, the society volunteered and provided Polio Salk vaccine immunizations. For the first time in the history of TCMS, an appreciation dinner for the auxiliary was held in December 1951.

"In September 1951, the Gold-Headed Cane Award was established with the recipient of this special award selected by ballot of fellow members."[1]

Drs. C. O. Terrell and May Owen, first and second recipients are profiled elsewhere.

* * *

Robert Joseph White, MD-1953

The doctors who knew and worked with Joe White held him in such high esteem their respect bordered on reverence. Dr. Dolphus Compere said of him, "Our greatest, best known surgeon. He was recognized by the Texas Surgical Association as one of the outstanding surgeons of Texas."[2]

White's interest in medicine harked back to the time in his youth when he assisted a doctor in a kitchen table operation. The Quannah native graduated from Yale in 1916 and took his medical education at Columbia College of Physicians and Surgeons. After his residency at St. Luke's Hospital in New York he moved to Fort Worth. The year was 1924 and he soon became the premier surgeon in the city.

Dr. White was an active member of professional organizations. He served as president of the Tarrant County Medical Society, the Texas Surgical Society, the Texas Society of Traumatic and Railway Surgeons, and the Southern Society of Clinical Surgeons. He chaired the Tarrant County American Cancer Society and was a member of the Southern Surgical Association. For fifteen years he was chief of staff at St. Joseph Hospital, and during World War II he served in that position at Harris Hospital. He was chief surgeon for the Fort Worth and Denver Railway for twenty-five years.

White's devotion to medicine went beyond scalpels and sutures. He considered surgery a religion in that it required total commitment and was his mission in life. The mission, he told *Star-Telegram* reporter Blair Justice, ". . . is to 'rescue' people—rescue them from sickness and, in some cases, from impending death."[3]

White recalled from his early practice one patient who asked permission to pray before surgery on his hand. Of course permission was granted. But White did not know the man was a camptown evangelist and when he prayed he shouted, perhaps giving God a better opportunity to hear him. "The halls of the hospital reverberated with the patient's voice as he invoked God's help. The prayer ended with 'Forgive them Lord, for they know not what they do.'"[4] White knew what to do and the surgery was successful.

The popular doctor expanded on his philosophy in a 1952 address to the Fort Worth Rotary Club.

He defined what a surgeon should be:

"If a surgeon is first a doctor and offers his people in trouble the support, encouragement and solace a good doctor should give,

". . . if he is diligent and persistent in his efforts to improve himself and the first to realize his limitations and errors,

". . . if he is eager to help the younger men about him and pass on whatever sound ideas he may have,

". . . if he has a fierce and instinctive personal and professional integrity, and is humbly grateful in his own way to his Creator for whatever talents for usefulness may have been given to him, I think he may hope to come to the end of the road serene, proud and happy to have spent his life as a surgeon."[5]

White's colleagues thought he met all of these qualifications and in December 1953 selected him to receive the Gold Headed Cane. In accepting the award, White told of his belief in the ethics of advising patients about the probability of recovery and the degree to which quality of life would be diminished. "If there is any chance of salvaging the person, or rescuing him, then certainly every means should be used. But when it is hopeless, the patient should be allowed to die with peace and dignity."[6]

Following his retirement, Dr. White and his wife, Marie, took an extended European vacation. While they were gone, friends in Fort Worth and Texas created the White Lecture Foundation to bring outstanding guest speakers to the city. The first year Dr. William B. Bean, Professor of Medicine at the University of Iowa, was guest speaker. He was followed by Dr. Denton A Cooley and other leaders in their fields.

Dr. White died December 17, 1976. He was eighty-two years old. The Fort Worth medical community lost a giant.

* * *

Robert G. Baker, MD-1954

Dr. Robert G. Baker never wanted to be anything except a doctor. Described as a very bright young man, he wasn't old enough to vote when he graduated from Baylor Medical School in Dallas. The twenty-year-old's father went to court to have his son's status as a minor removed so he could receive his medical diploma and license. Of his age, veteran physician Dr. S. J. R. Murchison said, "Bob Baker was born old," daughter Pat Baker recalled. "He was always accepted by his patients as a very mature individual, and had many patients that became personal friends,"[7] she added.

Baker entered Texas Christian University as a sixteen year old fresh man. After medical school he interned at Parkland Hospital, then returned to City-County (now John Peter Smith) Hospital for his residency. He later would serve twenty-five years as section chief of surgery there.

He officed on the seventh floor of the old Medical Arts Building in the early 1920s. He was well established in his practice, but the decade of the 1930s was difficult. During the depression he was often paid with black-eyed peas, if at all. "A lot of patients came back after they went to work in the war plant and pulled out a handful of money, saying 'Doc delivered my kid,'"[8] Pat Baker said.

For over forty years the general practitioner/surgeon served the community, gaining the devotion of patients and the respect of fellow physicians. When Baker was awarded the Gold-Headed Cane, reporter Blair Justice noted the doctor's first patient still came to see him. Not surprising, considering Baker's belief that a doctor must be more than a dispenser of medicine.

Justice characterized Baker as a kindly man who "feels that a doctor should never be in so much of a hurry that he can't sit down and talk with a patient about the patient's problems.

"By doing that, 'you grow into people's lives—you're their friend, their counselor. They turn to you in trouble,'"[9] he quoted the doctor. Baker felt this was part of being a family physician.

Pat and her sister, Beebee, in an interview, recalled some experiences growing up in the household of the popular doctor. "Friday night was our family night. We always went downtown and had dinner at the old Metropolitan Coffee Shop, in what later became the Milner Hotel." Then they went to a movie, often a western, at the New Liberty Theater. "He (their father) would tell the usher where he was (in case he was called to an emergency). He missed many a movie," Pat said. "There were times when he would go on whatever the call was and come back and get us—because it was usually a double feature,"[10] she added.

The Baker sisters remembered the war years as being difficult. Their father was one of the few doctors left to care for the growing civilian population. "He wouldn't have worked so hard if he had been in the service," they declared.

The war over, and more doctors to carry the load, Baker split his spare time between two main hobbies—fishing and golf. Beebee Baker Harrison reminisced, "He loved to fish, and with his deft surgeon's hands, he could filet a fish like none other. But, he didn't like to eat fish. He always gave them away."[11] One of Pat Baker's favorite photographs of her father shows him holding a massive double string of fish almost as long as he was tall.

By the late 1960s he was ready to relinquish his full time practice. He had already given up surgery, something that he prized, and now he spent only three days a week in the office. This gave him even more time to pursue his love of sports. Baker had lettered in college baseball and basketball, and of course he followed TCU football.

When Dr. Robert G. Baker died in 1980 the entire community joined the family in grieving for the loss of one of medicine's heroes.

★ ★ ★

THOMAS BURKE BOND, MD-1955

A fellow physician described Tom Bond as a radiologist a step ahead of most others in his field. So interconnected was he with radiology, Bond's life is profiled in the chapter on the Moncrief Radiation Center.

★ ★ ★

Edwin G. Schwarz, MD-1956

Lockhart native Edwin Schwarz gave no thought to becoming a doctor until he and a high school friend, nicknamed "Doc," spent a lot of time hanging around the local drug store. Both enrolled as pre-med students at the University of Texas. "Doc" flunked out and Schwarz graduated.

From Galveston he went to an internship at Bellevue Hospital prior to joining the Army Medical Corps. He was stationed at Carruthers Field near Benbrook. After the war he came to Fort Worth, via Cleveland, Ohio where he took post-graduate work in pediatrics. In 1919, he opened his office at the old Anchor Building at Ninth and Houston Streets. He told reporter Blair Justice, "I and the other early pediatricians here were what you might call trail blazers—we had to be . . . .Pediatrics had been taught at the old Fort Worth Medical College but no one was specializing in it."[12]

Most parents relied on family doctors to care for their children and some months Schwarz's income was less than twenty dollars. He augmented his fees by occasional poker games with old army buddies.

From the lean days of his beginning practice, Schwarz gained patients as mothers relied on his skill, but more importantly, they saw how he bonded with their children. Over the years he carved a niche in the hearts of Fort Worthians.

At the 1956 Gold-Headed Cane dinner, among the 300 guests were six doctors there to honor their "baby doctor."

A colleague praised Schwarz's dedication to three generations of Texans. His dedication was reciprocated, according to a quote in the *Star-Telegram*. "'Take my daughter. She's in California and she goes to her pediatrician and gets his remarks. Then she writes home and describes the visit and says "Ask Dr. Schwarz what he says." That's what they think of him.'"[13]

Tarrant County Medical Society President, Dr. Hobart Deaton, revealed Schwarz's achievements, including his authorship of a number of medical journal articles. "He was organizer of the Children's Clinic of Fort Worth Relief Association, which became the Children's Clinic of Peter

Smith Hospital; organizer of the Day Nursery, which later was taken over by the City Health Department; organizer of the original Baby Hospital, which is now Fort Worth Children's Hospital, and was chief of staff of Cook Memorial Hospital Center for Children."[14]

Accepting the accolades of his peers, Schwarz said, "I feel it a signal honor and it thrills and touches me more than I can tell,"[15] He gave credit to his wife and friends for any success he achieved.

In 1959 the Fort Worth chapter of the National Conference of Christians and Jews honored him. Dr. Frank Schoonover presented Schwarz with the traditional scroll. Reporter Ed Johnson quoted Schoonover's remarks about his longtime friend, ". . . he has worked in all kinds of homes in this community—Catholic, Protestant and Jewish. . . . he has brought great honor and distinction to his state and this community by his untiring devotion to the welfare of children . . . without regard to race, color or creed."[16]

Schwarz worked all day Sunday, October 14, 1962. He died at his home Monday morning. He would have wanted it that way. In his obituary, a *Star-Telegram* a reporter wrote, "Dr. Edwin G. Schwarz was a children's doctor—and a good one. It is probable that he will be remembered more for these evidences of genuine and unselfish concern for children than for his skill as a doctor of medicine, which was great."[17]

★ ★ ★

LOUIS OSCAR GODLEY-1957

The second pediatrician came to Fort Worth a year after Edwin Schwarz began his practice. Louis Oscar Godley built on the foundation of his predecessor. He had enough patients to earn $45.00 some months. In recalling his many years in medicine, he told reporter Maggie Droomgoole, "There was no specialist in anesthesiology here then and I made more by being an anesthetist that I did seeing patients."[18]

L. O., as he liked to be called, was born on a black land farm eight miles west of Corsicana, Texas July 12, 1885. He took classes at Summer Normal School in Corsicana and earned a teacher's certificate. From 1907 to 1909 he taught in the Navarro County Public School System.

Godley liked teaching school, but the plight of poor neighbors, racked by tuberculosis and malnutrition, spurred him to change careers. Reporter Blair Justice described the motivation behind it. ". . . Godley had 'always been interested in trying to do something for people,' [so] he decided to become a doctor. . . ."[19]

In an undated informal biographical sketch he wrote, "In Sept 1909 I entered The Fort Worth School of Medicine, which became The Medical Department of Texas Christian University, and from which I was graduated in May 1913. At the graduation I was awarded the Burt's Medal of Honor. Was also awarded a kit of surgical instruments; this award being given for the highest grade in surgery."[20] [Quoted as written, no editing]

To pay his tuition, Godley had gone back to the farm during the summers and picked cotton. Justice noted, "On a good day he could bag as much as 300 to 400 pounds."[21] At fifty cents per 100 pounds that was good money in those days.

From 1914 to 1920 he practiced in nearby Garland, Texas. While there, Godley's infant daughter became gravely ill and a pediatrician from Dallas had to be called in. She recovered and her father started to give serious thought to the need for specialists to work with babies. Years later he said to Justice, "I'd been told I had the disposition to be a pediatrician. I didn't know then it was about the hardest thing you can get into. You have to treat the mother and father and grandparents as well as the child."[22]

Again in his own words, "During the Summer of 1919 I did Post Graduate work at Harvard, and, right after Jan. 1st., 1920, I went to New York and did Post Graduate work at The Babies Hospital and Bellvue Hospital. . . . I then located in Fort Worth . . . . for the practice of Pediatrics."[23]

The early years were not easy. One winter he treated twenty-five children for diphtheria. Due to the lack of good sanitation, gastrointestinal diseases were common among his young patients. Before immunizations, treating smallpox, measles, whooping cough and lockjaw took much of his time. Reporter Dromgoole wrote, "Dr. Godley said the suggestion of sending a child to the hospital during the early days of his practice usually got this response from the parents: 'What's the matter, doctor, is he going to die?'[24]

When he was unable to get the child into a hospital, Godley gathered equipment and medications from the hospital and treated the child in the patient's home. Then he returned the equipment and continued making his rounds.

At the time of being named recipient of the Gold-Headed Cane, Godley for twenty-six years had been chief of the medical staff at Lena Pope Home. He served as chief of pediatrics at John Peter Smith Hospital, and on the staff of Fort Worth Children's Hospital for thirty-seven years.

Of his many experiences he once said, "I can't take them to the bank for collateral, can't eat them, can't wear them, but it sure feels good to do them."[25] And even today he is remembered for them. Dr. L. O. Godley died March 7, 1971.

★ ★ ★

DeWitt Neighbors, MD–1958

DeWitt Neighbors sang to his patients, familiar songs, ones they knew and could relate to. Colleagues said his songs did as much good as his medications.

He interned and did his residency at the hospitals of Johns Hopkins and Vanderbilt Universities.

In Fort Worth he shared an office with Dr. Sim Hulsey and the two became fast friends. Hulsey described his office mate as a "marvelous doctor and marvelous internist." After World War II they were among the first to leave the Medical Arts Building and buy a house on Fifth Avenue. They converted it to fit their needs as the patient load increased.

Dr. Neighbors served on the staff of City-County Hospital, now John Peter Smith, from 1931 to 1946. At the time he received the Gold-Headed Cane Award, he was on the active staff at Harris and the courtesy staffs at All Saints and St. Joseph's Hospitals.

In December 1958 friends and family gathered to honor the recipient of the Gold-Headed Cane. Dr. L. O. Godley said, "In Dr. Neighbors we have a man of high professional standing; a man of good citizenship;

a man from whom emanates good, personal friendship; a man of clear, strict personal integrity; a man of simplicity of heart and a man given to generosity. It seems to me that these qualifications eminently fit him to be our 'Doctor's Doctor' for 1958."[26]

After retirement, in addition to working on his farm, Dr. Neighbors played golf, with what he described as a "high handicap." At the age of eighty, he died in 1985 after a short bout with pancreatic cancer. Among the honorary pallbearers were Dr. Sim Hulsey and Dr. Nealie Ross, his former office mates.

★ ★ ★

CHARLES P. HAWKINS, MD-1959

Charles Pearre Hawkins wanted to be a doctor, but had to be a cowboy first. At five feet eleven, and weighing 125 pounds, the youth's family doctor deemed him too frail to withstand the rigors of medical school. Taking Dr. E. P. Hall, Sr.'s advice, Charles worked for a year on a ranch near Vernon. The physical labor and fresh air did the trick and the bigger, stronger twenty-one-year-old enrolled in the University of Texas Medical School at Galveston.

It was only his third school. His mother died when he was four, and an aunt and uncle, Mr. and Mrs. George Clark, raised him. The future cowboy/doctor received his elementary, high school and two years of undergraduate education at the old Polytechnic College, which taught all grades since there were no public schools in the area at the time. When that institution became Polytechnic Women's College, Charles transferred to Vanderbilt University. He graduated in 1914 with a B.S. degree.

Reporter Blair Justice noted, "Dr. Hawkins returned to Fort Worth to practice with . . . the same physician who prescribed ranching as a pre-requisite to medical school."[27] From 1921 to 1941 he was in general practice. With the advent of World War II, the forty-five-year-old was drafted into the military. He had been in the reserves, but still the call-up was unexpected. "I'd never been on a ship in my life, but I spent 2½ years in the South Pacific,"[28] he told Justice.

In 1946 he began to specialize in obstetrics and gynecology. He characterized getting up at all hours of the night to deliver babies as "routine."

That switch from general practice to ob/gyn caused at least one Fort Worth premed student to have some explaining to do. Hawkins delivered Don Boston and was their family physician for many years. When Don needed a letter of recommendation to enter medical school, he called upon his former family doctor. Hawkins wrote the letter extolling Boston's worthiness. "He has been my patient . . . ." The only problem, Hawkins used his office stationery—Charles P. Hawkins, MD, Obstetrics and Gynecology.

When not seeing patients, Hawkins enjoyed puttering in the yard. Interviewed by Jean Wysatta on the occasion of his being named president of the Tarrant County Medical Society, he told of a recent encounter as "yard man." It occurred in front of a big white house on Pruitt Street. A couple came up the walk and asked, "Is this Dr. Hawkins' office?"

"It is," replied the gardener with a smile. "But, the doctor is not in his office this afternoon. He takes off Wednesdays. Won't you go inside and make an appointment?"[29] Later, dressed in medical coat and not a trace of dirt beneath his nails, the "yard man" saw his surprised new patient and her husband.

After forty-four years as a leading obstetrician, Hawkins in 1964 moved to his retirement home in the Ouachita Mountains of Arkansas. He died in May 1978 at the age of eighty-three.

★ ★ ★

THE '60S

The decade of the 1960s was a turbulent one for the nation, but a productive one for Fort Worth doctors. According to Peschel:

"It was a decade of revolution. The baby boomers suddenly became a reverberating force for political and social change. It was the time of the New Frontier, the assassination of President John F. Kennedy, desegregation, Vietnam War and hippies.

"The society sponsored the Sunday Polio Oral Sabin Vaccine program. On four different dates, volunteer doctors provided the vaccine for all children in Tarrant County.

"The doctors conceived and helped develop the Child Study Center in 1963. The society sponsored the Heath Fair Sept. 14-22, 1963, at Will Rogers exhibit hall. More than 165,000 attended.

"The society aided its members to face the Medicare Law, which went into effect on July 1, 1966, and Medicaid which went into effect Sept. 1, 1967."[30]

★ ★ ★

Thomas H. Thomason, MD-1960

The first physician to receive the Gold-Headed Cane in the new decade was T. H. Thomason. "He was born March 2, 1895, the son of Dr. J. W. and Sue (Goree) Thomason. His paternal grandfather, like his father, was a physician, and his maternal grandfather, Major Goree, was a member of the staff of the Confederate Army's General Longstreet,"[31] according to the *Texas State Journal of Medicine*. Young Thomas considered becoming a college professor, but the pull of family ties was stronger. The third generation doctor graduated from the University of Texas, Phi Beta Kappa, in 1916. A scholar throughout his school years, the Huntsville, Texas native received his medical degree from Johns Hopkins Medical School. He graduated with Alpha Omega Alpha honors.

Thomason came to Fort Worth for a residency at Johnson and Beall Hospital. He began his practice of general medicine and surgery in 1923. When Frank Beall quit operating, he took over the surgery at Cook Hospital.

Thomason enjoyed growing camellias. Another hobby was boating. He was Commodore of the Fort Worth Boat Club in 1943.

Stricken at his home October 6, 1962, he died shortly after being taken to the hospital. The *Star-Telegram* obituary summed up his contributions and noted, "In 1960 the physician and surgeon was awarded the Tarrant County Medical Society's gold-headed cane and the title, 'A Doctor's Doctor.'"[32]

★ ★ ★

Joseph F. McVeigh, MD-1961

Joseph Fielding McVeigh stood tall among his associates. The 6'2" physician commanded admiration and respect for his artistic skills during college days. His drawings of complex cell structures in microscopic anatomy were the envy of premed peers at the University of Texas. And, he was a power to be reckoned with on the basketball court.

After graduating from Texas, he taught chemistry and zoology at Austin High School for two years. By 1915 McVeigh had saved enough money to continue his medical studies. He graduated from medical school at Galveston, then did postgraduate work at Barnes Hospital in St. Louis. Reporter Blair Justice wrote, "Dr. McVeigh said that by the time he finished a one-year internship at Charity Hospital in Cleveland there was a mild depression that made it inadvisable to start practice."[33]

He returned to teaching, this time at his alma mater. In addition to teaching anatomy at the university, he was interested in research. A project he did there later was cited by a Swedish doctor in a textbook on neurology.

In 1924 McVeigh felt the time was right to begin his practice. Specializing in internal medicine, he helped start the Coffey Clinic where he remained until his death.

He continued to teach and was dean of the St. Joseph Hospital School of Nursing for more than twenty-five years.

The doctor had many interests; one of them was politics. He headed a bipartisan committee to support the election of Dwight D. Eisenhower in 1952. The next year he ran, unsuccessfully, for city council. Gracious in losing, McVeigh told a *Star-Telegram* reporter, "My opponent . . . is a good man and should do a fine job on the City Council."[34] Among the sympathy calls he received after his defeat was one from a patient who ". . . expressed the idea that if he devoted enough of his time to do a good job for the city he may not have been available to them all the time."[35]

His colleagues considered him a winner and in 1961 voted him the recipient of the Gold-Headed Cane. Drs. R. J. White and DeWitt Neighbors escorted McVeigh to the rostrum. The 1960 holder of the cane, Dr. T. H. Thomason, presented the glittering symbol of acclaim.

McVeigh died in August 1966 at the age of seventy-six.

★ ★ ★

T. C. TERRELL, MD-1962

T. C. Terrell, from a long line of physicians, is profiled in the chapter "Family Practice."

* ★ ★

WALTER B. WEST, MD-1963

Walter West was almost a one-man *Dictionary of Occupations*. Prior to medical school he learned carpentry, served as chauffeur to exhausted doctors, taught typing and coached high school athletics. Each occupation added to his understanding of people, which helped him when dealing with patients. The son of a Hamilton, Texas carpenter, young Walter was an able apprentice by the time he finished high school. He told reporter Seth Kantor, "I used to drive the cars of two doctors at night.... They would get valuable sleep or rest while on the way to night calls as I drove."[36]

Upon graduation from North Texas Teachers College, he taught commercial subjects and coached in Kingsville. When the school board refused to name him principal, because some of the students were as old as he, West gave up teaching and went to medical school.

The Baylor Medical College alumnus was a fellow of the American College of Surgeons, but he preferred to call himself a family doctor. He came to Fort Worth in 1930 as John Peter Smith Hospital's first intern and resident doctor.

He steadily built a family practice which garnered the respect of both patients and fellow physicians. A nephew remembered his uncle as serious minded, but with glimpses of a sense of humor. One thing he was serious about was punctuality. "If he scheduled a surgery at 8:00 a.m., he had scalpel in hand at 8:01."[37] Dr. Doug Tatum said of Dr. West, "Some kids have baseball players as heroes—he was mine."[38]

When World War II broke out, he enlisted in a flight surgeon course. "During five years' military service, he spent two years as fleet surgeon with the South Atlantic Fleet,"[39] *Star-Telegram*'s Thayer Waldo wrote. A Lt. Commander, he was in charge of twenty-two hospitals spread from the British West Indies to Paraguay and several points in the South Atlantic. West visited each base weekly.

After discharge from the Navy, West returned to his Fort Worth practice. In 1960 he served as president of the county medical society. Three years later he was awarded the prestigious Gold-Headed Cane. Friend and longtime colleague Dr. J. A. Hallmark described the honoree as "a most invaluable associate, a rock of integrity, always available for help and ready with wise counsel."[40]

From his marriage to Madalyn Reed, he had two sons. Bill works with troubled youth and Britt is a physician. Dr. West enjoyed being a father. Not only did he make time to take the boys to local sporting events, he traveled with them throughout the United States. He and his sons also enjoyed the camaraderie of the many hunting trips they took.

In addition to his longtime dedication to John Peter Smith Hospital, Dr. West was on the staff at All Saints Hospital. Following his untimely fatal heart attack in 1965, that institution paid tribute to him by naming the auditorium in his honor. A 4-by-7 foot panel with an oil portrait hangs in the room where the hospital's business and scientific meetings are held. At the unveiling, Mrs. West told the assembled guests, "His love for All Saints was very great and we thank you from the bottom of our hearts." Nelson Scurlock, chairman of the board, conveyed his group's sentiments. "All of our trustees appreciated Dr. West when he was here. . . . Now that he is gone—as is true in the case of most great men—we appreciate him even more."[41]

★ ★ ★

SIMEON "SIM" HULSEY, MD-1964

Sim Hulsey played on the University of Texas 1920 championship football team and was still a winner—in medicine—until his retirement seventy-five years later.

Sim took his medical training at Galveston the first two years, then went to the University of Pennsylvania. That institution admitted only one or two students from Texas and he was selected to go after his sophomore year. "After graduation, I interned at the post-graduate hospital in Philadelphia,"[42] he told Dr. Bob Lanier in an interview for the *Tarrant County Physician.*

Dr. Hulsey regarded medicine as a service and never sought the limelight. He believed doctors should not drive flashy automobiles. His was always a black Ford coupe from Frank Kent. He did relent and buy Mrs. Hulsey a Buick—black of course. In his later years he loosened up somewhat; he bought a white Ford.

In addition to seeing patients, Hulsey gave a great deal of time to teaching and administration. He went once a week to see patients at the Elmwood Sanatorium. Hulsey taught at John Peter Smith Hospital, and later the hospital's Allergy Clinic awarded him a fifty-year service certificate. He gave time to the public health department and was in charge of pathology at St. Joseph Hospital for twenty years. In keeping with his love of teaching, and his fondness of students, Dr. Hulsey conducted clinical conferences for interns at St. Joseph every Saturday morning. "We had a good time and it was very informative and informal. I found this very gratifying, and the best way to keep up with medical developments,"[43] he said in an interview for the *Tarrant County Physician*.

As part of his pathology work he performed autopsies. Retired Bishop Sam Hulsey told of his father's occasional storing of body parts at home. "When it was more convenient than to go back to the office, he would sometimes wrap something up from the lab or autopsy and put it in our refrigerator. One time my mother opened the door and screamed, 'I told you, Sim Hulsey, not to put that stuff in our refrigerator!' He'd say, 'Oh, it'll be out early in the morning. I'll take it with me.'"[44]

Bishop Hulsey remembers his father working long hours. "He left every morning at 6:45 on the dot and often didn't get home until 7:00 in the evening. Then he might be on the phone or make night calls after that."[45] Mrs. Hulsey, trying to engage her taciturn husband in small talk, would ask how his day had been. His answer was usually something noncommittal. Once, her son recalled, his mother asked if anything interesting happened at the office, and Dr. Hulsey replied, "Nothing." In desperation Mrs. Hulsey said, "Well, make up something!"[46]

Dr. Hulsey and his wife, Ruth, enjoyed getting away for a weekend at their little farm in Parker County. He mended fences and worked in his blackberry patch. She raised cattle. One day he noticed a calf with a badly infected eye. Dr. Hulsey the allergist became Dr. Hulsey the veterinarian. He removed the eye and renamed the calf "Cyclops."

Bishop Hulsey described his father as a lifelong student as well as teacher. Dr. Hulsey attended meetings of the professional organizations to learn more about his work, and was meticulous in preparing papers for presentation at conferences or lectures to interns. "He would sit in his chair, medical books spread out all around him as he wrote his lectures,"[47] the son recalled.

In 1964 Dr. Hulsey received the Gold-Headed Cane. "I would like for you all to know how deeply appreciative I am of the honor you have just bestowed on me,"[48] he told the guests. As a young man, Hulsey considered becoming a missionary, but instead opted for medicine. He saw his choice as another way of service. The Gold-Headed Cane represented recognition of the reasons the healing arts were so important to him. Said Bishop Hulsey, "Daddy was really interested in medicine per se—medicine as a discipline and as a service; upholding the medical community and being supportive of other doctors. I think he felt it was such a wonderful thing for Porter Brown to start. . . .It meant a lot to him."[49]

After practicing almost seventy years, Dr. Hulsey retired in 1995. He caught up on his correspondence and reading, and kept in touch with friends and former patients by telephone. Asked about his retirement, he replied he was "enjoying procrastination."

He loved children and always had a set of tiny, stuffed toy animals in his office for them. It was only fitting that he requested his 100th birthday party last until 7:00 p.m. so the children could come after school. Seeing all the cars parked near his house, one child worried that he had died, but when she saw the balloons she exclaimed, "Oh, it's his birthday."

After a century of living and serving, Dr. Simeon Hulsey died August 9, 1999. And a legend died with him.

★ ★ ★

HOBART O. DEATON, MD-1965

Hobart Deaton underwent surgery for a blood clot on the brain March 28, 1955. His condition was so tenuous someone, probably Blair Justice, wrote a draft obituary.

"Dr. Deaton was not only a leader in state medical circles, he also was president-elect of the Tarrant County Medical Society. He would have become president in January 1956."[50] The unpublished story named a neurosurgeon and brother-in-law of the stricken man, Dr. Henry Dratz of Albany, New York as assisting in the operation. Deaton recovered and postponed the need for his obituary for fourteen years.

A published story, dated January 3, 1956, noted, "Dr. Hobart O. Deaton, who has practiced medicine here since 1927, will be installed Tuesday night as president of the Tarrant County Medical Society."[51] He was indeed installed, served, and later was awarded the prestigious Gold-Headed Cane.

After serving in the Navy for a year during World War I, the North Carolinian enrolled in Wake Forest College in the fall of 1919. Deaton worked his way through school by holding a variety of jobs. "I did just about everything from teaching school to digging ditches to carpentry," he told reporter Jon McConal. Once, he worked six months as a barber in Norfolk and earned enough to pay a year's tuition. "I've still got my (barber) license," he boasted.[52]

In 1924 Deaton received his medical degree from Washington University in St. Louis. Following an internship at Vanderbilt University Hospital, he began a practice in Fort Worth in 1927. His plan was to stay here a year or two and return to North Carolina, but there never seemed to be a convenient time to make the move. He stayed forty-two years.

In 1965 Deaton's peers voted him the "Doctor's Doctor." About the Gold-headed Cane Award he said, "I've had more honors than I deserve. . . .but, this award tonight is the greatest I'll ever have."[53]

Beside his talent as a physician, Deaton was a notable musician. He sang in the choir at Hemphill Presbyterian Church and played the violin. Describing himself as "a poor amateur violinist, but a good mountaineer fiddler,"[54] he acknowledged his love and level of playing.

On August 16, 1969, readers of the *Star-Telegram* saw a photograph of a smiling Dr. Hobart O. Deaton as they learned of his death eight months after his retirement. He was seventy-three-years-old, his "real" obituary disclosed.

★ ★ ★

C. S. E. TOUZEL, MD-1966

The only Canadian to be awarded the Gold-Headed Cane was Cecil Stuart Eugene Touzel. He answered to "Gene."

He worked laying steel for a railroad one summer when a fellow crew member, a medical student, encouraged him to consider medicine as a career. Gene had always admired their family doctor, but gave no thought to following in his footsteps. Now, comparing the backbreaking labor of building a railroad to the rigors of medical school, he decided long hours of study and lab work would be a cinch.

There was already a Touzel in school, a brother studying to be a dentist, but Gene's mother said they could borrow the money for one more Touzel. That fall he enrolled in college. With loans and help from his family physician, Gene earned his medical degree from McGill University in Montreal. Things were going well until he fell ill with rheumatic fever in 1930. Reporter Jon McConal quoted the doctor about it. "'I was flat on my back for six months. . . . I guess you could say I was in serious condition."[55]

After his health improved Touzel finished graduate school and did an internship at Montreal General Hospital, with further training at Children's Memorial Hospital there. He studied pediatrics for a year at Vanderbilt Hospital in Nashville, Tennessee. Explaining his move to the United States, he told McConal, "I came south to bake the fever out of me. . . .I've been baking it out of me ever since."[56]

Touzel was ready to go into private practice, but in 1932 the country was in the depths of the Great Depression. Employment was hard to find. A clinic in Fort Worth offered him a position and he gratefully accepted.

When Touzel received the Gold-Headed Cane in 1966, the tradition was to tell the winner, but not to make the name public until the awards dinner. Dr. Hobart Deaton introduced Touzel in this manner, as was written in the *Tarrant County Physician*: "Tonight's recipient, like so many others, came up the hard way. He is one of seven children. . . . He worked in the fields, in the woods, on the railroad, and on county roads, but I was unable to get the length of time he served. I personally know that whatever he works at he devotes himself to the job. He led his premed class in zoology. . . . He came to us a stranger but we liked him and he liked us. He has been chairman of the staff at four of our hospitals. He has been local and state president of his own speciality societies, and a past president of our own Tarrant County Medical Society and did a very good job."

Deaton spoke of Touzel's family, then said, "Will Gwendolyn and Dr. Cecil Stuart Eugene Touzel come to the front and center?"[57]

Touzel thanked the members for the honor, but added he suffered some anxiety the previous days. "All this week I have been sort of expecting Dr. [Emory] Davenport or Dr. [May] Owen [program chairs] to call me to tell me that it had all been a mistake. . . ."[58]

Touzel built a clinic at Pennsylvania and S. Adams, where he practiced until his retirement in May 1975. He died at his home six months later. He was seventy-two years old.

★ ★ ★

Louis J. Levy, MD–1967

The awards and commendations Dr. Louis Levy received for his outstanding work in the medical field could fill a room. In fact, they do. Among the most treasured is the scroll signed by his fellow physicians on November 2, 1967 as Levy was recognized as the recipient of the Gold-Headed Cane. In the twenty-five years between the beginning of his practice to the announcement naming him the "doctor's doctor" Levy racked up an impressive array of professional and civic achievements.

At the award banquet the modest orthopedic surgeon said, "It is difficult to express the gratitude and humility that I feel on being presented with this Gold-Headed Cane."[59]

This statement came from a man whose introduction to medicine was distinctly negative. When he was ten-years-old, Louis suffered a ruptured appendix. The antibiotic of the time was Mercurochrome. The organic mercury compound was given intravenously, hoping to counteract his peritonitis. Instead it induced a long-term coma.

The Fort Worth native interned and completed a residency in orthopedics at Michael Reese Hospital in Chicago. From there he went to Los Angeles County General Hospital and the Texas Scottish Rite Hospital in Dallas for further training.

Levy began his local practice in 1942. He had hardly begun to receive referrals when Uncle Sam tapped him on the shoulder. The young doctor, his wife and daughter moved to Abilene, Texas for his basic training, then he was shipped to North Africa, Corsica and Italy. He was in the Army Medical Corps for three years, serving as the orthopedist for the 40th Station Hospital. Danna Mehl Levy, reflecting back on those years, said her husband considered his military service as an excellent learning experience.

The war over, Levy returned to Fort Worth. At first he practiced alone, but in 1945 he founded the Fort Worth Bone and Joint Clinic, which is still in operation. In the years ahead he would become the role model for young doctors, surgeons and non-surgeons alike.

Much of his work involved correcting birth defects. One spina bifida patient stole his heart. He performed several corrective procedures on the little girl. "She had a disreputable stuffed animal named 'Henry.' She asked if Henry could go with her into the operating room. Louis said 'Yes.'" When she awoke she had a cast on one leg, and Henry had a cast on his leg too.

The patient's father was a peanut farmer. "Every Christmas she brought him peanuts," Mrs. Levy recalled. "She'd come to our house, we would invite her in, but she never said a word, just gave him the gift while her father waited out in the car."[60] The girl went on to college and Mrs. Levy still wonders where she is and how she is.

His work was not confined to children. Dr. Levy in 1946 adapted an operation for a seventeen-year-old high school football player. Ft. Worth *Press* reporter Jean Wysatta wrote of the procedure, "A muscle was transplanted, with the results giving the boy control of an arm that would have been useless for life."[61] The American Academy of Orthopedic Surgeons requested for their library a film of the operation.

Not only an academic film, but Levy's influence was seen on national television, the reporter noted. "Fans of the program 'Medic,' may remember seeing a two-part series based on an operation Dr. Levy and associates performed in Fort Worth. Dangerous, tedious surgery was done on a man completely bent over with an arthritic spine. The operation successful, the man was able to straighten himself to almost normal position."[62]

Levy and his colleagues at the Fort Worth Bone and Joint Clinic rendered invaluable service to TCU football players, according to

Wysatta. "And, as football trainer Elmer Brown puts it—'They've done $100,000 worth of work, and that's a conservative guess, and have never charged a nickel for it."[63] Mrs. Levy described this work as "Monday morning after a football game, there was a parade of beat-up players in his office."[64]

As busy as he was, Levy took time to relax by playing golf. He played with Gary Player and Jack Nicholas, "whom he tried to tell how to play," Mrs. Levy laughingly recalled. Guitar great Chet Atkins was another of his partners.

Levy took memberships seriously. For his efforts he received the Paul Harris Award from the Rotary Club, the Distinguished Alumni Award from the Fort Worth Independent School District, the Distinguished Alumni Award from Texas Christian University, and the Humanitarian Award from the National Jewish Hospital and Research Center in Denver.

Upon accepting the Gold-Headed Cane, he paid tribute to his family and partners, saying he could not have achieved such an honored status by himself. "My wish tonight is that you all could receive this Cane, so you could appreciate what a truly great emotional experience this is."[65]

Dr. Levy's poor health led to his retirement. Although he enjoyed time spent with his family, he missed his practice greatly. Levy died in 1993.

★ ★ ★

JAMES A. HALLMARK, MD-1968

Friendly, energetic James Hallmark was a product of Fort Worth's North Side High School. After three years at Texas Christian University he was accepted at the University of Texas Medical School. He graduated from the Galveston institution in 1936, a member of the elite Alpha Omega Alpha fraternity. Membership in AOA was reserved for the top twelve men in the class. Known for his sense of humor, Hallmark joked he was inducted because, "There were only twelve men in my class."

The general practitioner interned at the old City-County Hospital and began his practice in 1938. He officed with Dr. R. G. Baker for twenty years after he returned from the Army Air Force during World War II.

The 1968 Gold-Headed Cane affair was a light-hearted one. Dr. Louis Levy told of Hallmark's less than stellar foreign language studies at TCU. Said Levy, "While at T.C.U., among other things, he learned humility. He took a course in German under Dr. [Marguarita] Ascher—who was quite a character herself. She frequently brought her German police dog to class. This was the trouble—the dog was trained only to German commands, and it was humbling to realize that the dog understood German better than any of the students."[66]

But in his remarks that night Hallmark got even, saying about Levy, "I knew the guy when Dr. Marguarita Ascher's German police dog could outscore him in German grammar."[67]

After thanking his peers, Hallmark said, "I can only say that such an honor as this is unexpected, undeserved, happily acknowledged and humbly accepted."[68] He then gave a quick reflection of previous recipients of the cane.

"Cabe Terrell—that grand fellow's hold on Porter Brown's affection and admiration started this whole thing.

May Owen—a legend in her own time. For years I've been trying to prove her a myth. At least she is a 'Miss.'

Joe White—Nowadays the experts say doctors need more liberal arts education. That's so they can understand Dr. Joe.

R. G. Baker—He got me into this Medical Society mess, but don't hold it against him.

Tom Bond—Do you really believe there is such a guy?

Edwin Schwarz—A fine pediatrician and couldn't he be tough on occasion?

L. O. Godley—My privilege to tell him he had won the Gold-Headed Cane. The same day he won a radio. I'm not sure which thrilled him most.

DeWitt Neighbors—During my intern days, DeWitt was pretty austere. But when the TCU Frogs won, things were much more casual.

C. P. Hawkins—We didn't know until he retired and moved to Arkansas that he held his head on one side to offset a short leg.

T. H. Thomason—A gentleman and a scholar who once accused me of advertising when my picture was in the paper after returning from World War II.

J. F. McVeigh—Will St. Joseph ever produce another such courtly gentleman?

T. C. Terrell—Uncle Grumpy. Terrible, ain't he?

W. B. West—Some of his patients feel that he deserted them. (His untimely death) Sometimes I feel the same way.

Sim Hulsey—He spends so much time practicing medicine and farming that the ladies are having a hard time catching up with this handsome debonair widower.

H. O. Deaton—The strong and silent type.

C. S. E. Touzel—The only refugee from north of the border to win the CANE (sic)."[69]

Hallmark fondly recalled making the acquaintance of R. P. McDonald, now a longtime friend, on a train as the two young men headed for Galveston and medical school. He also remembered, not so fondly, Drs. Daly and Kingsbury and their 5:00 am surgery schedule at City-County. Other tasks involved boiling water and swatting flies as he and Dr. D. M. Rumph waited "for the stork to find the right house."

In a more serious vein, he thanked by name the many physicians whom he considered mentors and friends.

James Hallmark retired in 1984 after almost fifty years of practice. He died in February 1991.

★ ★ ★

John J. Andujar, MD- 1969

The 1969 Gold-Headed Cane recipient, Dr. John J. Andujar, speaks with great pride in the achievements of his late wife. Betty made history in 1972 as the first woman from Tarrant County, and the first Republican since the post Civil War period, to be elected to the Texas Senate. The internationally known pathologist is more reluctant to speak of his own achievements. Yet they are many.

The soft-spoken octogenarian, born in 1912 to missionary parents, spent his formative years in Puerto Rico. Early on both parents instilled in the youth a sense of service. A neighbor, Dr. Bailey K. Ashford, a tropical medicine pathologist, introduced young Andy to the laboratory. His interest in science grew with his purchase of an old monocular microscope. "When Andy 'discovered' an amoeba under the microscope, he was hooked!"[70]

He trained at Columbia University's School of Tropical Medicine under Dr. Ashford, his boyhood mentor. Next he studied with the famed James Ewing, Professor of Pathology at Cornell University Medical College. All through college he had planned to become a medical missionary, but it was 1934—the depth of the Depression. "Not only were they not sending missionaries to the field, they were calling some back,"[71] he said in an interview. Andujar heard of a position in pathology on the University of Arkansas Medical School faculty. He promptly applied and was accepted.

While there he developed the cardiolipin PCT (plasmacrit test on capillary blood) serologic test, the forerunner of the single-drop blood test for syphilis. In recognition of this advance in science, Andujar was given the Bryant Award from the Public Health Association. "That test is now included in the U. S. Public Health Service manual for standard serological procedures,"[72] Blair Justice wrote.

"In 1937 Harris Hospital announced they were looking for a young pathologist who would also be an organizer of internships and residencies."[73] Fort Worth had not had any approved internship or residency programs and Harris was looking to become the preeminent hospital in the city. The young doctor and his family—he and Betty married in 1935—moved to Fort Worth in 1938 and he became the pathologist and unofficial medical director. Andujar left Harris in 1949 when he established Fort Worth Medical Laboratories.

A quarter of a century later, Andujar recounted to *Fort Worth Star-Telegram* science writer Blair Justice some of his experiences, such as crusading for fluoridation of city water.

He also saw the need for medical examiners. "When I came here, the only pathologist was May Owen,"[74] he said in an interview. But she wasn't interested in doing autopsies, so the justice of the peace, who was not required to have medical training, certified the cause of death.

Andujar was convinced that homicides would go undetected under such a system. He worked for legislation to permit counties to hire medical examiners to determine causes of death. Such a law, requiring county coroners to be qualified pathologists, was carried by none other than Senator Betty Andujar.

Dr. Andujar served as president of local, state and national organizations. He was the first American to be elected president of the World Pathology Foundation. In that office he traveled over 100,000 miles to four continents presenting papers and meeting with local pathologists.

At the 1969 Gold-Headed Cane Awards dinner Andujar paid tribute to previous recipients of the prestigious award, citing pathologists May Owen and Truman C. Terrell as giants in the field. In his acceptance speech, entitled *Homo Sapens Medicus*, he painted a word portrait of a physician—idealist, scientist, and realist. Perhaps he was looking in the mirror as well as remembering those who had gone before him.

Thirty years later he was still being honored by his peers. On January 30, 1999, at a Texas Society of Pathologists luncheon, Dr. Vernie Stembridge announced,

"... that the Society's Citation of Merit Award be henceforth known as 'The Andujar Citation of Merit Award.'"[75]

★ ★ ★

THE '70s

Of this decade Peschel recalled:

"It was the decade for women's liberation. There was Watergate and the fall of Richard Nixon. The country became a nation of malls. We entered the world of high technology with pocket calculators and beepers.

"The society faced a serious issue. Medical malpractice and professional liability suits increased in geometric proportion. Insurance increased in cost, and some doctors could not buy professional liability insurance. The TCMS, TMA and the AMA actively pursued solutions for these problems.

"With a grant from the Sid Richardson Foundation, Tel-Med, a free telephone health informational service for the public, was made available. Tel Med was implemented and operated by auxiliary volunteers. Doctors reviewed more than 200 tapes. The Tel-Med service was a sweeping success, bringing a wealth of health education to the citizens of Tarrant County.

"PL (Public Law) 93-641, the Health Planning and Resource Development Act of 1974, was but one of the several major control systems put into place by the federal government to manage health care. . . .

"The first neonatal unit was established at Fort Worth Children's Hospital in July 1975 and expanded in 1977. . . . The first Cardiac Rehabilition Center opened in the spring of 1979 at All Saints Hospital to speed the recovery of patients who had heart attacks. Cook Children's Hospital opened a new children's Hematology/Oncology Clinic in 1979."[76]

★ ★ ★

WILLIAM P. HIGGINS, JR.,MD-1970

Bill Higgins was a warm, humorous and versatile man. He won acclaim for his medical skills and a medal for his charitable contributions. He decided early about his career goal. "I never considered becoming anything but a doctor."[77]

After a year at St. Joseph Hospital he established his office in general practice and surgery. World War II interrupted that practice and he served with the 4th Auxiliary Surgical Group in Europe. He received five Battle Stars, including one for the Omaha Beach landing.

Back from the war, Higgins became chief of staff at St. Joseph Hospital, and for more than twenty years he was on the staff of John Peter Smith Hospital, as Staff Secretary and Chief of Surgery there. For more than a dozen years he delivered babies for Catholic charities at no charge. For this and other humanitarian deeds he was named recipient of the Holy Trinity Award, the highest honor a Catholic bishop can confer. According to the *Star-Telegram*, "Dr. Higgins was cited for 15 years of outstanding service in Catholic charities and medicine. . . . The medal was presented by Rev. Charles L. Mulholland . . . at a St. Teresa Home banquet."[78]

Dr. John Andujar, in introducing Higgins at the 1970 Gold-Headed Cane dinner, amused friends and colleagues with tales of the honoree's medical exploits as an intern at St. Joseph Hospital. "Bill was noted for his ability to sleep . . . . [one night a new mother telephoned about her baby's colic] Bill muttered sleepily into the phone, 'give the kid 2 tablespoons of paregoric.' Horrified she wailed, 'to a tiny newborn?' Alarmed and now wide awake, and with rare presence of mind, our quick-witted hero quoth, 'I didn't say all at once, did I?'"[79]

Higgins became the twentieth doctor to hold the Gold-Headed Cane. In his remarks at the presentation he thanked those who had helped him, both professionally and personally. "We are all influenced by the older men of our profession, and I would like to name four whom I think have had the most influence on me: Dr. W. S. Lorimer, Sr., with whom I was associated for awhile early; then, the late Dr. Jack Daly; thirdly Dr. Bob Baker and then my very good friend and teacher, Dr. R. J. White. I want to thank all of you and say that I am pleased, excited and proud, but also very humbled by this wonderful honor."[80]

After fifty years of practice, Higgins' health failed. In his last months friends such as Dr. John Richards visited him regularly. He died October 25, 1988. It was his longtime habit to give out peppermint candy. At his Mass of Christian Burial a grandson placed a peppermint on the casket.

★ ★ ★

Emory Davenport, MD-1971

Dr. Higgins surrendered the Gold-Headed Cane to Dr. Emory Davenport. This outstanding internal medicine specialist inspired several family members to study medicine. His story is found in the "Family Practice" chapter.

★ ★ ★

William Crawford. MD-1972

William Massey (Bill) Crawford was born in South Carolina, but came to Texas in 1916 as a ten-year-old. He opened an office in 1933, not a good time to begin earning a living. He based his practice on a mix of sympathy and friendliness as part of any prescription for healing. In 1972 he told reporter Don Fisher, "I guess it's a matter of pride, but if I can't make emergency calls, I don't want to practice medicine. That's why I retired this year at 66."[81] In the intervening forty years Crawford made an indelible mark on Fort Worth medicine.

Like many others, Crawford put his civilian practice on hold in 1942. With the rank of Coast Guard Lt. Commander, he was stationed at Norfolk, Virginia and as a ship surgeon during World War II. One duty, in 1943, entailed accompanying a group of Japanese civilians to the Far East in an exchange of Americans civilians.

After the war Crawford returned to his practice. His emphasis throughout his career was the importance of the spread of knowledge. In August 1953, he and three other doctors, M. H. Crabb, Will Horn and May Owen attended the First World Conference on Medical Education in London.

Long a devotee of medical history, in 1957 Crawford was elected to the Harvenian Society of London. The society is a group made up chiefly of noted British physicians and surgeons. It is named in honor of William Harvey, the English doctor who discovered the circulation of blood. Crawford also was named to the prestigious Osler Society, made even more special in that he was the only United States citizen holding membership in both groups at that time.

William Crawford became the twenty-second doctor to receive the Gold-Headed Cane. In his response he outlined his philosophy of life. "I believe that order is better than chaos, creation better than destruction. I prefer gentleness to violence, forgiveness to hate. On the whole I feel that knowledge is preferable to ignorance. . . . We must try to learn from history."[82] These words were even more telling considering they were spoken in 1972 during a time of national upheaval.

W. S. Lorimer, Jr., in a 1989 *Tarrant County Physician* interview, introduced Crawford as an internationally noted and honored collector of the finest private historical medical library ever assembled. "When did your interest in the history of medicine begin?" he asked.

"It is always difficult to remember precise moments in time when an idea that may shape your future enters the mind. Perhaps, while in medical school. During a summer, I was working in the pathology department at Washington University to keep mice alive. In the department there was a partial Egyptian mummy. I was entranced. In reading about mummies, I encountered a book on paleopathology by Sir Mark Armon Ruffer. To make a long story short, I obtained a microtome and made some microscopic slides of this mummy and was surprised to find tubercles in the lungs, arteriosclerosis in the vessels, and nits in the hair! For me, the history of medicine had begun."[83]

Whenever he traveled, even in wartime, Crawford searched for priceless medical books. In 1972 he donated his library of rare books to the Texas Medical School at Galveston. Included was a 1628 booklet by Sir William Harvey which described blood circulation. A much rarer book was an original copy, one of twelve, of a 1543 text on anatomy. The doctor told reporter Blair Justice about it. "Andrea Vesalius, who taught medicine in Italy, gave doctors their first good lesson in anatomy. . . . when he published a book called *The Fabric of the Human Body*. The accuracy of Vesalius' work was astounding and is still used in medical textbooks. "Every time a doctor operates today," Crawford said, "he is paying tribute to Vesalius for giving surgeons the first knowledge of anatomy."[84]

After his retirement Crawford lectured on medical history at UTMS in Galveston. He died December 8, 1989.

★ ★ ★

C. HAROLD BEASLEY, MD-1973

Dr. William M. Crawford noted at the Gold-Headed Cane Award dinner, six general practitioners, four pediatricians, four internists, three pathologists, two surgeons, one gynecologist, one radiologist and one orthopedic surgeon had held the cane. On October 19, 1973 they recognized a new category—ophthalmologist—as they honored Harold Beasley.

In his response, the Arkansas native told of his involvement in a medical emergency. He and another ophthalmologist and their wives were on a flight to a medical meeting in San Antonio. Turbulent weather caused several passengers to become ill. One woman who had had recent heart surgery, needed aid. The stewardess asked if there were any doctors on board. "My friend and I waited the customary time for someone else to gct up." When no one did, "We went to the lady and she was pretty sick. Her color was not good, her pulse weak and fast, and she was a little cold and clammy." We made her as comfortable as possible, and my friend, who was always completely honest, said to the stewardess, "Miss, I think I should tell you that Dr. Beasley and I are eye doctors." This young lady stood erect and in a loud voice said, "Are there any real doctors on board?"

Beasley continued, "I tell you this tale so you will know that it is a genuine compliment to be honored by a bunch of real doctors."[85]

C. Harold Beasley practiced medical and surgical ophthalmology in Fort Worth from 1950 until his retirement in 1980. He practiced in Heber Springs, Arkansas for six years after leaving Fort Worth. Beasley kept his post as a consultant in research and development at Alcon Laboratories until 1997, an association which lasted forty-six years.

According to the *Star-Telegram*, "While in private practice in Fort Worth, Dr. Beasley, in cooperation with St. Joseph Hospital, was instrumental in developing the first inpatient facility in the Southwest devoted solely to ophthalmic patients. He was the first doctor in the Fort Worth area to perform corneal transplants, scleral buckling for retinal detachments and vitectomy."[86]

In addition to being honored by his peers with the Gold-Headed Cane, in 1976 he was honored with The People of Vision Award by Prevent Blindness Texas.

He loved airplanes. An accomplished pilot for sixty years, at age eighty Beasley was still flying. On his eighty-first birthday he became a member of the United Flying Octogenarians.

Although Beasley returned to his native state the last years of his life, and died in Heber Springs in 1999, Tarrant County Medical Society still has a Beasley on its membership list. Son, Dr. Cliff H. Beasley, Jr. is a retina specialist.

★ ★ ★

JOHN A. WIGGINS, MD-1974

John Wiggins and his brother Kenneth are profiled in the "Family Practice" chapter.

★ ★ ★

Frank Cohen, MD-1975

Doctor, lawyer, merchant, rabbi? Paraphrasing the children's game, those were the choices the deeply religious Frank Cohen considered. He could have chosen merchant, following in his grocer father's footsteps. But three generations who depended on him for health care are glad he chose doctor.

He enrolled in Waco's Baylor University in the fall of 1931. Baylor welcomed the few Jewish students in its predominately Baptist student body. Cohen remembered the dean told him he was exempt from going to the religious chapel required of other students. But when told the day's and week's activities were announced in chapel, he said, "Then that's where I ought to be."[87] He even attended two Baptist revivals while a student.

Cohen received his medical degree in 1937 and did an internship at Baylor Hospital, but this was back in his home town. His residencies were at Dallas' old Bradford Hospital, 1938-1939, then Cook County Hospital in Chicago the next year. For four years and nine months he served in the United States Army, rising in rank to Lt. Colonel.

In 1947 he saw his first Ft. Worth patient, Betty Marie Jones. By the time he retired in 1988 he had amassed folders on more than 26,000 infants and children. Over the years his "babies" had become parents and grandparents of his "babies."

In a reenactment of the television show "This Is Your Life," popular in the mid-1950s, Cohen was the surprised center of attention in 1954. The annual L. F. Shanblum Lodge of B'nai B'rith affair used humor and sentiment to detail the life of the popular pediatrician. Family members, old friends and colleagues told anecdotes and showed pictures of bygone days. Lowell Hudson, administrator of City-County Hospital, reviewed Cohen's many humanitarian services. Even two of his patients got into the act—his first patient, Betty Marie Jones was there to celebrate with him. Reporter Ida Belle Hicks wrote, "The other one in the review was Donna Kay Williams, a polio victim, who came through with her sense of humor still intact."[88]

Less than a decade later the Lodge named Cohen "Man of the Year." Edward Gaines, outgoing president, praised him for "'outstanding and meritorious service unselfishly rendered to community and fellowman,'"[89] a local daily reported.

Another of Cohen's many honors was the Fort Worth Sertoma Club's 1965 Service-to-Mankind Award. The *Fort Worth Star-Telegram* noted he was cited for "'his untiring and unselfish love for his fellow man.'"[90]

Cohen's work outside the office was considerable. He chaired the Public Health Advisory Committee and supervised the Salk and Sabin "Sugar Cube Sunday" polio vaccine drives. The "Worth Knowing" feature of *Fort Worth* magazine noted, He worked for the establishment of the Carter Blood Bank and the Fund for Nurses, which provided special nursing services for children in need. Cohen also helped establish quality day care centers in Tarrant County.

In an interview with *Tarrant County Physician* Dr. Cohen reminisced about his long and successful career. Polio was rampant when Cohen began his practice. He shared some of the misconceptions of the cause of the dread disease. "We stopped the children from going to parties, picture shows, and even going out in the mid-day sun for fear they might catch polio. For awhile we stopped them from eating bananas! Someone had written a story that there seemed to be a link with children consuming a lot of bananas and getting polio."[91]

Concerning his illustrious practice, "Is there one incident that stands out in your mind.?" Dr. Bob Lanier asked at the close of an interview. With typical grace Cohen recalled a patient from the day before. "There's nothing greater than to know the correct diagnosis was made, and the child's going to be well."

Lanier replied, "It's heartening that after almost a half-century of medicine, you choose as a memorable incident a case as recent as the day before."[92]

Patients and peers alike say that's what makes Cohen such a respected doctor. He considers every case important and is hard pressed to single out any particular one. It's all part of his goal to serve people. At the time he was awarded the Tarrant County Medical Society's Gold-Headed Cane, Cohen told reporter Jon McConal, "When I was a kid, I wanted to be either a rabbi or a doctor. That was definite. One or the other. I wanted to serve people."[93] His many awards and honors attest to the fact he has succeeded. Speaking of the prestigious award, he said, "This has got to be a highlight of my career."[94] Perhaps, but visitors to Cook Children's Medical Center might think having a wing of the hospital named in his honor "ain't exactly chopped liver."

★ ★ ★

GRANT BEGLEY, MD-1976

There was a time when Grant Begley couldn't wait to get out of Texas. The Kentucky native, stationed at Fort Hood, couldn't get back home fast enough to suit him. Fortunately for the Fort Worth medical community he came to realize it was Fort Hood he disliked, not Texas as a whole.

He graduated from Berea College, the famous Appalachian institution open to top scholars of all Kentucky schools. After Berea he enrolled in Tulane Medical School and graduated in 1944. Begley did both his internship and residency at Charity Hospital in New Orleans. Next came his unhappy years in Texas at Fort Hood. After his discharge, and back in Kentucky, he joined many other veterans looking for a start in the medical world. But things were tight.

Begley explained in an interview how he came to practice here. "In Lexington [another young doctor looking for a place] mentioned an opening for a urologist in Fort Worth. I got in touch with them and hired on with Harris Clinic."[95] He stayed with Harris, which later became Fifth Avenue Clinic, and began to build his reputation as a urologist. He later joined the Urology Clinic founded by Dr. Hub Isaacs and Dr. Dolphus Compere.

His speciality depended heavily upon referrals and he recalled the willingness of pediatricians to send him patients. Begley explained that one of the most common problems during gestation has to do with the urinary tract and much of his work was done with infants. Until pediatric surgery became a speciality, Begley repaired birth defects and other anomalies suffered by this population.

In the more than fifty years since Begley came to Fort Worth he has seen tremendous progress in medicine, including urology. "My generation has seen more innovations, more changes, more progress than all of medical history dating back to Hippocrates," he said in an interview. "No one has invented a sharper knife and human anatomy hasn't changed, but new ways to do things are making a difference."[96]

When not practicing medicine Begley kept busy with his many hobbies. Photography, gardening and woodworking helped him relax. The woodworking came in handy with his other hobby, hunting.

"A hunter and sportsman," the *Tarrant County Physician* noted, "Dr. Begley builds and decorates his own gunstocks."[97] Visitors to the home he shares with his wife, Joy, immediately notice the magnificent trophies from his hunting trips. He is a member of the Grand Slam Club. Membership is confined to those who have bagged all four species of Big Horn sheep that inhabit North American. Other mounted trophies include caribou, deer, elk, wolf and wild goat.

Characterized as a doctor who listens to his patients, Begley was tapped to be the 1976 holder of the Gold-Headed Cane. He confided to an interviewer, "It was the most surprising thing that ever happened to me." Accepting the honor, he noted with a typical touch of humor, "The two most important women in my life are here tonight, my wife and my mother. One is absolutely astonished and the other one thinks it's deserved—I'll let you decide which is which."[98]

★ ★ ★

BURGESS SEALY, MD-1977

Burgess Sealy was a "doctor in the making" at an early age as he went with his father on house calls in West Texas. His story is in the "Family Practice" chapter.

★ ★ ★

W. V. BRADSHAW, JR., MD-1978

Some physicians have hundreds of patients, some have thousands, but hundreds of thousands looked to W. V. Bradshaw, Jr. for health care. As director of the Fort Worth Public Health Department, he was the city's doctor.

In 1985 Phoebe Hummel, Director of Public Health Nursing said, "All of the good things that have happened in medicine the last 30 years he helped assure for Fort Worth."[99]

W. V. "Brad" Bradshaw, Jr. was born in Nansemond County, Virginia in 1911. He received his premed education at William and Mary College and M.D. from the Medical College of Virginia in Richmond. Bradshaw trained in Public Heath at Johns Hopkins in Baltimore.

During World War II he served as a medical inspector in Iceland for two years. His next assignment was Chickasha, Oklahoma. He arrived in the middle of summer, it was 100^0 at 10 o'clock at night. He thought he'd die, he complained to friends. In the Army Medical Corps for seven years, Bradshaw later served as surgeon for the 49th Armored Reserve.

Dr. Bradshaw came to Fort Worth as an assistant health director in 1947. He barely had time to get his feet wet after being named city health director. Then he *really* got his feet wet. In May, 1949—seventeen days after his promotion, much of Fort Worth was under water. He spent five days and nights on the job without going home. Son William V. Bradshaw, also a physician, recalled his father launched a motor boat to traverse the flooded streets. At the time of his retirement, Bradshaw recalled how he, his staff and volunteer doctors gave 121,000 shots for typhoid in the three weeks following the flood.

As director of Public Health, Bradshaw set up clinics for infants' preventive medical care. Over the years these clinics provided immunization for diphtheria, whooping cough, tetanus, polio and measles. For adults, he organized clinics for the treatment of tuberculosis and sexually transmitted diseases. At the latter, he attempted to curb the spread of venereal disease by asking patients to name their recent sexual partners in order that they, too, could receive treatment. One unhappy gonorrhea patient misunderstood the intent. Mack Williams noted, "The man threatened to beat up Dr. Bradshaw because the health director couldn't tell him where he got the disease. Finally Dr. Bradshaw told him: 'Look, I can't follow you around. I can only try to treat you.'"[100]

The medical community recognized his leadership by electing him president of the Tarrant County Medical Society in 1976. At that time no other public health director in a major city had ever been chosen by practicing physicians to represent them. Two years later he was awarded the Gold-Headed Cane. Hailed as a man with sunshine in his smile and goodwill in his heart, Bradshaw, with butter-smooth traces of a Virginia accent, thanked his peers for the honor.

Dr. Bradshaw retired in 1981 after seeing to the health needs of a growing city for a third of a century. He died of cancer four years later. His minister, Dr. A. M. Pennybacker of University Christian Church, summarized the doctor's dedicated life. "'Brad.' If the Lord himself welcomes him by some other name, he may not take up the option!'" He eulogized him: "People have been his business and health his trade. . . . He never got rich from his medical practice, but his wealth lay in the ties of life, the sharing and the friendship, of even those unknown whom he has touched."[101]

★ ★ ★

DURWOOD E. NEAL–1979

Durwood Neal was born in El Paso, not Texas, but Arkansas. He graduated from Hendrix College in Conway, before earning a medical degree from the University of Arkansas in Little Rock. He served in the Army from 1943 until 1945.

After his discharge Neal came to Fort Worth to intern at John Peter Smith Hospital. He stayed and became one of the city's most respected family physicians.

His volunteer activities were many, but Neal remained devoted to patient care. His colleagues named him recipient of the Gold-Headed Cane in 1979. At the awards dinner, Dr. W. V. "Brad" Bradshaw, Jr., told the assembled family and friends, "Durwood is receiving this honor from his peers because he is the kind of doctor who puts the care of his patients above everything else. He works hard to be a good physician. All that he does, whether medical or legislative or political, is with his patients' welfare in mind."[102]

He humbly and graciously accepted the Cane. And those were about the only serious moments in the ceremony. Neal was known for his sense of humor and love of a good joke, and his fellow doctors responded accordingly.

Bradshaw noted Neal's Arkansas hometown was so small, "Entering El Paso" and "Leaving El Paso" were on opposite sides of the same sign. He said the honoree claimed to be forty-nine, "That would make him starting college at seven and the University of Arkansas at the age of eleven."

Dr. Art Rutledge said, ". . . the only good thing to come out of Arkansas is Highway 67."[103]

Neal responded in kind, "The committee gave me some specific instructions, such as, 'Do not make a long, formal acceptance speech.' When I asked why . . .they said it might appear as though I deserved the award . . . . I wasn't sure whether Brad was going to relinquish the Cane or just give me the shaft." Of his wife, he said she loved antiques. "She buys anything two weeks older than I am." He promised to limit the introduction of family members to those who lived within a 300 mile radius. Speaking of family, he joked, "We've got so many children and grandchildren that some people say we have the only unfunded HMO in the country . . . . My sister's daughter-in-law lives in Lonoke. She's a doll. She is also known as the first girl in Arkansas to wear hot pants with orthopedic shoes."[104] Despite the wit and repartee, the family physician treasured the Cane.

Neal continued to be an advocate for patients until poor health forced him to retire in December 1990. He died in September 1992 at the age of seventy-one.

CHAPTER THIRTEEN

THE GOLD-HEADED CANE HONOREES: 1980-2000

THE '80s

Peschel started her account of the 1980s with a look at world events:

"The first U. S. space shuttle, Columbia, made its maiden flight. The Berlin wall was demolished. The first commercial product of generic engineering appeared when human insulin produced by bacteria was marketed. *Dallas fever swept the world* and everyone wanted to know who shot J.R.

"Health maintenance organizations (HMOs) and physician provider organizations became a rapidly growing, but solidly established, part of the health system.

"The TCMS and TMA worked to pass a Medical Practice Act. The act, signed into law in 1981, recreated the Texas State Board of Medical Examiners.

"In 1983, there was a downturn of the economy and unemployment rose. The society offered professional care at no charge to citizens of Tarrant County who were temporarily without work or health insurance.

"The physicians and auxiliary sponsored a Health Fair in 1988 and 1989. More than 30,000 people visited the health fair, which provided free health information and screens to the public.

"Volunteer physicians performed meritorious community service for health care to the homeless at the Presbyterian Night Shelter and Union Gospel Mission. Every year, volunteer physicians minister to the medical needs of the contestants and visitors of the Fort Worth Stock Show and Rodeo."[1]

★ ★ ★

DRUE O. D. WARE, MD-1980

The evening meal was family time at the Ware household, even if the busy doctor had to go back to the hospital after dining with his wife and children. And busy he was—shortly after World War II, Ware opened an office in a neighborhood of veterans and their wives who were just starting families. A general practitioner, his caseload was heavy with obstetrics and pediatrics.

Drue Ware was born in the tiny town of Jermyn in Jack County to a school teacher mother and rancher father. Ware didn't take to the land as did his father and grandfather. He announced at the age of six his intention to become a doctor. The youth took all the science classes his small school offered. It piqued his interest and kept his dream of medical school alive. He attended Baylor's medical school in Dallas and earned his degree in 1941.

During World War II he saw 167 days of front line combat duty as a Navy medical officer. He was attached to Carlson's Second Marine Raider Battalion, and involved in beachhead landings on Bougainville, Emerau and Guam during 1943 and 1944. Later he served as chief of surgery at the West Coast Marine Aviation Depot Hospital, San Diego, California. Ware held the rank of Lt. Commander when discharged in 1946.

As a civilian, he responded to a call from a Bridgeport, Texas physician. That doctor had built a small hospital and needed someone with surgical experience to compliment his practice. Drue and wife Mary liked living in the little town, but he was frustrated because he could not do simple procedures such as blood transfusions at the hospital.

In 1948 the Wares moved to Fort Worth where he practiced until his retirement in 1995. In the intervening years the tall man with the trademark silver gray mustache and dark, closely cropped hair, when not doing surgery, delivering over 5,000 babies or seeing patients, enjoyed hunting and fishing. Trout fishing in cold Colorado streams or hunting deer in the Texas hill country helped him recharge his batteries.

Ware exhibited a delightful sense of humor, but was deeply serious when the occasion demanded it. As he accepted the Gold-Headed Cane in 1980, he proclaimed the difficulty of expressing his gratitude. Jon McConal of the *Star-Telegram* quoted him as saying, "I've known all of the previous recipients and how outstanding they were. My colleagues have put me into a position where I feel wanting."[2] Those colleagues honored him because of his pleasing rapport in regard to patient care. They said after forty years he still felt a closeness to his patients, and they looked to him as friend as well as physician.

In 1993 the Texas Medical Association presented Ware with the Distinguished Service Award. Dr. Margie Peschel, in making the presentation, included the doctor's wife. "Drue Ware is married to the former Mary Helen Neeley. I know of no spouse more supportive of her husband than Mary Helen."[3]

Drue Ware was awarded emeritus membership in the Texas Medical Association in 1997. The news release listed many of the doctor's outstanding contributions as a physician, but his own words convey what a doctor was to him.

> "If first a doctor offers his patients the support,
> encouragement and solace they need. . . .
> If he has professional integrity, and is humbly
> grateful for those talents of usefulness given him,
> I think he should be serene, proud, and happy to
> spend his life as a physician."[4]

Dr. Drue O. D. Ware died February 18, 1988 after a long illness. His legacy to the profession he loved is a loving family, a host of patients who also call themselves friends, and a son who followed in his father's footsteps.

★ ★ ★

JAMES W. SHORT, MD-1981

The 1981 Gold-Headed Cane Award dinner was both a somber and joyous occasion. James Short died just nine days after he was named to receive the accolades of his fellow physicians.

The popular editor of the doctor's monthly magazine, the *Tarrant County Physician*, was born in Helena, Arkansas November 1, 1914. He graduated from the University of Arkansas Medical School in 1943. During World War II he was with the 5th Marine Division and participated in the invasions of Saipan, Tinian, and Iwo Jima.

After the war he accepted a surgical residency at Hartford Hospital in Hartford, Connecticut. In 1948 he opened his Fort Worth office and for twenty-five years he built a reputation as an adept surgeon. Heart disease caused him to curtail operating and led to his second successful career.

In 1974 he accepted the position of Executive Director of the Tarrant County Medical Society. He held that post until 1980. His third career was editing the *Tarrant County Physician*. His friend, Dr. Durwood Neal, described Short as ". . . a frustrated journalist who was widely known and respected at the TMA and American Medical Association level."[5] The *Tarrant County Physician* grew to a readership of 1800 under his tutelage. He wrote and encouraged others, such as Dr. Sam Jagoda, Jr. to take up the pen.

In May 1981 polyradiculoneuropathy, more commonly known as Guillian–Barre syndrome, was diagnosed. It led to his death in September of that year.

With the approval of Short's family, the Gold-Headed Cane Award Dinner was held as scheduled. Reporter Carolyn Ondrejas quoted Dr. Drue Ware's characterization of the late honoree. "Dr. Short was a man with a remarkable sense of humor, who was sympathetic, patient and loving."[6] Ware presented the Cane to Dr. Durwood Neal, who in turn presented it to Mrs. Short.

"The tenor of this evening is one of honor and dignity to commemorate and extol our departed friend's reception of the Gold-Headed Cane. The intent is not to eulogize, but to celebrate. This is the way he would have wanted it.   It may interest you to know that in 1974 he instructed the Tarrant County Medical Society to delete his name from the Gold-Headed Cane eligible list. This gesture draws a picture of his humility. Tonight, we wish to rectify this act.

"Our friend would want me to thank the Tarrant County Medical Society and the Auxiliary for their generosity in selecting him the 1981 recipient. With a twinkle in his eye, he would say—'A Cane winner will do well if he doesn't get carried away with himself,'"[7] Neal concluded.

★ ★ ★

WARREN MOORMAN, MD-1982

The years have slowed Warren Woodman Moorman physically, but mentally the retired internist hasn't lost a step. His interest in medicine stemmed from a visit as a four-year-old to a doctor. The physician repaired a cut eye, and Warren, pleased with the result, decided he wanted to become "a miracle worker."

The Fort Worth native was born February 27, 1919 and attended public schools here. In 1942 he received his medical degree from the Galveston Medical Branch of the university where he was a member of Alpha Omega Alpha honorary medical society. Moorman interned at Philadelphia General Hospital.

He joined the Navy and served aboard a Pacific transport for most of the war. Prior to his 1947 discharge he became a flight surgeon. During the Korean Conflict he served from 1950 to 1951, again as a flight surgeon. Between stints in the Navy Moorman did a three year residency in Internal Medicine at the veteran's hospital in McKinney. He wrote a book about his medical experiences.

In 1951 the Navy doctor said goodbye to military life and joined the Lorimer Clinic in Fort Worth. The clinic was located a couple of blocks from where he grew up and attended high school. "So I haven't gotten very far in my lifetime," he was fond of saying.

Dallas Morning News reporter Pat Gordon noted Moorman's gray hair, friendly eyes, and quick smile cast him instantly in the Marcus Welby role. But unlike the television doctor, he had practiced real medicine for thirty years at the time of the interview. The internist, named 1982 recipient of the Gold-Headed Cane, was asked if he made house calls. "You bet, I made one last night, and I enjoy them."[8]

In his book Moorman wrote about his first house call. It was to his grandmother. "I had just obtained my doctor's bag, of which I was very proud. I sat by my grandmother's bed to examine her, opened my bag to get out my new blood pressure cuff, and she leaned over the edge of the bed and vomited directly into my new bag. To this day I never leave an opened medical bag at the patient's bedside."[9]

Concerning house calls, he said, "There is no better way to get to know a family and what makes a patient tick than to see them at home."[10] He related memories of two patients who exemplified this concept. For months, several times a week, he called on two dying old men. One lived in an unpainted shotgun house, without electricity and the bathtub was used to store firewood. The old man was incontinent and an inveterate tobacco chewer with a poor aim. Despite the poor surroundings, his family hovered nearby and did all in their power to make him comfortable. Although he was dying, he seemed a happy old man.

The other patient sat in his palatial home, alone except for the servant who opened the door. The man's wife and daughters were away at some social event. This poor rich man was lonely and miserable in his final illness. Moreover, he was distressed because he was too ill and weak to leave his house and visit his mistress. "I thought there was some kind of lesson in the contrast between the two dying old men."[11]

He compared an internist to a detective who unravels an assortment of clues to solve a case. "Someone with a headache can go to an eye doctor, who says 'It's not your eyes'. . . and sends the patient to another specialist," he told Gordon. As an internist, Moorman said, "When someone comes in and says 'I hurt, doctor,' I have to find out why."[12]

One patient Moorman wrote about in his memoirs was "hurting, but feeling no pain."

"The most interesting patient I have ever known and the most memorable from my intern days was Jimmy Spillane, who was my patient on the psychiatric service at Philadelphia General Hospital. Jimmy had been brought to the hospital by police when he was apprehended carrying baseball equipment. . . . The police asked him where he was going . . . and he informed them he was going to work out at home. [In those days Philadelphia had two teams.] When I questioned him. . . he was proud to tell me that he was the star pitcher for both teams and admitted he was a superior player, but said I should meet his sister, who played catcher for him. He said she was 5 feet tall and weighed 200 pounds and could throw a baseball from home plate to the Gulf of Mexico.

"Jimmy had syphilis of the brain. . . . He had marvelous delusions of grandeur, which made him such a stimulating companion."[13]

Moorman detailed several more of Jimmy's delusions, such as thinking he was Jack Dempsey. "While leafing through a movie magazine, he saw a picture of Carole Lombard, whom he identified as his ex-wife, and for that moment he thought of himself as Clark Gable.

"When whiling away the time at a pretty nurse's desk, he promised to buy her a set of 'diamond-studded underwear' and told her that he thought I had potential to become a doctor, and that he was going to send me to Harvard next week."[14]

At Lorimer Clinic, Moorman learned a lot about physical pain. Interviewed by Carolyn Poirot, he said, "Arthritis pain is my special interest, but I'm a general internist. We serve as primary physicians to our patients. If it doesn't hurt or it doesn't show, most people put off going to the doctor. If it hurts or shows, it brings 'em in. So we see a lot of people with bone and joint pains."[15]

In 1982 a colleague told reporter Pat Gordon why Moorman was selected to receive the Gold-Headed Cane. "[He is] the complete physician, who epitomizes all the qualities that make a good doctor—intelligence, common sense and caring."[16]

"I'm surprised that many people knew my name,"[17] the internist told Gordon. At a Ridglea Country Club dinner, Moorman read from a 1927 *Journal of the American Medical Association*, "The good physician knows his patients through and through, and his knowledge is bought dearly. Time, sympathy and understanding must be lavishly dispensed. . . . The secret of the care of the patient is in caring 'for' the patient."[18] Holding the cherished cane, he concluded, "No other profession offers you the passport to all the echelons of society or allows you to come closer to really sharing the strengths and weaknesses of people than medicine."[19] Perhaps he was remembering the two old dying men from years ago.

★ ★ ★

MAL RUMPH, MD-1983

A colleague said of Dr. Mal Rumph, "He possessed this stentorian voice—every time he spoke it sounded like God talking."[20] The 1983 recipient of the Gold-Headed Cane came from a family deeply rooted in the tradition of medicine. His father, five uncles, and three great-uncles preceded him in the practice of medicine. Appropriately enough, his story is told in the "Family Practice" chapter.

★ ★ ★

Robb Rutledge, MD-1984

"I wasn't one of these people who wanted to be a doctor from day one,"[21] Robb Rutledge declared, some fifty years after he graduated from medical school. Math was his favorite subject in school and he toyed with the idea of developing games for Parker Brothers as he was growing up. But instead he kept a family tradition in tact; for three generations the second sons became doctors, and so did he. Now his second son, Dr. Peter Rutledge, extends the tradition to four generations.

Robb was born in Detroit Lakes, Minnesota and attended the University of Michigan at Ann Arbor. He graduated, *cum laude* from Harvard Medical School and did his internship and residency at Massachusetts General Hospital in Boston.

With his lofty credentials he could pick and choose where he would work. Fortunately for Fort Worth, he began his general surgery practice here in 1957.

The transplanted Texan views doctor/patient communication as a given for good medical care. One memorable patient showed his gratitude in a unique way. The man had severe ulcerative colitis which required an ileostomy. The patient left the hospital and Rutledge considered the relationship closed. Not so—when the surgeon suffered a broken wrist in a fall, he received a package from the former patient. It was a wood-carved statute of a balding doctor with his right arm in a sling. A year later the man was elected president of the local ileostomy association. Rutledge was there—to present him with a statute of an ileostomy survivor.

Rutledge received the 1984 Gold-Headed Cane. Some 400 family members and friends gathered at the Petroleum Club October 17 for the event. His remarks included the admission that his enthusiasm for the medical profession was as great as when he first began. He denied being a "workaholic" as his family described him—he preferred to think of himself as "positively addicted to medicine." In a more serious vein the surgeon ruminated, "If you can do what you're good at and what you enjoy doing, you're lucky."[22]

Despite his emphasis on interaction with patients, Rutledge during his career found time to publish fifty articles in such scholarly journals as the *Annals of Surgery* and *American Journal of Surgery*. "He was elected to the prestigious American Surgical Association, composed almost exclusively of surgeons in major medical schools, on the weight of his publications. That is a tremendous accomplishment for someone in private practice,"[23] reporter Carolyn Poirot quoted another surgeon in speaking of Rutledge. He also authored a widely known biography of the great surgeon Theodor Billroth.

Looking back on the many advances in medicine, he pegged the development of sophisticated uses of anesthesiology as one of the most important to surgeons. That, combined with the use of fiber-optic instruments have allowed surgeons to save lives that only decades ago would have been impossible. Looking to the future he sees improved transplantation as a major milestone. Dr. Rutledge predicted that when we get the problem of rejection licked there will be a much wider source of donors and transplantation will take off even more than it is now.

Now semi-retired, Rutledge teaches three and one-half days at John Peter Smith and the rest of the week enjoys being with his family. He leaves the doctoring to second son Peter, and who knows, maybe a second grandson someday.

★ ★ ★

DOLPHUS E. COMPERE, MD-1985

"War stories" from his Pacific tour of duty and from his Fort Worth medical practice reveal much of "Dolph" Compere's personality. He is entertaining in both fields.

A *Tarrant County Physician* profile stated, "From 1943 to 1945 he served, with the rank of Major, in the 3rd Air Commando Group of the United States Air Force, stationed in the South Pacific."[24] The article did not include any of his adventures, but in an interview he recalled some of them.

He was involved in invasions from the Philippines to Okinawa. "I landed with one aide and a first-aid kit. I told my commanding officer I needed a jeep, and he approved."[25] From then on he "lived in that jeep." Once, he survived a typhoon by clinging to the underside of the vehicle.

The only surgeon in the group, he patched up the wounded as best he could under battlefield conditions. He then went in his jeep to wherever there were casualties to do what he could to help them. "As time went by, living conditions improved, we got a tent, then we got a little Quonset hut, and in some places we actually took over buildings."[26]

He recalled an emergency night flight to Manila with a fighter pilot who was having difficulty breathing and exhibiting other signs suggesting either poliomyelitis or meningitis. During the next few days other suspicious cases were evacuated and he never did learn their final diagnosis. However, a few weeks later, a Colonel from Washington, D. C. came to further investigate these cases. To Compere's surprise and chagrin he was found operating, and because of the heat and humidity, wearing only shorts, a cap, mask and gloves! Fortunately for Dr. Compere, this Colonel turned out to be a fellow resident from the University of Michigan.

On January 30, 1945, Compere assisted the Marines in liberating 511 prisoners from Cabanatuan prison camp near Manila. Originally there were 16,000 in this camp who had survived the Bataan Death March. Among the fleeing Americans was Dr. Merle "Jim" Musselman, a fellow intern from Michigan. This was quite a joyous reunion! One of the many stories related to their long internment was the time a fellow physician prisoner, Dr. Charles Lewis, saved Jim's fate from being shipped to Japan. He told the Japanese commanding officer that Jim had "Tootsie Gamauchie Fever" which was a contagious fatal disease and all personnel on that ship would die. "Jim was removed from the shipping list and this probably saved Jim's life," Compere said.[27]

"After his discharge, Dolph returned to Michigan for an M.S. degree, which he received in 1948,"[28] according to the *Tarrant County Physician*. He joined Dr. Hub E. Isaacks in the practice of urology. Together with Dr. Grant Begley, they founded the Urology Clinic.

He also recalled an incident which could have sidetracked his medical career. "I almost got fired before I got started." He was operating at St. Joseph when a nun, in floor length habit, entered the operating room. "I ordered her out." He was told to report to the Sister Superior (the hospital administrator) the next day. Like a child sent to the principal's office, he sat and waited for his fate to be determined. After hearing his side of the dispute, he and the Sister came to an agreement. He would not order nuns out of the operating room and nuns would wear regulation appropriate clothing while there. "It wasn't very smart of me to do it, but it did change things,"[29] he reminisced.

One of Compere's patients suffered from ureteral colic. The man wanted immediate surgery to ease the pain. Compere urged patience and indeed the man subsequently passed the kidney stone. "Three or four months later on the first tee at Colonial Country Club, I was getting ready to hit the ball," the urologist said, "when a fellow came up to me and asked, 'What's your favorite animal?'" Somewhat irritated by the intrusion, he offhandedly relied, "Buffalo."[30] The result of that encounter is a large oil painting of a group of grazing prairie buffalo now hanging on Compere's wall. The patient happened to be Jack Bryant, renowned western artist. The physician also points with pride to a bronze statute of a mounted cowboy by the same artist. The miniature is so detailed one sees even the ashes on the rider's cigarette.

Another prized possession was the Gold-Headed Cane. This highest honor from his peers was awarded to Dr. Compere at a dinner October 1, 1985. Among the 400 family members and friends were two special guests—survivors from Cabanatuan prison camp, Dr. Merle M. Musselman, a retired professor of surgery at the University of Nebraska, and Dr. Charles Lewis, a retired obstetrician–gynecologist from Oakland, California. Carolyn Poirot, of the *Star-Telegram*, wrote that after completing their respective residencies at the University of Michigan Hospital the three ". . . had not been back together for more than 37 years."[31]

When accepting the Gold-Headed Cane, he commented, "More scientific progress has been made in my lifetime than at any time in the history of medicine, and I feel blessed indeed to have been in practice during this period."[32] While lauding scientific advancement, he cautioned, "But, no matter how far technology takes us, there is always going to be that special relationship between the physician and his patient."[33] And Compere has an oil painting to prove it.

★ ★ ★

MARGIE B. PESCHEL, MD-1986

Margie B. Peschel has as many hats as the late Hollywood gossip columnist Hedda Hopper, but the popular doctor's brain power is difficult to hide under a hat. Her story in found in the "Women in Medicine" chapter.

★ ★ ★

WILLIAM S. LORIMER, JR., MD-1987

Bill Lorimer's family tree is filled with doctors. His story is in the "Family Medicine" chapter.

★ ★ ★

JAMES D. MURPHY. MD-1988

Many people play golf. Many people would have liked to play golf with Ben Hogan and Byron Nelson. James D. Murphy has played with these two legends of the game. Retired, Murphy still shoots in the low seventies, but now he golfs with friends and other retired physicians.

The genial Irishman comes from a family of attorneys, but his junior high school days in the science lab whetted his appetite for medicine. "From age twelve I wanted to be a doctor,"[34] he said in an interview. Despite being a good student, he remembered the first year of medical school as a rude awakening. Probably speaking for many of his colleagues he recalled, "We thought we knew how to study, but we learned how to really study. That first year we had only two or three weekends without a lot of studying. . . but the second year was better."[35]

For five years, from 1942 to 1947 he was a Navy doctor. He shed his Lt. Commander rank and happily became Dr. Murphy again. Back in Fort Worth, he began his work in family medicine. It was May 1947 and making house calls helped establish his practice. "I'd cover for as many as fourteen doctors. I'd sometimes make as many as seventeen house calls in a day," he told Dr. Grant Begley in an interview for the medical society journal. "That's a lot of travel."[36]

Eventually his clientele numbered from seventy to one hundred families, most of whom stayed with him until his retirement. He counted among his patients Ben Hogan's family. "'I am very proud to be a family physician,'" he said when interviewed by *Tarrant County Physician*. "To me, it is the most rewarding form of medicine—you're taking care of people who know you and know you're doing the best you can."[37]

Murphy's talents were tapped beyond the local scene. In 1950 the Texas Academy of General Practice elected him vice-president, and president five years later. In that office one of his goals was to interest more young people in family practice. At every opportunity he outlined the advantages of getting to know an entire family.

Installed in 1966 as president of the 9,600 member TMA, he noted the newly legislated Medicare program would change the way physicians and hospitals cared for patients. He predicted, "There will be certain people who will have to be limited to the time they can stay in a hospital regardless of the amount of their hospitalization and their ability to pay,"[38] he told reporter Mabel Gouldy. That prediction is now a reality.

For his work in local, state and national professional organizations, for his efforts to improve the training program at John Peter Smith, and for his caring attitude toward patients, the Tarrant County Medical Society members voted him the "Doctor's Doctor" in 1988. In acknowledging the presentation of the Gold-Headed Cane, Murphy reflected back on his career. "Fort Worth has been a good place to practice for the past forty years,"[39] he said. His peers consider it a better place because of his efforts.

★ ★ ★

JAMES O. McBRIDE, MD-1989

Third generation Fort Worthian James O. McBride attended public schools here, graduating from the old Central High School. He studied premed at Texas Christian University before earning a medical degree from the University of Texas in Galveston. McBride returned to his home town to do an internship at City-County, now John Peter Smith, Hospital.

World War II interrupted his formal medical career. According to the *Tarrant County Physician*, "He then went on active duty with the U. S. Navy, serving in the Pacific Theater. . . . He made nine landings in an LST as a junior member of Surgical Team 17."[40]

Dr. Sam Jagoda, Jr. told of one of the Navy medic's experiences. Perhaps exaggerating a bit, he said, McBride ". . . was the only person who ever dug a foxhole on the deck of a battleship."[41] With a Japanese kamikaze headed directly toward him, it seemed like the prudent thing to do.

Colleagues described McBride as "probably the premier chest surgeon in town," but he also was a leader in the medical community. Dr. McBride's peers honored him in 1989 by naming him recipient of the Gold-Headed Cane. At the October 12 Award Dinner he said, "Medicine gives a person who has some scientific bent and who likes people a chance to combine these in one wonderful profession."[42] Friends and colleagues say he has done so in an extraordinary, yet modest, way.

★ ★ ★

THE 90s

Peschel continued her countdown of the decades.

"It has been the decade of the breakup of the Soviet Union. A truck bomb exploded outside a federal building in Oklahoma City. Mark McGwire set a new home run record of 70. The drug, Viagra, became a top seller.

"The 1990s will be remembered as the decade of change in health care. Physicians had to become involved in both the delivery and economics of health care.

"The Veterans Affairs Medical Outpatient Clinic opened in Fort Worth to serve the 19-county area of North Texas in 1992.

"The TCMS created the May Owen Award in 1992 to be given to nonphysician individuals, agencies or groups who have made outstanding contributions to health care in Tarrant County.

"In August 1995 the Tarrant County Medical Society was the first county medical society in the nation to have a home page on the

Internet. The home page provided a collection of medical information and community resources. What a tremendous resource to both the citizens and physicians of Tarrant County for years to come!

"The society joined the American Cancer Society, the American Heart Association, American Lung Association and other health-related entities in the Fort Worth Tobacco-Free Coalition. Work included a City Ordinance to prohibit smoking in public places and restrict minors' access to tobacco."[43]

★ ★ ★

THOMAS L. SHIELDS, MD-1990

Most people have heard of the love bug, and its "bite" is no cause for a visit to the doctor, but the kissing bug? Ann Landers deals with the former, and Dr. Thomas L. Shields is an authority on the latter.

The dermatologist's interest in medicine and healing germinated at the age of twelve when he was a patient at Parkland Hospital. "I got hit in the face with a baseball bat and was unconscious for a few days,"[44] he recalled in an interview. "And a lot of people say that's what's wrong with me today," he laughed.

Shields received his medical education at Baylor Medical School and did his internship and residency at Parkland.

Like many other young doctors in the 1940s, his medical career was interrupted by World War II. He served in the European Theater, then was stationed in Japan with the Army of Occupation. "Dr. Shields was awarded the Bronze Star and held the rank of Lieutenant-Colonel when discharged."[45]

Returning to civilian life, Shields studied dermatology at the University of Pennsylvania and in 1948 he joined the Southwestern Medical School faculty as an associate professor. A year later he began his Fort Worth practice.

At that time dermatology and syphilogy were a joint domain and he is board certified in that speciality. Today dermatologists see more skin cancer than syphilis, but that was not always so. Shields recalled, early in his career, treating an entire family, including young children, for the once dreaded disease. The father passed the infection to the mother, and as all drank out of a common long-handled cup and water bucket, the children were infected. He cured them, and while syphilis is usually a sexually transmitted disease, he noted there are tragic exceptions such as this case.

Shields lauds the development of antibiotics as a great advance in medicine. Sadly he remembered the days before antibiotics. "At Parkland little kids would come in with pneumonia and be dead the next day. Now two per cent of pneumonia patients fail to recover,"[46] he said.

He and fellow Fort Worth dermatologist E. N. Walsh, in 1954 presented a seminal paper on the "Kissing Bug Bite." The whimsical name belied the seriousness of the malady. Shields and Walsh told the assembled doctors the bites were multiple and often grouped on the forearm, hand, feet, and face. "To find the kissing bug on or about the bed is truly big game hunting in the general field of bug hunting when applied to bites observed by dermatologists in humans,"[47] the two noted.

The report grew out of case histories and their own experiences. "During the past two years we have seen 45 patients who presented themselves because of lesions which were caused by the bite of Triatoma sanguisuga, an insect commonly known as the 'kissing bug.'"[48] To learn more about it, Shields and Walsh allowed the bug to bite them. Walsh seemed immune, but Shields suffered a reaction. "In 25 hours an erythematatous, pruritic papule developed, which reached its maximum size of 8mm. in 72 hours."[49] The bite did not blister and the red "bump" scaled off in about four weeks. He still has one of the bugs mounted and encased in glass.

The doctors found only two references to the bug bite in the English medical literature and the purpose of their paper was to bring attention to this little known insect and its effect on patients.

Dr. Shields served as chief of dermatology at Harris-Methodist Hospital and for twenty years held a skin clinic at John Peter Smith, where he was a former chief of dermatology. For many years he was a consultant for the United States Public Health Service, and is a former president of the Fort Worth unit of the American Cancer Society.

In addition to recognition for his work on the kissing bug bite and holding professional offices, Shields is no stranger to honors and awards.

In 1990 he was designated the recipient of the Gold-Headed Cane. His acceptance remarks reflected a genuine regard for his fellow physicians. "It has indeed been a pleasure to practice medicine in Fort Worth. The high standards and moral tone exemplified by our distinguished medical forbearers continues today in the professional demeanor of my peers."[50]

Shields is quick to give credit to those who have helped him along the way. His father died when he was seventeen months old, leaving his mother to raise three children. It is from her that he learned self-discipline and the value of hard work. He praises Pauline, his wife of more than fifty years, for the sacrifices she willingly made while he finished his medical training and pursued his career goals.

To cap his untiring devotion to medicine he was honored in February 2000 by his alma mater. "In recognition of his decades of service to the Dallas/Fort Worth medical community and generous philanthropic efforts, the Department of Dermatology at UT Southwestern Medical Center has established a professorship in honor of Dr. Thomas L. Shields."[51]

Well said and well deserved.

★ ★ ★

Stephen Eppstein, MD-1991

One might say Stephen Eppstein grew interested in medicine from the ground up—as a teenager he helped his father make arch supports. He met many physicians, including Dr. Louis Levy, who became a good friend and role model.

In 1963, the articulate internist joined three other doctors at the Lorimer Clinic, but from 1966 to 1968 he was in the Air Force, stationed at Amarillo, Texas. By the time he returned the clinic had grown to six physicians—four internists and two surgeons. Except for the two years in the service, Eppstein was with Lorimer for twenty-eight years. He considers that time as memorable because of the relationship with outstanding colleagues, such as the Lorimers, Dr. Warren Moorman, and Drs. A. R. Daniel, Robert Ward, Richard Penny, James Davidson and Roger Eppstein.

Dr. Eppstein is now with the Medical Clinic of North Texas. His encyclopedic knowledge of his field leads many Fort Worth physicians to refer their family members to him. As an internist he frequently sees the same patients year after year, which to Eppstein is one of the most satisfying aspects of his practice.

Concerning hospitals, as a new doctor in town, he recalled Dr. Lorimer, Sr.'s reading of hospitals. "'Let me tell you about the hospitals in Fort Worth—Harris is run for the nurses; All Saints is run for the doctors; St. Joseph is run for the patients,'" he quoted the retired doctor as saying. "I enjoyed my association with St. Joseph for thirty years,"[52] Eppstein said in an interview.

Teaching others has been an important way in which he gives back to the community. For many years he volunteered as a clinical professor at Southwestern Medical School. He also volunteers at local Critical Care Nursing Courses and has been a volunteer instructor at Tarrant County College and Texas Wesleyan University.

In 1991 Eppstein was tapped as recipient of the Gold-Headed Cane. One of the youngest to receive the honor, he was described by Dr. Richard Penny, TCMS president as one who ". . . personifies what doctors think is important about being a doctor—honesty, integrity, clinical ability, trustworthiness. He represents the kind of doctor we all want to be, the kind of doctor we would want to take care of our families." He went on to say, "I can't think of a more deserving recipient,"[53] Penny told reporter Carolyn Poirot.

"I am proud to be a physician and am optimistic about the future of medicine. It has been my privilege to practice in this fine medical community and to live in a city where I spent my childhood,"[54] Eppstein said when learning of the award. Almost ten years later, when interviewed for this book, Eppstein was still proud to be a physician. "I think that for me I can't imagine any other professional choice that would or could have been better. The challenges and rewards are still there and I don't think the political scene or the economics of medicine alter that a great deal."[55]

Would he encourage a young person to enter the medical profession? Perhaps his son, Dr. Roger Eppstein is the answer to that question.

★ ★ ★

John W. Freese, MD-1992

If he had followed in the family business John Freese might be reading blueprints today instead of X-rays. The physician did share with his late father Simon, an engineer, a love of books and history. Simon Freese wrote a chronicle of his company, Freese & Nichols, entitled *100 Years in the Works*. Outside the medical field, John has been involved in Friends of Tarrant County Junior College, Historic Southside, Inc., and is an active member of Broadway Baptist Church.

He majored in biology at Williams College in Williamstown, Massachusetts. Many of his biology classmates were premed students and it was during college that Freese decided to study medicine. After his 1952 graduation he spent a year at Massachusetts Institute of Technology. He entered Johns Hopkins University Medical School in 1953.

Johns Hopkins is a proud school that boasts such faculty members as the great Canadian, Sir William Osler. Freese considered himself fortunate to be able to take a class in the history of medicine which emphasized the traditions of the famous Baltimore institution. Graduating in 1957, he interned and did a residency in general and thoracic surgery at Duke University Medical Center in Durham, North Carolina.

He returned home in 1964 to practice surgery. Freese has seen many improvements since then, including open heart surgery—a new technique when he began his practice. "Heart surgery at that time was mitral valve surgery, not truly 'open heart.'"[56] He credited colleague Dr. Clive Johnson with pioneering cardiovascular surgery in Fort Worth.

In the area of improvements in the overall health care system, Freese recalled the decrease in infectious diseases when a pure water system was installed. Notes from his father's *100 Years in the Works* revealed a drop from 235 cases of typhoid a year to practically none. They could pinpoint which city wells contained typhoid germs.

Until a pediatric surgeon was available, Freese saw both children and adults. Later he confined his practice to adults. In 1990 he again limited his practice, this time to surgical oncology. He has seen progress in this speciality as it changed from gross anatomy to the subcellular level of today. All this Freese finds tremendously exciting. In early 2000 he joined the University of Texas Southwestern Moncrief Cancer Center as Medical Director of the Diagnostic Center.

Freese's strong voice and commanding presence belie his gentle concern for patients. Regarding the doctor-patient relationship, he told reporter Lou Chapman, "It means not only giving them health care, but helping patients as they relate to the hospital, or the X-ray clinic or whatever—to act as the patient's advocate as they move through the health-care system."[57]

Freese's interest in history led him to write a feature for the April, 1990 *Tarrant County Physician*. In it he urged doctors to contribute medical memorabilia to the Fort Worth Heritage Center. "Many of our members have family ties that go well back in Fort Worth's 140 year history, and many 'newcomers' would like to have access to the source material that documents the history of Fort Worth's government, businesses, people, and families."[58] The surgeon's scientific articles have appeared in *The Journal of Thoracic and Cardio-Vascular Surgery*.

Freese has been chief of surgery at All Saints and chief of staff at Cook-Fort Worth Children's Medical Center, and on the staff of four other hospitals. In 1992, the year he was awarded the Gold-Headed Cane, Dr. Freese commented that he is known because of his work at so many hospitals. Gratified to be honored by his peers, he nevertheless said, "But by the same token, the ones most likely to be chosen are the ones that may work at more than one hospital or come into contact with other physicians regularly."[59]

In this case, his peers would argue, many more knew of the fine work he was doing and for that reason he was chosen.

★ ★ ★

G. Douglas Tatum, MD-1993

"I'm not a research scientist, and I'm not a teacher, per se, although I teach. My work is the patients. That's what I do,"[60] Dr. G. Douglas Tatum told a *Star-Telegram* reporter on the occasion of his receiving the Gold-Headed Cane. Fort Worth colleagues recognize his competence and compassion as evidenced by the many who refer their own family members to the gynecologist.

Tatum's interest in medicine grew out of extraordinary personal experiences. His father's work necessitated long absences from home. His mother suffered from Class A diabetes, and depended on young Douglas to take care of her. "She was very brittle and very prone to episodes of hypoglycemic insulin reactions. And I had to deal with that as a ten-year-old,"[61] he recalled in an interview.

At Texas Christian University, Dr. May Owen gave him a night job at the All Saints Hospital Laboratory. He considers her mentoring as one of the highlights of his college years.

The 1957 Suez Canal crisis caused Uncle Sam to interrupt his residency for two years. As an Air Force reservist he was called up and worked in a Roswell, New Mexico hospital. "The aliens had come and gone," he laughed. His tour ended, Capt. Tatum returned to Parkland and finished his residency.

For many years he practiced both obstetrics and gynecology. Looking at women's health historically, Tatum noted those of child-bearing age have benefited tremendously from sterile techniques we now take for granted. In the late 1800s a Vienna physician, Ignaz Semmelweis, saved the lives of thousands of women by a simple edict, "Wash your hands between patients."

The invention of the sonogram, more than the ability of a pregnant woman to show "pictures" of her baby, enable obstetricians to observe the development of the fetus. This, plus monitoring during parturition, allows for intervention if needed, to save both mother and baby. These, according to Tatum, have revolutionized obstetrics. But, he maintains, the doctor/patient relationship is still the most important

Family dinner-table conversation is stimulating, as his wife, Barbara, is the daughter of Dr. Judge Lyle and daughter Leslie is a pathologist. If the conversation turns to legal matters sons Stephen and Daniel are there to advise—perhaps on the oil business, son Scott's domain.

Tatum's family, including his thirteen grandchildren, celebrated with him when he was named the 1993 recipient of the Gold-Headed Cane. His initial reaction was one of astonishment and a feeling of being tremendously honored. Of that award, he said, "It is a means of accepting the kind of medical practice I've always believed in—and that is patient care." This practice involves prevention and communication. "'If you don't communicate with them,' he said, 'you can't help them at all,'"[62] he explained to reporter Lou Chapman.

What advice would he give a young doctor just starting out? "Maintaining a caring relationship between doctor and patient."[63] That is what the well-respected Tatum has used as his guide for almost forty years in medicine, and hundreds of patients heartily concur he has succeeded.

★ ★ ★

John M. Richardson, MD-1994

John Richardson is the son of an EENT specialist, and there are two dentists and one medical technician in the family. Where else but the "Family Practice" chapter would one put Dr. Richardson's profile?

★ ★ ★

Bohn D. Allen, MD-1995

Bohn (it rhymes with John) D. Allen was named for an Alpine, Texas friend of his father's. Years later Dr. Bohn Allen met and became the physician of the man with whom he shares the name. But all of this aside—the 1995 Gold-Headed Cane recipient's friends call him Dick. At the October award dinner, Allen, the only Arlington doctor to receive the honor, said, "I am humbled and gratified that my peers would seek me out and give me this award. . . . I was shocked to receive it. . . .No. 1, that someone from Arlington would be chosen and secondly, that it would be me."[64]

Allen's father owned a dry cleaners next door to a small private hospital in that Davis Mountains city. As a boy, Bohn made friends with the doctors and decided that was what he wanted to be when he grew up. The conviction strengthened as he worked summers in the hospital. By the time he began his studies at the University of Texas Medical School in Galveston, he was experienced in laboratory and X-ray work.

He did his internship at FitzSimmons General Hospital, a U. S. Army facility in Denver, Colorado. The training he received there would come in handy later. For twelve years he was an Army surgeon, three of which he spent in Japan. "I did more surgery there than the rest of my lifetime,"[65] he said in an interview. Perhaps a slight exaggeration, but working with the multiplicity of battlefield wounds from Vietnam war victims certainly gave him a wide range of surgeries, both life-saving and reconstructive.

The friendly Arlington physician has seen many changes in medicine in his years of practice. "In the last fifty to sixty years we have moved away from studying medicine from the gross anatomical standpoint and have begun to understand the body from a subcelluar level. This enables us to operate on the carotid artery to prevent strokes," he noted as an example. "Up until the early 1950s patients who had aneurysms died. Now we do surgery to prevent complications."[66]

Even more than his surgical skills, his caring for the total well-being of patients is evident from listening to him. He feels education of patients is vital to their successful recovery. And patients leave his office knowing they are his number one priority. Dr. David Russell said of his cohort, "He makes sure that every patient understands what is happening and is comfortable with all their available options."[67]

"The well-being of the patient must always be foremost in the minds of all physicians. When we place the needs and interests of our patients before all other considerations and we reassure ourselves of the essential and inherent virtues of the practice of medicine, we will once again find peace and satisfaction in our life long endeavor of service to mankind,"[68] he wrote in 1993.

What do others think of the this hard working, down-to-earth surgeon? One woman, after hearing Dr. Allen espouse his medical philosophy, said "If I ever need surgery, he's the one I want to do it." Perhaps his professional and personal life is best summed up in a comment made by a peer. "What a great guy he is."[69]

★ ★ ★

DICK G. ELLIS, MD-1996

Does a pediatric surgeon remove tiny tonsils? No, an eye, ear, nose and throat specialist does that. Then what *does* a pediatric surgeon do? A lot, if he is Dick Gibbs Ellis, M.D. The personable physician estimates he has done over 3,000 hernia repairs in children.

There were enough doctors in his family to operate their own hospital had they chosen to do so. His mother's uncle was a pioneer doctor in Oklahoma, in fact the first to be licensed after statehood. This uncle, Charles Bobo, became the first dean of the medical school at the University of Oklahoma. Ellis had three uncles who were physicians; two were his mother's brothers and one was married to his aunt. They were all in Baylor Medical School in Dallas in 1922. One uncle, Zack Bobo, Jr. practiced in Fort Worth until he moved to Arlington in 1931. Young Dick planned to go into general medicine, but his uncles advised him to get additional surgical training as well.

Dick Ellis, the 1996 holder of the Gold-Headed Cane was born in Muskogee, Oklahoma April 24, 1928. Following a 1952-53 internship at St. Louis City Hospital, Ellis did a two year residency in general surgery there the next year. "Those were great years,"[70] he recalled, great because he met and married Kay Kolisek while an intern.

In 1954 Ellis joined the United States Air Force and spent two years in England. This assignment, near London, led to a lifelong interest in Anglo/American medicine and he is a member of the British Association of Pediatric Surgeons. After his military service he returned to St. Louis and completed his surgical residency at City Hospital.

Ellis began his Fort Worth general surgery practice in 1960. More and more he came to realize the need for a surgeon to care for the special needs of newborns and infants. While in St. Louis, he recalled in an interview, "There was a doctor, J. Eugene (Gene) Lewis, a pediatric surgeon by training, who was almost like an evangelist about it."[71] He remembered his father's advice, "Before you wish yourself off on the public, go get yourself well-trained."[72] That admonition, and Lewis's zeal caused Ellis, although certified by the American Board of Surgery, to take leave of his practice and do an eighteen month "fellowship" in pediatric surgery at Columbus Children's Hospital. The hospital was affiliated with Ohio State University Medical School.

Asked the difference between general surgery and pediatric surgery, the former Fort Worth Children's Hospital chief of surgery explained, "The diseases are different. First of all, you don't have an adult without a rectum or a swallowing tube, or has his intestines on the outside, but you do have newborn babies with these things."[73] Thus corrective surgery on newborns is a big part of pediatric surgery, on infants that in a previous era almost certainly died within days of birth. In July 1965 Ellis introduced the new speciality to Fort Worth.

Dr. John Dalton said, "Dr. Ellis paved the way for a tertiary care children's medical center in our county. Without him, it would not have happened when it did, if at all."[74]

He is past president of the Texas Society of Pediatric Surgeons, and past president of Pediatric Surgical Associates of Fort Worth, which he founded in 1965. "He was a member of the elite Lilliputian Surgical Society and was elected chairman of the Surgical Section of the American Academy of Pediatrics. . . . Ellis is especially proud to have held this position as the first and only private-practice, non-academic president of the American Pediatric Surgical Association."[75]

The surgeon received the highest honor bestowed by his peers in 1996. "For the past 30 years, Dick Ellis has exemplified the ideals of the Gold-Headed Cane throughout his stellar, sometimes visionary, career. While he's no stranger to awards and accolades, Ellis feels particularly proud of this most recent honor,"[76] according to Leslie Senevey of the *Cook Medical Staff News.*

Without false modesty, he proclaimed that a physician doesn't receive the Cane without deserving it, but he lamented the fact there were so many who are worthy, but because of only one being honored, others must go unrecognized. In the year Ellis was tapped for the award 490 candidates were eligible.

As pleased as he was of the Gold-Headed Cane award, Ellis told Senevey, "My children, grandchildren and marriage are absolutely the best and most important accomplishments of my life. . . . My oldest son is an oral surgeon, my youngest son is an urologist and my daughter is an attorney. I give their mother most of the credit."[77]

It's not surprising that the much-traveled physician served part-time at the American Airlines industrial medical clinic or that he was for a time a ship's doctor. He wrote about one such sea-going voyage, "Adventures on the *Sea Cloud*," a yacht formerly owned by Margorie Merriweather Post and her husband E. F. Hutton.

Ellis has more time for his children and grandchildren, but he has not abandoned his professional calling. He continues to write professional papers, and co-authored a chapter on pediatric urology problems in Halle's *Pediatric Surgery*.

★ ★ ★

VAL F. BORUM, MD-1997

Val Borum is a poet, a deep-sea diver, a former submarine officer, a former Texas Medical Association delegate to the American Medical Association, grandfather and great-grandfather, and a retired anesthesiologist—all with a twinkle in his eye. The poet gene perhaps came from his mother. There are doctors and dentists galore in his family tree, but how did a West Texas boy wind up at Annapolis and then the submarine base at Groton, Connecticut?

Val played in the Midland High School band and "toured" such places as Abilene and Lubbock, but also took an interest in science. After high school he attended and graduated from Centenary College in Shreveport, Louisiana, the city of his birth. He entered Vanderbilt Medical School in the fall of 1941. The December 7 events of that year put any immediate plans on hold. A deeply religious man, and son of a Baptist preacher, Val determined, "If it was intended that I should be a doctor I could always come back to it."[78] He joined the Navy and trained at the Naval Academy and Cornell Diesel School. Borum saw wartime service as a submarine deck and engineering officer in the Southwest Pacific.

Interest in college physics came into play during this second tour. The *USS Nautilus*, the first nuclear powered submarine, was being built three miles away. In a cogent article for the *Tarrant County Physician*, Borum wrote, "I was the medical consultant on the construction committee of *Nautilus*, a ship that would help preserve the peace for more than 25 years until it would be retired as a museum."[79]

Borum's medical rotation in the submarine infirmary is when he became interested in anesthesiology. A civilian again, he returned to New Orleans for further study.

At the invitation of a friend, he moved to Fort Worth in 1958. The seventh anesthesiologist in the city, Borum considers members of his speciality a vital part of the operating team, because as he puts it, "the patient's life is in the hands of the anesthesiologist."[80] He remembered a patient who feared she would die on the operating table. He asked if she had had surgery before. "Yes," she answered. He asked if she felt fear then. "Oh, yes, every time." He assured her he had never lost a patient yet and he didn't want her to be the first one. "You have to take seriously what your patients are feeling and deal with it,"[81] he said.

He compared anesthesia to different levels of sleep. With that twinkle in his eye he recalled a patient who was on the table, under sedation, but not in deep sleep. "The OR nurse dropped a surgical tray. Retrieving the instruments she muttered, 'This is not my day.' Whereupon the patient declared, 'I'll come back when it *is* your day.'"[82]

At the 1993 Annual Session of TMA, the Young Physicians Section selected Borum to receive its "Young at Heart" award. Dr. Susan Cribbs thanked him for the guidance and support he had given young doctors during past years.

"This award was especially meaningful to me," Borum said, "because my wife and I have a son, a granddaughter and a granddaughter-in-law in medicine."[83] The anesthesiologist exhorted the group, which makes up 40% of TMA's membership, to help each other. He urged local medical societies to encourage and support young leaders. They are ". . . our hope for the future of our profession."[84]

For these contributions, and his caring attitude toward patients, Borum's peers voted him the "doctor's doctor" in 1997. He thanked his colleagues for allowing him to hold the prestigious Gold-Headed Cane. He noted previous holders of the cane shared a common trait with most physicians, "They are devoted to service to other people. To me, service to our patients is what the profession of medicine is all about."[85]

In his acceptance speech Borum rebutted the contention that Dr. Crawford Long administered the first anesthetic in 1842. With his droll wit, he announced, "Actually, Adam was the first to receive an anesthetic, and has been ribbed about it ever since."[86]

Now in retirement, the always devoted family man spends time with his wife, his three sons, eight grandchildren and two great-grandchildren.

Not ready for the proverbial rocking chair, Borum is active in his church and the Retired Physicians of the Tarrant County Medical Society.

★ ★ ★

JOHN H. SMITH-1998

A man who names his monthly column "Notes from the John" must have a sense of humor. And so he does. Typical of items in the column is the question, "Do pediatricians play miniature golf on Wednesday afternoons?"

"For more than fifteen years, Dr. John Smith's wit and humor have been reflected in the pages of the *Tarrant County Physician* magazine," Cathy O'Neal wrote in a tribute to the 1998 Gold-Headed Cane recipient. He confessed that he couldn't remember jokes and relied on jotting them down for future use. Those jokes then show up in his column. "My claim to fame—plagiarized material."[87]

It's no joke that Dr. Smith takes his profession seriously. "When I'm in surgery, I'm very demanding, but outside of the operating room, I tend to be less serious,"[88] he told O'Neal. Outside the hospital or office, he enjoys art, museums, light reading, travel and working in his yard.

As a senior at Polytechnic High School, John's part time job was mopping floors in the operating rooms at St. Joseph Hospital. "Some surgeons were kind enough to let me watch the operations,"[89] he told an interviewer. That whetted his interest in medicine.

Dr. Susan Wynn credits Smith with her coming to Fort Worth. They met during an AMA party in Chicago. "If you can imagine these Yankees having a country-western party. . . .I had my 2-month-old baby son . . . with me. . . . The hour was getting later, and the music was loud, and the baby started to get fussy. John picked up the baby and held him and began to dance with him. We had just met, but here this man was so sweet and so kind. I thought right then that the doctors in Tarrant County were my kind of people. . . ."[90]

Concerning Smith being named the Gold-Headed Cane "Doctor's Doctor" Wynn characterized him as representing everything that's good about the practice of medicine. "Not only is he very much a physician's advocate and is willing to speak out and be a leader, he's also a very dear and caring physician one-on-one with his patients,"[91] she told *Star-Telegram* reporter Laura Vozzella.

Sometimes his advocacy is wrapped in humor, as in:

> "The Rules
> "The HMO always makes the rules.
> "The rules are subject to change at any time
> without prior notice.
> "No doctor can possibly know all the rules.
> "If the HMO suspects that the doctor knows all the rules,
> they are changed immediately.
> "The HMO is never wrong. . . ."[92]

After thirty years in private practice, Dr. Smith joined the Veterans' Administration Outpatient Clinic in Fort Worth as surgeon in 1993. When Leo Benevides, TCMS's Executive Director, was killed in an automobile accident, Smith divided his time between the VA and the medical society until a new director came on board.

Dr. Smith enjoys teaching family practice interns at John Peter Smith Hospital. Would he encourage a young person to go into medicine today? Yes, and the proud father has four daughters in health care to prove it. One is an ophthalmologist, one a family practitioner, one a nurse midwife, and one a physical therapist. He is also proud of his son—a lawyer.

★ ★ ★

M. DWAIN McDONALD, MD-1999

Dr. M. Dwain McDonald's voice sings with enthusiasm when he talks about the next generation of physicians. He finds the prospects for today's medical students and what they can look forward to in the way of advances invigorating—yet medicine was not his first career choice.

"The young doctors are so smart. It's just a thrill to be around them. They're bright and well trained. It's thrilling to think these are the hands medicine will be in in the future,"[93] he said in an interview. The general practitioner had ample opportunity to be around young doctors. Son,

Stuart, is a pulmonologist, daughter, Cheryl, works in infectious diseases, and her husband, Kevin Connelly, also is a pulmonologist.

Coupled with his excitement for the newcomers is a reverence for the doctors who helped establish him in the medical community. In his office McDonald proudly displays portraits of Dr. R. J. White and Dr. W. P. Higgins, Jr. Of Dr. Higgins, he fondly remembers the times he would scrub with him prior to surgery.

McDonald was the first in his family to study medicine. Cathy O'Neal wrote in the *Tarrant County Physician*, "He didn't know any doctors, and in fact, he doesn't remember even seeing a doctor until he was a student at the University of Texas in Austin. He broke his foot, and a doctor examined him and put his foot in a cast."[94] He hobbled to his chemistry classes and graduated in 1954.

For a short time he worked as a chemist for Shell Oil Company. Next he labored for Uncle Sam as a Marine for two years. When considering prospects for his civilian life, McDonald realized employment as a chemist deprived him of the opportunity to be with a mix of people, something he enjoyed in the Marines. "Then I thought about how a doctor deals with people, and I decided to be a doctor,"[95] he told O'Neal.

Today his patients definitely see him as a people-friendly doctor. Fort Worth resident Margie Skidmore recounted to reporter Charlotte Huff, an incident thirty years ago, when her husband, now deceased, was stricken with kidney stones. They called Dr. McDonald who told them to go to the hospital. "In just a little bit, we heard these footsteps coming down the hall—and this was 2 or 3 in the morning. And there was Dr. McDonald."[96]

Shortly after medical school, McDonald planned to establish a practice in Austin, but found his home city "too wonderful to leave." During the first twelve years in private practice he officed in the Polytechnic Heights neighborhood where he grew up. When the Professional Building, built just across the street from St. Joseph's Hospital, was finished, McDonald moved to his present location.

He believes in giving back to the city that has supported him in his almost forty years of medicine. He was a volunteer doctor at the Presbyterian Night Shelter when that facility's clients had no other opportunity for medical intervention. That has changed, but he still volunteers, now helping serve meals rather than medical attention.

In a preface to the *Tarrant County Physician* story on the occasion of McDonald receiving the Gold-Headed Cane, an example of his caring about others is detailed. "In 1957, things weren't great financially for Tarrant County Academy of Family Practice. They couldn't afford to buy their president, John H. Richards, MD, the traditional pin that went with the office. Flash forward to an evening in 1991, when Dr. Richards is working in his yard with no plans to attend the academy's first meeting of the year for the first time after many years of service."[97]   McDonald persuaded Richards to go. "At the meeting, they presented me with the pin I never got. He knew I didn't have one and got the society to buy me one and present it to me," Richards said.

This typical act of kindness, plus his deep respect for his peers and for medicine itself, as well as his love for tradition and his patients, led his colleagues to award him the coveted Gold-Headed Cane. "It scares me to death, it's just so overwhelmingly humbling. It becomes such an emotional thing that it leaves me without knowing what to say,"[98] he confessed. Co-workers see no need for words—McDonald's actions say it all.

Retirement is not in Dr. McDonald's immediate future, but he enjoys getting away to his farm with wife, Rev. Jane McDonald, and their three grandchildren. There he relaxes by riding his tractor and looking after his cows and eight donkeys.

★ ★ ★

THE NEW MILLENNIUM

The new decade, 2000–2009 was in its infancy when this book went to press. Based on the rapid developments of the previous half century, it is probable that great strides will be made in medicine. Futurists predict body part replacements will be common, diseases will be understood and conquered, and the life span will increase. Physicians will be needed to minister to an aging, but healthier population. It is hoped that the golden age of medicine is yet to come. And the Gold-Headed Cane will be treasured in the future as it has been in the past.

* * *

John H. Richards, MD-2000

Family practitioner John H. Richards was the first in the new millennium to receive the Gold-Headed Cane. Eighty-eight years young and going strong, Dr. Richards has no plans for retirement. "All of my colleagues that retired ended up dying,"[99] he quipped when interviewed by *Star-Telegram* reporter Paul Bourgeois.

The Weatherford native was introduced to medicine the hard way; his appendix ruptured February 2, 1928. During the hospitalization he got well acquainted with his doctor, J. M. Givens.

After graduation from Polytechnic High School, Richards worked for Dr. Givens as "office boy, bill collector and 'nurse'" for $7.00 a week. It was 1932 and money was scarce. Richards sometimes received money and sometimes chickens or produce as he balanced Givens "accounts receivable."

Knowing the young man's interest in medicine, Givens allowed Richards to work part time and go to Texas Christian University. The premed student worked in the university's Clark Hall Infirmary for part of his tuition. Even with two part time jobs there was never enough money. "When I went to a dance, I had to borrow my roommate's suit,"[100] he told reporter Jean Wysatta about those days.

In 1939 Richards was accepted into medical school at Galveston, but with only $300 in his pocket, and unable to raise the rest needed, medical school was postponed. He went to work as a pharmaceutical salesman. Richards' degree in chemistry, plus his experience in Dr. Givens' office made him popular with doctors and within three years he had saved enough money to pursue one year of his dream.

He was admitted to the 1942 class of the newly opened Southwestern Medical School in Dallas. It was wartime and the Air Force paid his tuition in exchange for what would have been medical services after his 1946 graduation. They sent him to McKinney at the end of his junior year for a physical prior to commission. An x-ray showed a spot on his right lung and he was released from the Air Force. (Civilian doctors failed to find any problem with the lung and Richards feels the Air Force erred in its findings.)

With one more year of medical school to go, the administrator at Parkland Hospital allowed him to live there as an intern and complete his senior year of medical school. Richards did his "real" internship at St. Joseph Hospital.

Student loans had not come on the scene, and mindful of the difficulties of his own education, Richards has since been generous in helping others pay for medical school.

In 1947 he began his practice in the old Medical Arts Building. There was just one problem; there wasn't space for a regular office. Wysatta noted he ". . . contracted to sub-lease store rooms and other space from doctors in the building, with the result he hop-scotched from one floor to another."[101] To get his practice established, Richards took home and night calls, and other less desirable referrals. He bought a car and put 38,000 miles on it that initial year.

His first patients paid $3.00 for an office visit, if they had it. Others paid with produce. Through the years patients remembered him at harvest time. "People still bring fresh garden vegetables–just a month

Dr. Margie Peschel congratulates Dr. John H. Richards, 2000 Gold-Headed Cane honoree. Courtesy Tarrant County Medical Society archives

ago someone brought me a plastic bag of blackberries,"[102] he told this interviewer.

The happiest part of his practice was delivering babies, sometimes as many as eighteen in one month. He prized watching "his babies" grow up and have babies of their own—and he took care of them, too.

His compassion extends to non-patients as well. A ninety-two-year-old woman, his neighbor for many years, was a patient at St. Joseph Hospital. After his rounds, he stopped by to see her. In a gentle voice he recalled, "She said, 'Doctor, I'm so glad you came to see me. Thank you for being such a good neighbor and taking care of me when I couldn't get my regular doctor. We're such friends—I've just waited all morning for you to show up.'"

"'How did you know I was coming?'"

"'I just knew you would come by.'"

"She took her last breath as I held her hand."[103]

Richards considers communication one of his most important duties as a doctor. He not only tells patients what prescription they should take and why, he writes it out for them.

Mary Schwartz, his office nurse for twenty-five years, describes her boss as an old-fashioned country doctor. "His patients are his family. They aren't just in and out of the office. He listens to them. He's interested in them. He even calls them sometimes, just to see how they are doing."[104]

For these reasons and as a tribute to his long service to the community, Richards was selected by his peers to receive the Gold-Headed Cane. Reporter Bourgeois quoted him as saying, "An award for doing what you love is almost embarrassing."[105] Despite his early brush with death, the struggles to obtain a medical degree, and establish a practice, Richards' response reflects his positive outlook. "I've had a charmed life . . . . To start out with nothing and get to practice medicine, which is something I love to do, is a blessing."[106]

CHAPTER FOURTEEN

THE HUMANITARIAN AWARD: CAST YOUR BREAD UPON THE WATER

Tarrant County Medical Society President Raymond LeBlanc believed there were many physicians who donated time and talent beyond the care of their patients. He proposed to the board that those who, as he said, "went above and beyond" warranted public acclaim. The board agreed. In 1999 the Tarrant County Medical Society Humanitarian Award, also called the Physicians' Humanitarian Award, became a reality.

Recipients are selected from a pool nominated by their peers. Criteria for selection states, "A physician member of the Tarrant County Medical Society who provides exceptional service to others."[1] The nomination form requests information on the nominee's service to others, and how these services significantly benefited or affected humanity.

Dr. Valentin Gracia was the first recipient. The plastic surgeon was born in the small farming community of Panuco, thirty miles from Tampico, Mexico. Cathy O'Neal, wrote in the *Tarrant County Physician,* "His mother was a nurse, and he often watched her work with patients at the charity hospital. It was there that he saw first-hand the particular birth defect of cleft palate and how these indigent children were forced to deal with their defect in an unforgiving society that ridiculed them for their differences. He vowed that he would become a doctor and return to help people like them."[2]

Dr. Gracia took his medical training at the *Universidad Nacional Autonoma de Mexico Escuela Nacional de Medicina,* graduating in 1951. He interned in Mexico City and Long Branch, New Jersey. His residencies were in surgery at St. Luke's Hospital in Bethlehem, PA, and at Scott and White Hospital in Temple, and in plastic surgery at Baylor Hospital in Dallas. He came to Fort Worth in 1959 because he saw the need for a specialist in plastic surgery here.

Gracia shared his dream of helping cleft palate children with friends in 1964, and the next year he returned to Panuco. He performed eighteen operations, and learned the job was too big for one man. He raised funds, solicited medical supplies, and recruited volunteer teams.

Since 1972 he has led a group of doctors and nurses on "an around-the-clock surgical marathon." Prior to their arrival, Gracia's brother-in-law, Dr. Jose Christen of Mexico City, and sister, Dr. Olinda Gracia, supervise local doctors in making arrangements and examining the children receiving the life-changing operations.

Reporter Betty Cook, in a 1975 feature entitled "The doctor who fixes faces," described one of the procedures. ". . . Gracia marked the boy's lips on both sides of the gaping cleft with line-connected dots traced in sterile purple dye. . . . He checks the z-shaped lines with a small steel ruler, then with his scalpel delicately follows the pattern he has drawn. Ultimately, the lip halves will fit together as closely as if the z-cut had been made in a whole upper lip—but not until several hundred minute stitches have been tied by hands which work with dipping, butterfly grace, sewing the living flesh into a symmetrical upper lip,"[3]

For the first time in the boy's life, his upper lip will fall cleanly into place, covering his teeth, and when the Ace bandage is removed, he will be able to smile like other boys.

Dr. Gracia calls his project, *Proyecto Huasteco—Sonrisa Alegre*, which means "Happy Smile." It is a non-profit, charitable organization named for the area on Mexico's east coast where Gracia grew up. By 2001 he had made fifty-two trips back to his native land, and he estimated that 3,100 Mexicans have benefited from his deft hands. Regarding that trip, Gracia wrote in the *Proyecto Huasteco* newsletter, "Trip 52 . . . to the city of Guanajuanto, Gto. Mexico during the last week of June was a great success. In 4 days . . . we completed 63 operations on children and adults with cleft lip and cleft palate deformities."[4]

Accepting the Humanitarian Award, he said, "'I'm not seeking awards. . . . I appreciate it, and I appreciate recognition for something close to my heart.'"[5]

Gracia's numerous awards and recognitions, both in Mexico and the United States attest to his medical skill and to his compassion. And because it is close to his heart, "the doctor who fixes faces," is preparing for yet another trip to help poor children smile.

★ ★ ★

JAN D. COCHRUM, MD

Jan Cochrum read *Death Be Not Proud* while in high school. It told of a journalist's son who was dying of a brain tumor. "I decided I would be a neurosurgeon,"[6] he told an interviewer. Jan graduated from Texas Christian University in 1957, then attended UT Southwestern Medical School in Dallas for four years. He returned to Fort Worth for his internship at St. Joseph Hospital, not in neurosurgery, but in family practice.

Following a tour of Air Force duty, Dr. Cochrum practiced in Austin for twenty-eight years, including caring for students at the University of Texas. He became interested in medical missionary work when he and his wife attended a meeting of the Intervarsity Christian Fellowship in Urbana, IL. "We caught the mission bug."[7]

The physician, moved by the needs of natives living in the mountains of Central America, first did medical missionary work in Honduras. Then he heard of Helps International. According to their brochure, "We are a philanthropic, international, non-governmental, Christian organization committed to assisting the indigenous people of Guatemala through programs in . . . medicine and health care, and projects of practical social concern."[8]

In 1992 Cochrum returned to Fort Worth, and continued his Central American work. In 2000, a team of medical caregivers, some sixty-five to seventy-five physicians, nurses, and technicians, traveled to Guatemala to provide elective and urgent medical care to hundreds of indigents of Nebaj. Despite communication barriers—the Americans needed to have their medical questions and instructions translated into Spanish and then into Ixil, the native tongue— successful surgeries and procedures were performed at a dizzying rate. "If they (the natives) hear an American doctor is there they will walk for a day or two to get medical help,"[9] Dr. Cochrum explained.

In each of his pilgrimages, Cochrum and his colleagues, volunteers from throughout the United States, stay one to two weeks. Helps International provides equipment, and the team supplies medical samples and other necessities.

Marjorie Creigh nominated Dr. Cochrum because of his role in "saving the lives of the people of Guatemala for several years." In graphically describing the caregiving of Dr. Cochrum's team, one associate said, 'Operating from an old hospital shell, the medical care they (the Cochrum team) are able to provide these people pushes the delivery of sophisticated medicine to the brink.'"[10]

After receiving the award at the February 5, 2000 dinner, Cochrum said, "'I realize how much what we are doing is worth every time I look into the faces of those we have helped, . . . and, when I witness all the obvious satisfaction derived from the caregiving by our physicians and aids (sic) who are first-time team members.'"[11]

Dr. Cochrum and his wife, Billie, have led four expeditions to Guatemala, the most recent one in February 2001. After flying to Guatemala City, the team rode eight hours over barely passable roads up into the mountains. They worked in a regional hospital, built by the United States in the 1950s, and poorly maintained. Mrs. Cochrum handled the administrative details, which were many. The team carried in their food and bedding plus the medical supplies. It wasn't unusual for her to oversee the loading and unloading of thirty to thirty-five bags of supplies, in addition to personal baggage.

Why do they do it? Dr. Cochrum told of a little boy who had been hit in the face. To repair his badly injured eye, he needed to be taken to a Guatemala City specialist. At the same time, a little girl was brought in with half her scalp peeled away. To save her life, the surgeons needed a dermatome to do a skin graft. It happened that a missionary was going to the capitol for a meeting, and a small plane was there for him. The pilot took the youth to the specialist and returned with the surgical instrument for the physicians to use on the little girl. Coincidence, or God's providence? Dr. Cochrum believes it was the latter.

★ ★ ★

DON BOSTON, MD

In a sense Don Boston entered into medicine because of his injured dog. It was a convoluted path. He took the animal to a vet, and although the doctor was unable to save the pet, Boston decided "right then and there" to become a veterinarian. After graduation from Polytechnic High School he entered Texas A&M. Belatedly, the aspiring doctor discovered grades counted. Unable to enroll in the veterinary program, he joined the Army. Quite by accident, assigned to the base dispensary at Camp Zama, Japan, he came to realize people patients were more intriguing than animal ones.

Army medics taught him how to care for patients, and during his tour he decided to pursue a medical career. After his discharge he again enrolled at A&M, this time a more mature, serious student. Recalling those days, he said, "In medical school they asked why I wanted to become a doctor. I told them I was either going to be a preacher or a doctor and reasoned God could use a doctor more than another preacher."[12] After completing pre-med at A&M, Boston entered Southwestern Medical School in Dallas.

One incident he remembered with a touch of irony. He and another medical student were having coffee in a small restaurant across the street from Parkland Hospital's Emergency Room. Two lab techs came in and lit cigarettes. One blew smoke directly in Boston's face. He took his handkerchief and dramatically waved the smoke away. Many years later he would be widely recognized for his stop smoking campaign.

In 1956 he began his practice with Dr. DeWitt Claunch on Travis Avenue. The young doctor liked the idea of treating the whole person and family practice seemed a good fit. In his thirty-four year career, until health problems forced him to retire, Boston made an impact on the community. He told reporter Paul Bourgeois, "I delivered babies and they grew up, and I took care of their children. It's nice to be able to follow people throughout their lives."[13]

He loved family practice, but he is better known for his efforts to persuade people to stop smoking. In the 1960s, information flooded across doctors' desks about the damage cigarette smoking did to the heart and lungs. "Then I began to realize the habit retarded the healing of ulcers, and the connection to smoking and cancer—not only lung cancer but bladder cancer as well," he said in an interview. "I began to realize damage was possible wherever in the body blood goes... because it carries carbon monoxide to every tissue."[14]

Not only was he seeing the ill effects of tobacco use in his patients, his brother died of lung disease brought on by fire fighting and cigarette smoking. Boston worked with the North Texas Tuberculosis and Respiratory Disease Association to make the public aware of the the dangers. In 1970 he organized the first "Stop Smoking Week" in Tarrant County. He enlisted print and television media to help publicize the event. He wrote ministers, asking them to urge their congregations to participate. "I don't know if we made a big dent in smoking, but we made a big splash,"[15] he told Bourgeois.

In 1971 the family practitioner secured a patent for, and the gratitude of thousands of women with his invention of a limited conveyer belt devise for pelvic examination tables. "Often in performing a pelvic exam, saying repeatedly 'Scoot down one more time, please,' I mused aloud to my nurse and patient, 'If you can move groceries, you should be able to move patients.'"[16] Challenged by nurse and patient, he enlisted the aid of two relatives for help with the mechanics and electronics. Together they invented the Subo Automatic Pelvic Examination Table. The result— doctors were able to control the positioning to an exact degree and patients didn't have to "scoot down one more time."

Prior to 1982, each of the eight Fort Worth hospitals had separate parking lot gate cards used by doctors. Valuable time was lost in finding the right card for the gate at hand. Boston's innovative thinking came up with a simple solution. He suggested all hospitals use the same key code, requiring physicians to use only one card. Both hospitals and Medical Society members unanimously adopted the concept.

Boston contributed to the welfare of the community in many ways. For thirty-four years he volunteered as director of medical services for Christ Haven Home for Children. Like the physician/Gospel writer Luke, Boston considered the contributions he made to his church as important as his medical practice. A part-time minister for the Church of Christ, he taught, preached, led song services, performed weddings, and conducted funerals. One of the most far-reaching enterprises was his leading his congregation in the memorization of the entire New Testament.

In the 1970s he helped organize Teen Enterprises, a program to help youth. Cathy O'Neal wrote, "This nonprofit group helped troubled teens, particularly those with drug problems. Through the program, Dr. Boston took the teens out of the city for a week to a camp in Colorado, where troubled kids spent their time with strong youth role models. The program lasted for 10 years."[17]

For five years in the late 1980s and early 1990s Boston and his wife, Mary Lee, participated in the Engaged Encounter Program. They opened their home to engaged couples and shared with them spiritual and practical considerations of marriage.

After retirement he was first appointed to fill a vacancy, then elected to the Forest Hill City Council.

Dr. Boston received the 2000 Physician Emeritus Award from the 50,000 member Texas Academy of Family Physicians. Dr. John W. Freese, spoke for his colleagues in saying, "Don Boston is an excellent role model and example for all physicians. His practice has exemplified our best traditions."[18]

A page-long listing of accomplishments and publications is part of his curriculum vitae. Honors continued to come his way. In January 2001 he received the Humanitarian Award for his work. Despite the publicity concerning the stop smoking campaign and other strictly medical endeavors, Boston prefers to think of himself as a physician who brought as much of his Christian ministry as he possibly could to the medical care and treatment of his patients and community. Those who know the man who chose to become a Christian doctor rather than a full-time minister are reminded of the scripture "Well done, thy good and faithful servant."

CHAPTER FIFTEEN

EPIDEMICS AND ADVANCES: KILLER DISEASES AND DISEASE KILLERS

Since the beginning of recorded history there have been accounts of epidemics. In the early fifth century the Greek physician Hippocrates described a respiratory illness that wiped out an entire Athenian army. The Black Plague killed an estimated twenty-five million people in Europe and another thirty-seven million in Asia. Nine out of ten people afflicted with this disease died in the Middle Ages.

★ ★ ★

INFLUENZA–1918

In 1510 two Italians gave us the name "influenza" meaning influence, because they believed the malady was influenced by cold weather. Doctors had little understanding of the mystifying disease and even less knowledge of successful diagnoses and cures. Iezzoni, in *Influenza 1918* wrote, "Patients were treated with lime juice, tobacco juice, emetics . . ., purgatives . . ., or the ever-popular venesection: bled until they were pale, limp, and anemic."[1]

Influenza arrived in America in 1647, brought by sailors from Valencia, Spain. Over the next 250 years North Americans suffered periodic outbreaks, but none so devastating as the 1918 epidemic. That year the United States fought two wars, one in the trenches of France and one in the make-shift hospitals set up in every major American city.

Lethal influenza, called the "Spanish flu," spread terror throughout the country. In September 1918, 12,000 Americans died.

So rapid was the contagion, communities staggered to cope. According to the *Fort Worth Record*, "Never in the history of the city has the situation been worse than it is at present in regard to nurses and physicians. In all Fort Worth if there is a woman who has had training as a nurse or who has any idea of practical nursing, (please help). . . . There are hundreds of families in the city who are absolutely unable to get trained assistance. . . ., for there are no nurses to be had."[2]

The city received as many as fifteen requests a day for nurses. One reason for the lack of available help was the nurses themselves were ill. While none of the sisters at St. Joseph's Infirmary died, twelve had been stricken. At All Saint's Hospital eight nurses caught the disease and the *Fort Worth Record* noted, ". . . there are only two or three patients in the hospital at present who are not victims."[3]

The Fort Worth Relief Association begged for donations of mattresses, blankets, cots and bedding of all kinds. "Two of the four nurses employed by the Relief Association are sick with the influenza and this puts a double duty on the other two, but they and all other members. . . are doing their utmost to answer every call for help,"[4] according to a newspaper source. In Fort Worth and elsewhere, doctors, nurses, and even the civilian population wore gauze masks at all times. Gymnasiums became hospitals as cots, with bed sheets hung between them, housed hundreds of sick people.

Heart-tugging stories abounded in the chronicles of the Writers' Project. ". . . every member of a family of seven, except one, had been taken to the hospital suffering from influenza. The baby had died and another of the children was near death.

"Another case coming to the attention of the Fort Worth Relief Association . . . . A 12-year old boy without any relatives, so far as he knows, has been making his own living by working in a dairy. He became ill very suddenly in the city two nights ago and was taken in by charitable people."[5] The account did not reveal the boy's fate.

At the county orphan's home one-fourth of the children were bedridden at one time. The only employee well enough to care for them, a Mrs. Easley, tended the little ones round the clock. The physician assigned to the home was himself a victim of the malady, and the male attendant, Mrs. Easley's assistant, remained at home to care for his ailing family.

On October 19, 1918 the *Record*'s lead story noted, "Reports from the health department Friday were that fourteen deaths had occurred from pneumonia during the day—a larger number than occurred Thursday, but a much smaller number than Wednesday's report showed. In addition to the seven deaths from pneumonia, Thursday there also were seven deaths from influenza."[6]

Local doctors, and their counterparts across the nation, frequently stated the cause of death as pneumonia. It was a known killer, and "the flu" was not. Iezonni stated their dilemma, "If influenza resulted in pneumonia, and the pneumonia proved fatal, had the victim died of influenza or pneumonia?"[7] Without an autopsy it was difficult to tell, and with the number of victims there was no time for autopsies.

A later review of death certificates for fifty cities, mostly on the East Coast, revealed widespread influenza among the civilian population in 1918. The *Journal of the American Medical Association* made no mention of it in its 1918 issues, owing to the perception that influenza was not a killer disease.

Military camps across the country suffered towering losses. The *Record* reported that in sixteen camps 80,000 men were ill and 1,877 died by October 2, 1918. Camp Bowie's Maj. Gen. Edwin Greble, quoted in the Writers' Project, said, "During November . . . 6,000 men or about one-third of his command, passed through the hospital with deaths from pneumonia, measles or other diseases averaging sixteen daily. At one time 1,600 men were crowded into a hospital built to accommodate 600 and that without a sewerage system."[8] Two weeks later, Dr. John Mahoney of the United States public health services stated Camp Bowie benefited from a drop of 200 new cases a day the previous week to sixty-seven new cases reported on October 18, 1918. Seven hundred and sixty men were in the base hospital at the time of the report. Nationwide, according to Iezonni's figures, in the fall of 1918, 621,000 American servicemen fell sick with influenza. In a matter of hours they were prone, delirious invalids.

By the end of the year the epidemic tapered off, with only a slight recurrence, the "spring wave" in 1919. Before Spanish flu spent itself, more than 650,000 Americans died. Texas historian Pat Ireland Nixon noted, "In the November issue of the *Texas State Journal of Medicine*, there were notices of 11 (doctors') deaths, all due to influenza. In two issues of the *Journal of the American Medical Association*, there were 255 notices of death, and influenza was the cause of death in at least 154."[9]

Yet Americans were lucky by comparison—in the crowded and war-torn cities of Europe, influenza struck over one billion people, killing an estimated thirty million.

As the epidemic subsided, researchers throughout the world's laboratories hunted the elusive germ. By the process of elimination bacteriologists invented the field of virology. Dr. Richard Shope, an American, hypothesized a deadly, synergistic relationship between bacterial and viral agents. This theory was disproved, but he identified the source of swine flu. Building on his meticulous research, three Englishmen went one step farther. In 1934 the Smith-Andrews-Laidlaw team isolated the first human influenza virus. Thirty years later, with the use of a powerful electron microscope, scientists saw for the first time the deadly virus. Innocent looking, twelve million of the fluffy, cloud-like creatures can fit on the head of a pin. And bring nations to their knees.

★ ★ ★

POLIOMYELITIS

"Acute paralytic poliomyelitis is a very old disease that probably dates back to 1500 B.C.,"[10] begins a monograph in the *Annals of the New York Academy of Sciences*. A photograph in *A Summer Plague: Polio and its Survivors*, of "an Egyptian stele, dating from the eighteenth dynasty (1580-1350 BC) depicts a man with a withered leg, evidence of the antiquity of polio as an endemic disease."[11]

Dr. Judge Lyle, writing in *The Fading Family Physician*, described the dilemma of Fort Worth doctors. "At the time of the polio epidemic . . ., we did not have antibiotics or sulfa drugs. In fact, we had to depend upon our own idea of treatment for we did not know much about polio. Many of the doctors did spinal punctures on their patients, others did not." Lyle's patients were treated at home due to the lack of hospital space. "I kept them packed in ice and insisted that a member of the family stay right with the patient until the temperature went down. Then, after a few days we gave the patient the same as the Kenny treatment (named for Sister Elizabeth Kenny), which we had never heard of at that time. In other words, we put hot applications to their legs and back and massaged them."[12]

The *Annals* monograph noted, "The source of infection was the subject of much debate in the early part of the twentieth century. Initially, it was believed that the virus gained entrance to the nervous system by way of the olfactory nerves. It was demonstrated later that the virus could be found in the gastrointestinal tract and could be disseminated by secretions and feces. The discovery of poliovirus in flies and in sewage in the area of an epidemic led to strict quarantine of patients."[13]

Most Texans over the age of sixty remember the days of swimming pool shutdowns, and the summer closing of movie houses. Some parents took extra precautions such as sending city children to relatives who lived on farms or in small towns.

When children were stricken, too often there was an emotional tug of war between parents and care providers. City health workers, when space was available, wanted the children hospitalized and isolated. At times families of infants and very young children were not allowed to see patients for days and weeks. This traumatized both, and other families, hearing horror stories, were reluctant to allow their children to be taken away from them "to die in a strange bed."

Treatment of poliomyelitis made a significant advance with the development of the iron lung in the 1930s. Earlier treatments consisted of splinting affected limbs or encasing them in plaster casts. Once the crisis period ended, most patients were outfitted with leg braces or crutches. Donald Mulder, in *Annals* wrote, "In 1940, an Australian nurse named Sister Kenny came to the United States and advocated more active treatment for patients with poliomyelitis. . . . The treatment proposed . . . was the application of warm moist heat (wool packs) to the affected areas in combination with early activity. . . . (Her method) was severely criticized by the medical profession, and she began a worldwide crusade to advocate her system of treatment."[14]

Reporter Eleanor Wilson, in *In Old Fort Worth*, recounted her coverage of the Fort Worth polio epidemic.

"It was the summer of 1943.

"Hot. Seemingly endless.

". . . Fort Worth had its first big epidemic of infantile paralysis. Our city was 'off limits' to enlisted men and officers from nearby Camp Wolters in Mineral Wells unless on 'official business.'. . .

"First recorded cases of poliomyelitis (we were just beginning to use that strange, hard-to-spell word in our news stories) began May 22. By July 13 when I was assigned to cover the story of the epidemic as a cub reporter, there were 49 known cases of infantile paralysis in Tarrant County. The next day six more cases were reported.

"My last story on Oct. 18 listed a total of 186 polio cases in Fort Worth hospitals in 1943. . . .

"Those stricken ranged in age from a 10-month-old boy to a 55-year-old man. The majority were children.

"It was a fearful time. No one knew just what caused the dread crippling, killing disease or how it was transmitted.

"At the height of the epidemic in late August there were 82 polio cases under treatment at one time at Harris (then usually called Methodist) and City-County (now Peter Smith) Hospitals. Those two hospitals were selected by Fort Worth doctors to handle the cases which were confined to isolation wards, thus centralizing treatment. Iron lungs and patients' beds overflowed into the halls.

"There was always a shortage of nurses due to so many serving in the armed forces. . . .Mrs. W. J. Danforth, then a volunteer with the (Tarrant County Infantile Paralysis) association, recalls making appeals on radio for washing machines with wringers and blankets needed in this (Sister Kenny) treatment. The blankets were cut up, soaked in hot water, run through the wringers and then applied to afflicted limbs. . . .

"'Sister Kenny spent only one day in Fort Worth, but to the children undergoing treatment . . . and the doctors and nurses helping to combat the disease in our hospitals, she left new hope and courage,' I wrote on Aug. 25.

"I followed the remarkable woman on her rounds here— holding clinics at both Harris and Peter Smith Hospitals where she went over the patients, speaking softly to them and manipulating their weakened limbs with big, gentle hands. Then in terse, technical terms she would give her directions for treatment to doctors and nurses. As one doctor put it, 'She sure knows her bodies.'

"It is all so long ago now. Since the breakthroughs in preventing polio with the Salk and Sabin vaccines it is rarely heard of. City health authorities can't remember when the last case was reported here—the records kept on hand only go back five years."

Wilson concluded, "But those who were stricken and their families and friends and the gallant medical and nursing staffs who worked those long, hot hours will always remember the summer of '43."[15]

One of the physicians who worked the epidemic was Dr. Porter Brown. Since he had polio as a child, he was immune from catching the disease. But as his daughter, Isabelle Newberry, recalled, he feared for his children's health. "Daddy always changed every shred of clothing before coming home after he had been at the hospital."[16]

Subsequent summers were not without their toll. In 1948 readers of the *Star-Telegram* learned that an infants' respirator had been flown to City-County Hospital. The following year hospitals reported they were full and over-flowing. Breckenridge firemen rushed an iron lung to City-County' Hospital to meet the needs there. In June of 1950, 106 patients had been diagnosed for the year. City-County turned a serving pantry into a two-bed ward to help alleviate the shortage of space. The beds bordered a refrigerator, gas stove and a sink.

A new polio wing opened in August, 1951, providing care for forty-eight patients, three of whom were in iron lungs. Mrs. Hazel Jay, director of nursing, reported that six additional nurses from the Red Cross arrived to help with the patient load. Every year health officials eagerly awaited the onset of cool weather, because as author Tony Gould wrote, polio was a summer plague.

Virologists conducted animal experiments in the 1930s, trying to find a cure or vaccine. Although some progress was made, the breakthrough eluded them. All research halted during World War II, but in the 1950s

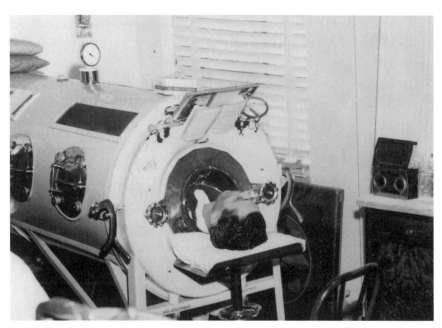

Iron lungs like this one pictured in 1951 filled every available space at City-County Hospital. Courtesy Fort Worth Star-Telegram Photograph Collection; Special Collections Division, The University of Texas at Arlington Libraries

two researchers, Jonas Salk and Albert Sabin, strong personal rivals, put together the pieces of the puzzle. In 1955 Salk introduced the first, but less effective vaccine. It contained three types of formalin-inactivated viruses and after injection, produced immunity. As 1955 ended, a survey reported by Fishbein[17] revealed the number of admissions of children to hospitals for infantile paralysis dropped fifty-two per cent among eight-year-olds and forty per cent among seven-year-olds.

Sabin perfected an oral vaccine using live, but weakened viruses. Because of its ease of administration, the Sabin vaccine soon became the preferred one. Almost every member assisted in the Tarrant County Medical Society Sunday Polio Sabin Vaccine Program held on July 29, August 5, September 16, and September 23, 1962. Thousands of residents, many still in their church finery, went to nearby schools or other public gathering places for their lumps of sugar which contained the vaccine. Those who could, made a small donation to defray costs, those who couldn't weren't turned away.

The use of the vaccine led to the virtual disappearance of polio in the United States and other developed countries.

★ ★ ★

Acquired Immune Deficiency Syndrome (AIDS)

Some health experts predict that before a common vaccine is found for AIDS, one-fourth of subsaharan Africans will die of the disease.

The first citation about AIDS in the *Reader's Guide to Periodical Literature* was in Volume 42, March 1982-February 1983. Jean Marx's *Science* article entitled "New Disease Baffles Medical Community" alerted the general reader to what would become a world-wide epidemic. She wrote, "Within the past 4 years, a new disease of unknown cause and high virulence has afflicted more than 470 people, killing almost half of them."[18]

According to 1999 United Nations data 35,300,000 people have been infected with the virus. By September 1999 2,940 cases of AIDS had been recorded in Tarrant County.

At first, Marx noted, as many as 75 per cent of patients were homosexual males, usually confined to large cities on the East or West Coast. The next largest sub-population, intravenous drug uses, made up 12 per cent. Many Americans viewed the problem as a moral one, but health care workers saw hemophiliacs and others dependent on blood transfusions infected by the mystery disease, unrelated to their behavior.

In 1984 Dr. C. L. LaGrone updated local doctors in the July issue of *Tarrant County Physician*. He explained how humans naturally in the course of growing up, develop an immune system. "Now, there comes along a new disease that destroys this resistance that we have suffered a lifetime to build."[19]

The virus, named HTLV-3 (human T-lymphotropic virus type III), researchers found, could contaminate blood, be passed from infected heterosexual as well as homosexual partners, and infect infants born to HIV (human immunodeficiency virus) mothers. "The National Institute of Allergy and Infectious Diseases recognizes this *EPIDEMIC* (stress LaGrone's) as the worst in modern times. They, and others are working frantically and feverishly on a cure and a vaccine."[20]

The following year an update in *Science News* reported, "The CDC (Center for Disease Control) says that as of July 8, the number of persons diagnosed as having AIDS in the United States is 11,505. More than 5,700 have died, almost 1,000 since April."[21] These figures show the dramatic increase over the reported 4,400 in July 1985.

Other statistics were equally grim. James W. Curran, et.al., writing in *Science*, predicted a doubling of reported cases by 1986. They did give some hope, however. "The screening of donated blood and plasma for antibody to HTLV-III/LAV (lymphadenopathy-associated virus) and use of safer clotting factor concentrates should greatly reduce HTLV-III/LAV transmission through blood and blood products."[22]

Curran and his associates urged a continued search for a cure and vaccine. The 1985 issues of *JAMA*, the journal of the American Medical Association, were filled with articles and reports on AIDS cases and research.

The *Tarrant County Physician* kept doctors up-to-date on the local epidemic with monthly figures of new cases. In "Public Health Notes," Nick Curry, MD, reported a steady increase of cases year by year. In 1983 to 1989, 122 deaths from AIDS occurred. This compared to no deaths from polio reported in this same period.

At the Fifth International Conference on AIDS in 1989, physicians and others in the health care industry, heard promising news about a new drug, AZT (azidothymidine). B. D. Colen, writing in *Health*, explained, "Some of the most heartening findings concerned the drug . . ., which was originally used to treat full-blown AIDS cases but now seems effective in the early stages as well. While not a panacea, AZT does appear to help HIV-infected people live longer, healthier lives before succumbing to the diseases that eventually overwhelm their ravaged immune systems."[23]

In light of this, he also urged a shift in thinking from acute to chronic care. "What these advances appear to indicate is that AIDS is becoming a treatable—though not yet curable—condition."[24]

Hugh T. Lefler, Jr., MD, made the abstract concrete, in terms of the AIDS situation locally. "In Tarrant County alone, as of October, 1990, 576 cases have been reported. Roughly half of these people have died, and most of the remaining AIDS patients will probably die. For every diagnosed case of AIDS, there are at least 5,000, and probably more like 10,000, people who carry HIV in Tarrant County."[25] He urged his colleagues to stress education and prevention, as they, and the Public Health Department, battled the disease.

Susan Wetzel, MD, put a human face on the problem when she announced she was HIV positive. In a statement in the May 1992 *Tarrant County Physician* Wetzel wrote poignantly of how, in treating a patient, she suffered a life changing accident.

". . . I felt drawn to (AIDS patients). . . . I found that I had much to offer in terms of both medical information and treatment, and emotional support and caring.

"In September, while drawing blood from a HIV infected patient, I had an accidental needle stick. At the time, I was stunned and frightened—common emotions experienced by anyone who has had an occupational exposure."[26]

In December Dr. Wetzel's HIV test proved positive. The results made her more determined to help others. She continued to work in the outpatient Infectious Disease Clinic at John Peter Smith Hospital. "I have the opportunity to develop a national program for women infected with HIV. It is my hope that I will become a spokesperson and educator for both women and health care workers who are HIV positive,"[27] she said.

Charles A. Oke, issued information gathered by the Office of Epidemiology of the Fort Worth/Tarrant County Health Dept. which showed of the 1,419 cases of AIDS (Nov. 31, 1993), 142 were women. More than half, 53%, were intravenous drug users, 18% were infected from heterosexual contact, 11% from infected blood products, and the remaining infections resulted from occupational or non-identifible sources.

"The most common manifestations of HIV infection in women, namely gynecological infections, may frequently not be recognized in the early stages of the illness," Oke wrote.

Because of this delay, for diagnosed women the survival time is half that of men. "In Tarrant County the average survival time for women is approximately eight and a half months."[28]

As Americans moved closer to the end of the twentieth century, the disease continued to cut a wide swath in the nation. A March 1995 statistical report revealed the following:

>One of 250 persons in the U.S. is infected with HIV.
>HIV infection/AIDS is the third leading cause of death among adults ages 25-44.
>The percentage of AIDS cases attributed to heterosexual contact has increased by 21% from 1990 to 1991.
>By the end of 1994, the cumulative number of diagnosed AIDS cases will be between 415,000-535,000.
>The Public Health Service projects through 1994, 320,000-385,000 cumulative deaths.[29]

Two years later the Tarrant County surveillance report, cumulative from January 1982 to December 1996, showed 2,388 patients with a 54.9% mortality rate. The number had risen to 2,690 by February 1998.

As this book went to press, 2,940 Tarrant County infected patients had been identified (Jan. 1982-Sept. 1999) and were receiving treatment. This is a downward trend from the previous two years. People are living longer, the quality of life is better than fifteen years ago, but until a cure is found, the prospect of an early death is always with them.

★ ★ ★

DISEASE FIGHTERS

When asked to name the most important achievements of medicine in the past 100 years, many doctors said, "Good public health." So common-sense, it tends to be overlooked, but its benefits are enormous. In 1876 the American Medical Association adopted a resolution promoting sanitary municipal water supplies and sewer systems. In 1899 the association created the Council on Education to promote public health education. That same year it urged local boards of health to adopt laws requiring compulsory smallpox vaccinations. From then to the present the AMA actively supports good public health through education.

At the 1912 meeting, doctors approved a report on standard methods for prevention and control of tuberculosis. Two years later they adopted a resolution approving establishment of uniform milk standards. Using the latest in media, in 1924 the AMA began broadcasting public health messages on radio; in 1946 television spots on health were initiated. A web site (http:\\www.ama-assn.org) was launched in 1995.[30]

Dr. W. P. Burts, Fort Worth's first mayor, recognized the relationship between the spread of disease, unclean drinking water, and improper disposal of wastes. One of his first official acts was to establish a board of health. This board served as a policing agency to ensure quarantines, and water purification. It also established regulations for sewer building. Over the years, crude cabins were replaced by "modern" homes with running sanitized water and indoor toilets. Window screens to protect inhabitants from disease-carrying house flies and mosquitoes became the norm.

As the population grew, the public health department launched education programs and conducted vaccination drives. City health officers, at the dawn of the twentieth century, participated in a national effort to disseminate information about preventable diseases such as tuberculosis. Public health workers taught prenatal care and infant hygiene to expectant mothers. In 1922, the American Medical Association, in conjunction with the National Health Council, developed guidelines for official and volunteer agencies to promote regular physical examinations for all age groups.

Local and state governmental bodies passed laws enacting standards for businesses whose products impacted public health. For example, grocery stores, meat markets and restaurants had to pass regular cleanliness inspections. Food handlers were required to be free of tuberculosis and sexually transmitted diseases.

These measures resulted in drastic reductions in the death rate from communicable diseases. Death from diphtheria, diarrhea, entritis, tuberculosis and typhoid fever, all ravagers of the young, practically disappeared by the 1940s.

Antibiotics deserve a front line place in the fight against killer diseases. Before penicillin and other antibiotics, doctors had little in their medical bags to suppress infections. Arsenic, quinine and sulfa quelled the bacteria somewhat, but these were toxic to humans as well as to microbes. Because there was no sure way to curb some infections, all too often, a patient with a wound on an arm or leg faced amputation or being made as comfortable as possible as he awaited death.

The decade of the 1950s saw the development of vaccines for polio. These were followed in the 1960s by a vaccine for measles. Smallpox was declared eliminated in the 1970s.

Improved procedures, including the use of safe anesthetics, led to new thresholds in surgery. Open-heart and cardiovascular surgery, organ transplants, and less invasive techniques made the surgical suite an exciting place to be.

These scientific advances, coupled with the art of medical care, made for practices beyond the wildest dreams of pioneer doctors. Yet one thread has remained constant. Dr. Val F. Borum expressed it well: ". . . service to our patients is what the profession of medicine is all about. . . . That is, to aid in the process of healing, and to offer hope and alleviate pain and suffering whenever recovery is prolonged or elusive. Cicero in the first century B.C. said: `There is nothing by which one approaches nearer to the perfections of Deity than to restore the sick to the enjoyment of the blessings of health.'"[31]

CHAPTER SIXTEEN

THE TARRANT COUNTY MEDICAL SOCIETY: 100 YEARS OF MEDICAL HISTORY

In 1984 staffers Leslie Cormier Alcorn and Kathy Andrews discovered a bit of history in a storage room in the Academy of Medicine. Dr. Frank Sanders, secretary from 1911 to 1915, penned it—and who better than he to tell of the early history of the society? Titled "The Tarrant County Medical Society; Its History, Purposes and Membership," he wrote:

"I was asked by the chairman of the program committee to read a paper before this body. . . . The society was organized August 6th, 1903, and grew out of its predecessor, 'The Tarrant County (Sic) Medical Association. . . . in April 1902, Drs. C. P. Brewer and Lyman Barber issued a call for a gathering of the physicians and surgeons of Tarrant County, and this call stated the purposes of the meeting. The first meeting was held April 14, 1902, and twenty-nine physicians are recorded as being present. A permanent organization was formed with Dr. Julian Field as president, and Dr. Lyman Barber as secretary.

"The records show that this organization held seventeen regular meetings, and that at the last, which was held July 27th, 1903, Dr. I. L. Van Zandt introduced the following resolution:

"Whereas, Representation in the State and National Medical Association is dependent on membership in a County Medical Association,

"Resolved, That the Secretary of the Association be instructed to notify every regular physician in the county that on Thursday, the sixth day of August, 1903, at 8:30 p.m., (meet to organize) the Tarrant County Medical Association."[1]

The motion carried and the Fort Worth Medical Association had a new name in order to be in compliance with the state and national guidelines.

Dr. Van Zandt was chosen as the first president of the county medical society. Sanders listed the presidents up to 1915. He continued:

"The purposes of the society are practically the same as those of all other medical societies, and the constitution and bylaws begin by saying that it is designed to bring into one organization the physicians of the community, so that by frequent meetings and full and frank interchange

Dedication of the Fort Worth Academy of Medicine. From left Drs. W. G. Cook, May Owen, William Crawford, president of the Academy of Medicine, Amon G. Carter, Sr., Drs. L. H. Reeves, *(continued page 273)* R. J. White, Porter Brown, W. F. Ossenfort of Dallas, Amon G. Carter, Jr., and Dr. Tom B. Bond. Courtesy Fort Worth Star-Telegram Photograph Collection; Special Collections Division, The University of Texas at Arlington Libraries

of views, they may secure such intelligent unity and harmony in every phase of their labor as will elevate and make effectual the opinions of the profession in all scientific, legislative, public health, material and social affairs, to the end that the profession may receive that respect and support within its own ranks and from the community to which its honorable history and great achievements entitle it."[2]

Under the leadership of involved, caring doctors the society grew as it met the changing needs of the profession. One change was finding a place to meet. For years they met in the auditorium of the Medical Arts Building, but in 1950 that space was leased to an oil company. Not only was the society without a place to meet, records and memorabilia were housed in various offices and no one really knew all the depositories of important documents.

Dr. I. L. Van Zandt III, in his history of the society, noted the origin of the Academy of Medicine. "In 1951 Dr. L. H. Reeves, Dr. William Crawford and other medical leaders talked of a library and meeting hall . . . and in June of 1952, the Fort Worth Academy of Medicine was

incorporated with Drs. Joe McVeigh, Hub Isaacs, May Owen, Porter Brown and William Crawford as incorporators."[3]

Crawford gained support from the Amon G. Carter Foundation, and construction began the following January on a sloping lot on Tulsa Way. Over 600 people gathered for the September grand opening. Dr. D. E. Compere, wrote about that event. "Mr. Carter attended and noted that the building had no furniture, particularly chairs for the meeting hall. The next day 500 chairs were delivered to the Fort Worth Academy building. Mr. Carter remarked, 'When you give a person a suit, you should include a hat.'"[4]

Today the academy houses the Tarrant County Medical Society offices, the Alliance (formerly called the Woman's Auxiliary) and provides space for various medical-related and community meetings.

As the membership grew, and the organization became more service oriented, the society hired staff to handle the myriad of details and publish *The Bulletin*, which became the *Tarrant County Physician*. Under the leadership of Executive Director Leo C. Benavides, TCMS made

A well-attended meeting at the new Fort Worth Academy of Medicine, circa 1953. Courtesy Tarrant County Medical Society archives

important strides toward reaching out to the community at large. He worked to bridge TCOM students with TCMS students. Through his efforts the Auxiliary was included in strategic planning of events. Benavides worked to ensure the representation of the Arlington branch of TCMS. Dr. Bohn Allen in 1993 noted, "He enabled us to go from a Society of slightly over 1100 members in 1980 to over 2,000 today."[5] Allen's comment was part of a tribute to Benavides, who died in an automobile accident August 21, 1993.

Robin B. Sloane, the current executive director, sees the TCMS as a vehicle to serve its members. She supports advocacy for professional stature by linking medicine to the community through working with the public schools and other organizations for the mutual benefit of both. By strengthening relationships between various county groups, she believes both physicians and the public will gain a greater understanding of members' contributions to the community. TCMS, according to Sloane, should advocate for professional policy relating to legislation and regulations affecting the practice of medicine. "The Tarrant County Medical Society is your advocate in the place you live and work,"[6] she wrote in the February 2001 issue of the *Tarrant County Physician*.

The Alliance, since its inception in 1920, has been supportive of Tarrant County physicians. Brenda Pender recounted the history in a recent *Tarrant County Physician*. "Before there actually was an Alliance, the wives . . . were ready and able to assist their husbands. For instance, in 1853, Mrs. Peak stepped in to teach women . . .how to care for the sick."[7] . . . .

"Today, the Alliance consists of men and women, spouses and families involved in our community and its health care. The projects and contributions are as varied as its membership, from health fairs to legislation and education on health issues. And the Alliance remains a powerful force," she concluded.[8]

In addition to opportunities for professional growth and continuing education, TCMS sponsors programs to recognize outstanding achievements. The Gold-Headed Cane and the Physicians' Humanitarian Awards honor physicians. The May Owen Award goes to non–physicians whose contributions enrich the community. Providing scholarships, and volunteering at athletic events are two of the many ways the society participates in helping students.

* * *

Dr. Bobby Q. Lanier, Tarrant County Medical Society's 2000/2001 president, is an allergist by profession and a communicator by choice. He views technology as an aid to better communication. Dr. Lanier describes himself as a futurist with computers, the internet and web pages as tools for better information sharing among physicians. He consults with the American Medical Association for website development and computer related ethical issues.

Dr. Lanier is the medical director of Lanier Education and Research Network, a corporation devoted to educational technology and pharmaceutical research.

Concerning the Academy, in his President's Paragraph January 2001, he noted in 1952 there were 400 members and two employees of the

The Fort Worth Academy of Medicine has been home to the Tarrant County Medical Society since 1953. Courtesy Fort Worth Star-Telegram Photograph Collection; Special Collections Division, The University of Texas at Arlington Libraries

society. Those numbers have grown to 2500 members and a staff of eight. Lanier used humor as the means to communicate the need for larger quarters for TCMS.

"'Leslie, do you know where the Board agenda is?' I recently asked the director of operations, Mrs. Alcorn. 'DO YOU KNOW WHERE THE AGENDA IS?'

"'WHAT?' yelled Mrs. Alcorn.

"'THE BOARD AGENDA,' I repeated. 'DO YOU KNOW WHERE IT IS?'

"'I CAN'T HEAR YOU,' Mrs. Alcorn replied.

"It's like that in the backstage area of the Medical Society Building when the last wood-fired envelope stacker is in full motion—rattling, vibrating, grinding, crashing, sealing and folding. It's an industrial-aged nightmare confined to a hallway just big enough to let a skinny person pass—the reason I was yelling from down the hall."[9] He made his point and discussion of the problem will spill over into the next administration.

★ ★ ★

Dr. James L. "Jim" Norman, 2001/2002 president of the medical society, performed the first laparoscopic gall bladder operation in Fort Worth.

The general surgeon came here in 1978 because of the welcoming spirit he found among physicians. He attributed the help of Dr. Burgess Sealy and Dr. Fred Aurin to his making a smooth transition from residency at Parkland Hospital in Dallas to private practice in Fort Worth. Twenty-five years later he still sees the spirit of cooperation and camaraderie among members of the Tarrant County Medical Society as one of the great strengths of the organization.

Norman belongs to the Fort Worth Surgical Society, which recently celebrated its seventy-fifth anniversary. "The society," he said in an interview, "was founded for the purpose of the exchange of ideas and to provide a means to promote the advances in surgery in an organized manner."[10]

As president of the TCMS, Norman stresses the need for organized medicine, such as local, state and national bodies, to protect the doctor/patient relationship. "Organized medicine is the only way we will be able to survive against the power and the disruptive force of the insurance industry. If we don't have the strength to fight back, the industry and managed care systems will further insinuate themselves between us and our patients. That is a tremendous disservice to us, but more importantly to our patients," he told an interviewer. "We must have a presence in Austin and in Washington in order to preserve the practice of medicine as we would like to see it,"[11] he continued.

Dr. Norman is upbeat about the future of health care. He sees many and undreamed of advances in medical and pharmacological technologies. Concerning the future of medicine, he said, "If we keep the patient the focus, the satisfaction we get from treating someone at death's door, healing them, and seeing them recover will always be the greatest satisfaction one can derive from one's work. That satisfaction is beyond comparison."[12] And his colleagues in the Tarrant County Medical Society agree.

EPILOGUE

Fort Worth's pioneer doctors treated diseases caused in part by the lack of modern sanitation. In 1977 Mack Williams quoted Sam Smith, who at the age of eighty-two, wrote of his youth in the city. "I can remember seeing on lower Main Street, in front of a meat market, rabbits, squirrels and prairie chickens hanging out on the sidewalks and flies swarming like bees. Hardly anything was sanitary then, with no refrigeration and no screens on the houses and places of business. . . . No water system existed then, as water was carried from the Trinity River. In later years, W. J. Gilvin made, or had made, a wooden tank and fitted it to a wagon and hauled water. Everyone had a barrel in their yard and Mr. Gilvin would deliver water to those who were his customers."[1]

Today, public health regulations protect against such conditions. Instead, physicians and researchers deal with two equally important aspects of health care: improvement and prolongation of the quality of life, and basic research into causes and cures for diseases.

Much progress has been made by the physicians chronicled in this book. They spoke of practicing medicine in the "best of times." Yet the new millennium promises to be a remarkable time for medicine. The potential for bettering human health will be unequaled in history.

In 1893 the United States experienced a financial panic. A well-meaning congressman put forth a bill to close the U. S. patent office as a cost-cutting measure, because, as he told his colleagues, "Everything has already been invented."

Fortunately, for physicians and all of us, his bill did not pass, and today the patent office is still open.

Appendices

APPENDIX A

FACULTY OF THE
FORT WORTH UNIVERSITY MEDICAL SCHOOL

Elias J. Beall, M.D.; Emeritus Professor of Principles and Practice of Surgery and Clinical Surgery.

Amos Clark Walker, M.D.; Professor of Clinical Surgery.

Johann W. Irion, M.D.; Professor of Principles and Practice of Medicine and Clinical Medicine.

Frank D. Thompson, M.D.; Professor of Gynecology and Surgical Diseases of Women.

Julian T. Feild, M.D.; Professor of Obstetrics and Clinical Gynecology.

Bacon Saunders, M.D., LL.D.; Professor of Surgery and Clinical Surgery.

William A. Duringer, M.D.; Professor of Genito-Urinary and Rectal Diseases.

Edgar Doak Capps, M.D.; Professor of Physiology and Diseases of the Brain and Nervous System.

Ira Carleton Chase, A.M., M.D.; Professor of Anatomy.

Frank Gray, M.D.; Professor of Diseases of the Eye, Ear, Nose and Throat.

William R. Howard, A.M., M.D.; Professor of Histology, Pathology and Bacteriology and Curator of the Pathological Museum.

William Beverly West, M.D.; Professor of Dermatology and Syphilogy.

F. D. Boyd, M.D.; Lecturer on Hygiene and Physical Diagnosis.

Ernest L. Stephens, M.D.; Professor of Materia Medica and Therapeutics and Lecturer on Clinical Medicine.

James Anderson, M.D.; Professor of Diseases of Children.

William Robert Thompson, M.D.; Clinical Lecturer on Eye, Ear, Nose and Throat, and Lecturer on Anatomy of the Special Senses.

Hon. George T. West; Lecturer on Medical Jurisprudence.

David R. Fly, M.D.; Lecturer on Anatomy.

Goodridge V. Morton, A.B., M.D.; Lecturer and Assistant in Obstetrics.

Willis G. Cook, B.S., M.D.; Professor of Chemistry and Toxicology.

John D. Covert, M.D.; Demonstrator of Histology, Pathology and Bacteriology.

Rufus Chambers, M.D.; Lecturer on Minor Surgery and Bandaging and Assistant Demonstrator of Anatomy.

W. Ernest Chilton, M.D.; Demonstrator of Anatomy.

Roy S. Loving, M.D.; Asst. Demonstrator of Anatomy.

Lyman A. Barber, M.D.; Asst. Demonstrator of Anatomy.

Claude O. Harper, M.D.; Lecturer on Physiology.

Leonidas A. Suggs, M.D.; Lecturer on Histology. And,

C. B. Van Horn, M.D.; Lecturer on Materia Medica and Pharmacy.

APPENDIX B

"A called meeting of the Fort Worth Osteopathic Hospital, Inc. was held at 1402 Summit Ave., Fort Worth, Texas on the 15th day of August A.D. 1946 at 8 o'clock pursuant to regular business. The meeting was called to order by Dr. V. L. Jennings at 8 p.m.

Purpose of the called meeting was to put before the hospital incorporators the issue of an increased fee basis to stabilize revenues:

Obstetrical Cases: Delivery room from $7.50 to $10.

If used: Anesthetics $7.50 and up.

Hospital Beds and Care: From $5 to $6 per day.

Anesthetics: $10 and up; Labor and Delivery, $7.50

Major Surgery Procedures: Operating Rooms, $10;

Local Anesthesia-General Anesthesia $7.50 and up.

Tonsil and Adenoid Operations: Special Operating Room-$7.50 plus day's hospitalization and general anesthia (sic), if used.

Medication: Charges listed for medication, tablets, ampules, dressings, IVs will be added to patients' bills.

Meeting adjourned.
Roy B. Fisher, D.O. Secretary" [1]

APPENDIX C

1902-2001 PRESIDENTS OF THE TARRANT COUNTY MEDICAL SOCIETY

1902 Julian T. Field, MD	1907 R. B. West, MD
1903 R. E. L. Miller, MD	1908 E. D. Capps, MD
1904 I. L. Van Zandt, MD	1909 W. G. Cook, MD
1905 J. R. Frazier, MD	1910 William Rounds, MD
1906 Bacon Saunders, MD	1911 Lyle Talbot, MD

1912 I. A. Withers, MD

1913 K. H. Beall, MD

1914 S. A. Woodward, MD

1915 J. A. Gracy, MD

1916 C. O. Harper, MD

1917 Wilmer L. Allison, MD

1918 S. J. Wilson, MD

1919 J. H. McLean, MD

1920 Kent V. Kibbie, MD

1921 T. C. Terrell, MD

1922 L. A. Suggs, MD

1923 W. R. Thompson, MD

1924 Edwin Davis, MD

1925 Charles Clayton, MD

1926 T. L. Goodman, MD

1927 E. P. Hall, MD

1928 F. D. Boyd, MD

1929 Charles H. Harris, MD

1930 M. E. Gilmore, MD

1931 L. H. Reaves, MD

1932 Tom B. Bond, MD

1933 Jack E. Daly, MD

1934 Frank C. Beall, MD

1935 Will S. Horn, MD

1936 S. J. R. Murchison, MD

1937 Harold L. Warwick, MD

1938 R. G. Baker, MD

1939 J. M. Furman, Sr., MD

1940 L. O. Godley, MD

1941 R. G. Gough, MD

1942 R. J. White, MD

1943 Porter Brown, MD

1944 Frank G. Sanders, MD

1945 T. H. Thomason, MD

1946 E. L. Howard, MD

1947 May Owen, MD

1948 X. R. Hyde, MD

1949 Burt C. Ball, MD

1950 Sim Hulsey, MD

1951 J. F. McVeigh, MD

1952 Hub E. Issacs, MD

1953 William M. Crawford, MD

1954 W. P. Higgins, MD

1955 C. S. E. Touzel, MD

1956 Hobart O. Deaton, MD

1957 J. A. Hallmark, MD

1958 William E. Flood, MD

1959 Robert D. Moreton, MD

1960 W. B. West, MD

1961 C. P. Hawkins, MD

1962 John J. Andujar, MD

1963 Louis J. Levy, MD

1964 John H. Richardson, MD

1965 H. W. Anderson, MD

1966 Emory Davenport, MD

1967 Robert Stow, MD

1968 Charles J. Terrell, MD

1969 James D. Murphy, MD

1970 James O. McBride, MD

1971 C. Harold Beasley, MD

1972 Drue O. D. Ware, MD

1973 Dewey W. Johnson, MD

1974 Durwood E. Neal, MD

1975 Val Borum, MD

1976 W. V. Bradshaw, Jr., MD

1977 Frank Cohen, MD

1978 Grant F. Begley, MD

1979 Charles A. Rush, Jr, MD

1980 George H. Sullivan, MD

1981 Dolphus E. Compere, MD

1982 John W. Freese, MD

1983 Margie B. Peschel, MD

1984 Lynn C. Perkins, MD

1985 Bruce K. Jacobson, MD

1986 Hugh Lamensdorf, MD

1987 G. Douglas Tatum, MD

1988 John H. Smith, MD

1989 M. Dwain McDonald, MD

1990 Desmond B. Corbett, MD

1991 Richard E. Penny, MD

1992 Ladon W. Homer, MD

1993 Bohn D. Allen, MD

1994–1995 James F. Herd, MD

1995–1996 Robert W. Sloane, Jr., MD

1996–1997 Susan Rudd Wynn, MD

1997–1998 Lee S. Anderson, MD

1998–1999 Raymond LeBlanc, MD

1999–2000 Larry E. Reaves, MD

2000–2001 Bobby Q. Lanier, MD

2001–2002 James L. Norman, MD

Six presidents of the Tarrant County Medical Society have also been president of the Texas Medical Association.

T. C. Terrell, MD

May Owen, MD

James D. Murphy, MD

Durwood E. Neal, MD

Val Borum, MD

Hugh Lamensdorf, MD

Endnotes

CHAPTER 1: THE TRAILBLAZERS: HOUSECALLS ON HORSEBACK

1. Mae Benson, *Fort Worth Record*, "Dr. Van Zandt Vigorous at 88." 1/10/28, Second Section 1.

2. *Federal Writers' Project*, microfiche #1132.

3. Nassie Watson Cook, "Pioneer Doctors."*By the Way*, A Biweekly Publication for the Employees and Friends of the Osteopathic Health System of Texas, Lewis Library Special Collections, 1977.

4. Julia Kathryn Garrett, *Fort Worth: A Frontier Triumph* (Ft. Worth: Texas Christian University Press, 1996 reprint), 154.

5. Garrett, *op. cit.* , 311.

6. Oliver Knight, *Fort Worth: Outpost on the Trinity* (Fort Worth: Texas Christian University Press, 1990 reprint), 70.

7. *Fort Worth Gazette*, "Death of Doctor S. P. (sic) Burts: The Veteran Physician Called Away," 9/6/1895, 6.

8. Sam Jagoda, Jr., MD, "Those Bright Bealls" *Tarrant County Medical Society Bulletin* Vol. 48, No. 11 (1976): 17.

9. L. H. Reeves, *The Medical History of Fort Worth and Tarrant County* (Fort Worth: Tarrant County Medical Society, 1955) 71.

10. C. L. Douglas, and Mrs. J. W. Poindexter, *Doctors of the Frontier Days*, reprinted in the *Fort Worth Press*, 11/25/33, "Theodore Feild Won Fame as Early Day Surgeon Here," 8.

11. Bennett Smith speech at unveiling of historical marker at Flatiron Building (from Jagoda personal papers) 2/13/71, 3.

12. L. H. Reeves, *op. cit.* 65.

13. Ibid

14. Mrs. George Plunkett Red, *The Medicine Man in Texas* (Houston: Standard Printing & Lithographing Co., 1930) 311.

15. Mack Williams, *News Tribune* 1/18/80, "The Biggest Building in Town,"10.

16. Jane Ann Gaines, Chairman of the Medical Auxiliary's Research and Romance of Medicine Committee,*et al*, "Notes on Dr. Bacon Saunders and the Flatiron Building of Fort Worth," (Collected by Mrs. Saunders Jary, granddaughter of Dr. Saunders) *Tarrant County Physician* Vol.60 No.5(May 1988): 66.

17. "History of Surgery," *Bulletin of the History of Medicine* Vol. 1, (1972) 316.

18. Bennett Smith speech, *op. cit.* 11.

19. Bess Stephenson, "Fort Worth's Oldest Physician Nearing 93," University of Texas at Arlington Special Collections Library, Van Zandt file

20. *Fort Worth Star-Telegram* "Ages of Five Children of Isaac Van Zandt, Who Negotiated Texas Annexation, Aggregate 401 Years," 1/11/20, 9.

21. *Op. cit. Fort Worth Star-Telegram* "Ages of Five" 9.

22. "Dr. Van Zandt Will Be 92 Years Old Tuesday," UTA Special Collections Library, Van Zandt file.

CHAPTER 2: THE EARLIEST HOSPITALS: NO MORE KITCHEN TABLE SURGERY

1. L. H. Reeves, MD. *The Medical History of Fort Worth and Tarrant County: One Hundred Years 1853-1953,* 44.

2. Ibid

3. Ibid

4. Reeves, *op. cit.*70.

5. Reeves, *op. cit* 46.

6. *Fort Worth Star-Telegram* "St. Joseph Will Mark 74th Anniversary" 4/22/63 pm, Section One 11.

7. "Saint Joseph Hospital 100 Years of Community Service 1889-1989," *Tarrant County Physician* Vol. 86 No. 11 (1989): 29.

8. "Old Records at St. Joseph's Reflect City's Early Days," UTA Special Collections Library, St. Joseph Hospital file.

9. Ibid

10. Dr. Ruth Darnell, Personal interview

11. Seth Kantor, "Charity of Sisters Is Strain on Budget," *Fort Worth Press* 5/18/60, 13.

12. Ibid

13. *Fort Worth Star-Telegram* "Pastel Shades Ease Eye Strain for Patients, Doctors,"5/14/48 pm, 32.

14. *Fort Worth Star-Telegram* "St. Joseph's New Psychiatric Unit Completed, Early Opening Planned," 7/15/59 pm Section One 5.ß

15. *Fort Worth Press*, "St. Joseph's to Dedicate New Wing with 11 Operating Rooms," 7/12/59: B8.

16. Billy Glenn Marsh, "Bishop Gorman at Groundbreaking Ceremony," St. Joseph *Newsartery* 6/65: 1.

17. Ibid

18. W. S. Lorimer, Jr. (news release) "Centennial Celebration Inspires Insights into Advancement in Medicine," University of Texas at Arlington Special Collection Library, copy of news release, 3/30/89: 1.

19. Seth Kantor, "Charity of Sisters" *op. cit.*

20. St. Joseph *Newsartery* "St. Joseph to Get 1.5 Million Hill–Burton Grant," 10/23/61: 1.

21. Glen D. Bunn personal papers, UTA Special Collection Library. (no date, no page number)

22. Beverly Robb, Manager/Pub. Rel."St. Joseph Hospital: Highlighting Areas of Excellence," copy of news release, 3/30/89: 1.

23. Jim Fuquay, *Fort Worth Star-Telegram*, "Changing Prognosis" 5/13/94: B1.

24. Michael Denis, Exec. Dir. of the DFW Area Health Education Center, Personal interview

25. Ibid

26. Ginger Richardson, *Fort Worth Star-Telegram*, "Workers Grieve for Hospital," 7/31/95: 11.

27. Linda Campbell *Fort Worth Star-Telegram*, "St. Joseph Hospital Closes Doors," 9/29/95: A 1.

28. Sarah Lundy, *Fort Worth Star-Telegram*, "Nursing Home to Lose State Funding," 2/8/00: B 1.

Chapter 3:
The Professors: Medical and Nursing Schools

1. Ann Arnold, *History of the Fort Worth Legal Community* (Austin: Eakin Press, 2000), 17.

2. Mack Williams, *In Old Fort Worth* (Fort Worth: Mack and Madeline Williams, 1977), 110.

3. L. H. Reeves, *Medical History*: 36.

4. *Fort Worth Star-Telegram*, "Dr. I. C. Chase Dies 24 Hours Before Luncheon Planned to Honor Him," 6/21/33: 1.

5. Mack Williams, *op. cit.*, 110.

6. L. H. Reeves, *op. cit.*, 37.

7. Mack Williams, *op. cit.*, 111.

8. "Dr. Isaac A. Withers," *Texas State Journal of Medicine* Vol. 37 (June 1941): 131.

9. *Fort Worth Star-Telegram,* "Funeral Planned Today for Dr. W. E. Chilton, 78," 10/28/55 am, 5.

10. L. H. Reeves, *op. cit.*, 51.

11. *Fort Worth Press,* "Dr. Webb Walker Funeral to Be Held Here at 3 P.M. Wednesday," 12/12/62: 11.

12. Abraham Flexnor, "Medical Education in the United States and Canada: A Report to the Carnegie Foundation for the Advancement of Teaching," reprinted in the *Bulletin of the History of Medicine* Vol. 1 (1972): 545.

13. Flexnor, *Op. cit.* : 310, 311.

14. Katie Brown, *Fort Worth Star-Telegram*,"Nurses Pleased with Pantsuits," 7/14/70 am, B1.

15. Ibid

16. Ibid

17. Ibid

Chapter 4: The Pioneer Doctors: From Horseback to Horseless

1.   Tony Slaughter, UTA Special Collections Library. Draft of story prepared for *Newsweek* 11/15/58: 1.

2.   Slaughter, *op. cit.*: 2.

3.   *Fort Worth Star-Telegram,* "Dr. Cummins, 91, Hearty Supporter of TX Academy," 9/26/50: 14.

4.   Blair Justice, *Fort Worth Star-Telegram*,"Meningitis Epidemic 'Hero' Alert at Near 92," 1/26/58, Section Six 18.

5.   "Dr. Harold L. Warwick," *Texas State Journal of Medicine* Vol. 37 (July 1941): 266.

6.   Ibid

7.   Mabel Gouldy, *Fort Worth Star-Telegram*,"50 Year Doctor Firm in Beliefs," 7/12/59 am: Section Two 1.

8.   Ibid

9.   John Milner, Personal interview

10. *Fort Worth Star-Telegram*"Dr. Jack Daly Dies at 71; Longtime Physician Here" May 6,1967 am, B4.

11. Horace Craig, *Fort Worth Star-Telegram*,"Veteran Medical Examiner Recalls Flunking Wiley Post," 10/28/62 pm: Section One 17.

12. Ibid

13. Mrs. Burgess Sealy, Personal interview

Chapter 5: Doctors as Authors: They Wrote More than Prescritptions

1.   Charles H. McCollum, MD. *Pills and Proverbs* (Boston: Meador Press, 1941) 5.

2.   McCollum, *op. cit.* 41.

3.   McCollum, *op. cit.* 61.

4.   Reeves, *Medical History* 54.

5.   William C. Duringer, MD, J'Nelle Pate, editor. *A Pioneer Doctor's Story* (Ft. Worth: W. C. Duringer, 1965) 9.

6.   Duringer, *op. cit.* 10.

7.   Duringer, *op. cit.* 11.

8. Duringer, *op. cit.* 12.

9. Duringer, *op. cit.* 13.

10. Ibid

11. Duringer, *op. cit.* 18.

12. Duringer, *op. cit.* 21.

13. Judge M. Lyle, MD. *Life of Judge M. Lyle: An Autobiography* (Ft. Worth: Henry L. Geddis Co., 1964) 3.

14. Judge M. Lyle, MD. *The Fading Family Physician* (Ft. Worth: Henry L. Geddis Co., 1965) 11.

15. Lyle, *Fading* 21.

16. Lyle, *Fading* 25.

17. Lyle, *Fading* 26.

18. Lyle, *Fading* 42.

19. Lyle, *Life of Judge M. Lyle* 62.

20. Reeves, *op. cit.* 43.

21. Lyle, *Fading* 49.

22. Lyle, *Fading* 51.

23. Zack Bobo, *Ramblings of a Country Doctor* (Dallas: Southwest Offset Inc., 1977) 51.

24. Zack Bobo, *Ramblings* 61.

25. Reeves, *op. cit.* 2.

26. Ibid

27. Reeves, *op. cit.* 22.

28. Albert Goggins *Keep Well* (Ft. Worth: Albert Goggins, Word processing, graphics and layout by: Bob Ballew & Associates and Main Station Advertising, Inc., 1994) vii.

29. Goggins *op. cit.* 21.

30. Goggins *op. cit.* 92.

CHAPTER 6: THE OSTEOPATHS:
FROM HUMBLE BEGINNINGS TO TCOM

1. Jean L. McKechnie, editor, *Webster's New Universal Unabridged Dictionary*, Deluxe Second Edition (New York: Simon & Schuster, 1983), 1267.

2. Abigail Zuger, *New York Times* "Scorned No More, Osteopathy Is on the Rise" 2/17/98, F1

3. Russell, Phil R. DO, with Judy Alter, *The Quack Doctor* (Fort Worth: Branch-Smith, Inc., 1974), 2.

4. Russell, *op. cit.* 14.

5. Russell, *op. cit.* 3.

6. UTA Special Collections Library (untitled biography of Dr. Phil Russell, dated 12/1/60, unpublished):1.

7. Thayer Waldo, *Fort Worth Star-Telegram*, "Honored Doctor Due More Laurels," 6/25/64: 2.

8. Russell, *op. cit.* 36.

9. Russell, *op. cit.* 37.

10. Russell, *op. cit.* 1.

11. UTA untitled Russell biography *op. cit.*: 1.

12. *Fort Worth Star-Telegram,* "Doctors Urged to Give More Time to Patients" Sun 1/26/58, 6.

13. UTA untitled Russell biography *op. cit.*: 2.

14. Fort Worth Osteopathic Hospital Brochure, undated: 1.

15. Russell, *Quack Doctor*: 177.

16. *Fort Worth Star-Telegram,* "Osteopathic Hospital Open House Set Today," 4/16/50: Section One 12.

17. Russell, *op. cit.*: 167.

18. *Fort Worth Star-Telegram,* "Osteopathic Hospital Fulfills 30-Year Dream," 7/29/56: Section One 6.

19. Fort Worth Osteopathic Hospital Brochure, undated: 3.

20. "Osteopathic Hospital Fulfills 30-Year Dream," *Fort Worth Star-Telegram*, 7/29/56: Section One 6.

21. George Luibel, Personal interview

22. Ibid

23. Richard Scott Rafes, *The Historical Development of the Texas College of Osteopathic Medicine as a State Medical School 1960-1975* Ph.D. dissertation, 1990, 31.

24. Luibel, Personal interview

25. Luibel, Oral history tape transcription, Lewis Library Special Collections, 4.

26. Ray Stokes, and Judy Alter, *Texas College of Osteopathic Medicine: The 1st 20 Years.* (Denton, TX: Texas College of Osteopathic Medicine with the University of North Texas Press, 1990) 9.

27. Carl Everett, Oral history tape transcription, Lewis Library Special Collections, 4.

28. Luibel Oral history, *op. cit.*, 10.

29. Ray Stokes, Personal interview

30. Stokes and Alter, *op. cit.* 14.

31. Stokes, Personal interview

32. Luibel, Oral history, *op. cit.* 28.

33. "Texas College of Osteopathic Medicine," unpublished paper, Lewis Library Special Collections, 2.

34. Everett, oral history *op. cit.*, 6.

35. Everett, oral history *op. cit.*, 8,

36. Elizabeth Harris Oral history tape transcription, Lewis Library Special Collections, 9.

37. Stokes and Alter, *Texas College of Osteopathic*, 14.

38. Elizabeth Harris oral history *op. cit.* 4.

39. Elizabeth Harris, Personal interview

40. Luibel, Oral history *op. cit.*, 23.

41. Everett, Oral history *op. cit.*, 14.

42. Elizabeth Harris, Oral history *op. cit.*, 13.

43. Stokes and Alter, *op. cit.*, 48.

44. Everett, oral history *op. cit.*, 16.

45. Everett, oral history *op. cit.*, 18.

46. Stokes and Alter, *op. cit.*, 64.

47. Craig Elam, Personal interview

48. Paul Bourgeois, *Fort Worth Star-Telegram*, "A College Flourishes," 12/14/99, B6.

49. *The New Handbook of Texas in Six Volumes Vol 6* (Austin: Texas State Historical Association, 1996) 641.

50. Lou Chapman, *Fort Worth Star-Telegram*, "Health Science Center Program Receives Accreditation," 9/5/96 B4.

51. Charlotte Huff *Fort Worth Star-Telegram*, "New President Has Big Plans for UNT Facility" 8/15/00, B7.

52. Crystal Yednak *Fort Worth Star-Telegram*, "Ex-Army Surgeon General Has a New Mission" 4/1/01, B1.

CHAPTER 7:
THE HOSPITALS: MODERN HALLS OF HEALING

1. Sam Jogoda, Jr., "The Major Hospitals of Fort Worth (Third of a Series) All Saints Episcopal Hospital" *Tarrant County Medical Society Bulletin* Vol. 47 No. 12 (12/77): 80.

2. Quay Lutrell, Personal interview

3. Jim Fuquay, *Fort Worth Star-Telegram*, "All Saints Hospital Starts Expansion," 2/12/93, 1.

4. Lutrell, *op. cit.*

5. Federal Writers' Project microfiche #17688

6. Texas Radiologists," *Texas State Journal of Medicine* Vol. 49 No. 5 (6/25/53): 306.

7. *Fort Worth Star-Telegram* "Tom B. Bond Is Chosen Tarrant Doctor of the Year," 12/9/55 pm, 8.

8. *Fort Worth Star-Telegram*,"Tarrant County Medical Society Bestows Honor on Dr. Tom B. Bond," 12/9/55 am, 5.

9. Nancy Kincheloe, *25 Years of Service:One Day at a Time* (Ft. Worth: Radiation & Medical Research Foundation of the Southwest, 1985), 56.

10. Kincheloe, *op. cit.*, 3.

11. Blair Justice, "Super X-Ray Tube Installed," *Fort Worth Star-Telegram* 4/1/58, reprinted in *25 Years of Service*, 7.

12. Kincheloe, *op. cit.*, 13.

13. *Dallas Morning News*,"Spirits Are Lifted at Radiation Center," 10/26/69, reprinted in *25 Years of Service*, 38.

14. Kincheloe, *op. cit.*, 68.

15. John D. Scott, *True Legacy: The Biography of a Unique Texas Oilman... W. A. "Monty" Moncrief* (Authorized biography, limited edition, privately published, not for sale to the public) 184.

16. Charlotte Huff, *Fort Worth Star-Telegram*, "Moncrief Cancer Center Enters into Partnership with UT Southwestern," 10/4/99, B3.

17. Jeffrey Bernard, Personal interview

18. William H. Craig, Personal interview

19. Kincheloe, *op. cit.*, *v.*

20. William T. Harris, Jr., "Hospital Growth Not 'Abortive,'" *The Tower* (Employee Edition Reprint) Southwest & Genealogy Department, Fort Worth Public Library vertical files, 4/1967, 1-4.

21. Ibid

22. Blair Justice, *Fort Worth Star-Telegram*,"Peter Smith Hospital Troubled Since Birth," Ft. Worth Public Library, John Peter Smith Hospital vertical files, 1955 (No month or day) 1.

23. Blair Justice, "Peter Smith" *op. cit.*, 2.

24. Dr. James A. Hallmark, *Fort Worth Press*, "Peter Smith Hospital Ills Diagnosed by Chief of Staff," 11/26/56, 19.

25. William T. Harris, *op. cit.*, 3.

26. "Hospital Campus Nearing Completion," *Tarrant County Physician*, Vol. 51 No. 8, (8/89) 41.

27. Dr. Will S. Horn, "Response to the Toast: 'The Surgeon' at a Dinner Honoring Dr. Chas. H. Harris," UTA Special Collections Library, Harris personal papers, 4/20/42, 1.

28. Horn, *op. cit.*,2.

29. Horn, *op. cit.*, 3.

30. Ibid

31. Author's personal experience

32. Sam Jagoda, Jr. "The Major Hospitals of Fort Worth (second of a series) Harris Hospital," *Tarrant County Medical Society Bulletin* Vol. 47 No.11 (11/77) 56.

33. "SMMI-Harris' Careflite-E.R.," *Scanner* (Harris Methodist Health System) Vol. 1, No. 1 (Fall 1981) 2.

34. "A Great Medical Center for a Great City," Supplement to *Fort Worth Star-Telegram*, 5/11/80, 1.

35. "Harris on the Grow,"*Focus* (Quarterly magazine for employees and friends of the hospital) Spring 1985, 13.

36. "Harris Center," *Focus* (Summer 1986) 20.

37. Barclay Berdan, Personal interview

38. "Bridge to the Critical Care Tower," *The Monitor* Vol. 20 No.1, (Jan/Feb 2001) 1.

39. Federal Writers' Project microfiche # 17766

40. Federal Writers' Project microfiche # 11767

41. Federal Writers' Project microfiche # 17769

42. Pauline Naylor, *Fort Worth Star Telegram*,"Childrens' Hospital Event Recalls History," 10/11/59, Section Three 20.

43. Federal Writers' Project microfiche # 17772

44. Sam Jagoda, Jr., "Major Hospitals of Fort Worth (Fourth of a series) W. I. Cook Children's Hospital," *Tarrant County Medical Society Bulletin*, Vol. 48, No. 3 (3/78) 40.

45. Ibid

46. Riley Nail, *Per Stripes: The John Nail Family in Texas: 1839-1995.* (Private printing, no city, no date, 281.

47. Ibid

48. Jagoda, Cook Children's *op. cit.* 41.

49. "Cook-Fort Worth Medical Center,"*Fort Worth Star-Telegram* Advertising Section I, 4/20/86, 10.

50. www.cookchildren.org 2/21/01, 1

51. Ibid

52. "Providing a Critical Resource for the Referring Physician: Cook Children's Talks with Dr. David F. Turbeville," *Tarrant County Physician* Vol. 71, No. 1 (1/99) 16.

CHAPTER 8:
"FAMILY" PRACTICE: SONS, DAUGHTERS AND SIBLINGS

1. Ted Terrell, Personal interview

2. Ibid

3. Ibid

4. Larry E. Reaves, "The Gold-Headed Cane," *Tarrant County Physician* Vol. 71, No. 10 (10/99) 7.

5. L. H. Reeves *Medical History op. cit.* 38.

6. "M. E. Hospital Sues Terrell," *Fort Worth Star-Telegram*, 7/22/37 pm, 3.

7. Ibid

8. "Winner of Gold Cane Still Full of Zip at 72," *Fort Worth Press*, 12/2/62, A10.

9. Blair Justice, *Fort Worth Star-Telegram* "Dr. T. C. Terrell, Who Never Gives Up, Recipient of Cane," 12/1/62, Section One 2.

10. Lee S. Anderson, Personal interview

11. Jean Wysatta, *Fort Worth Press* "New President of Doctors Likes Jazz, Children, Aids Baby Gorillas," 1/5/65 p. B9.

12. Ibid

13. Lee S. Anderson, "We Must Reconnect," *Tarrant County Physician* Vol. 69, No. 6 (6/97) 7.

14. Lee S. Anderson, "Me, A Contrarian?" *Tarrant County Physician* Vol. 69, No. 8 (8/97) 7.

15. Lee S. Anderson, "What Will Our Legacy Be?" *Tarrant County Physician* Vol. 70, No. 1 (1/98) 5.

16. Gracie Bond Staples, *Fort Worth Star-Telegram*, "Family Doctors," 4/10/94, Section A 8.

17. Ibid

18. Staples, *op. cit.*, A9.

19. Hollace Weiner, *Fort Worth Star-Telegram*, "Event Will Salute Pair of Black Doctors Who Blazed Trails as Fort Worth Doctors," 10/24/91, A18.

20. Jon McConal, *Fort Worth Star-Telegram*, "Cane Honor to Internist Here," 10/30/71, A1.

21. Sam Jagoda, Jr. "The Great Detroit Riot," personal papers, no date, unpublished

22. McConal, "Cane Honor" *op. cit.* A1.

23. Emory Davenport, Personal interview

24. All Saints Hospital video 1998

25. McConal "Cane Honor" *op. cit.* A2.

26. Davenport, Personal interview

27. Ibid

28. Edward Guinn, Personal interview

29. Jacquielynn Floyd, *Dallas Morning News*, "Lone Doctor in Poor FW Area Turns No One Away," 2/15/92, A 1.

30. Ibid

31. Guinn, Personal interview

32. Ibid

33. Ibid

34. Hollace Weiner, *Fort Worth Star-Telegram*, "Event Will Salute Pair of Black Doctors Who Blazed Trails as Fort Worth Doctors," 10/24/91, A 18.

35. Thomas Kleuser, Personal interview

36. "Rosary Tonight for Dr. Kleuser," *Fort Worth Star-Telegram*, 8/31/71, A12

37. Kleuser, Personal interview

38. Ibid

39. Ibid

40. W. S. Lorimer, Jr., Personal interview

41. Ibid

42. Ibid

43. "Remarks by W. S. Lorimer, Jr., M.D. Upon Acceptance of Gold-Headed Cane," *Tarrant County Physician*, Vol. 59 No. 12 (12/87) 57.

44. Ibid

45. Ibid

46. "Gold-Headed Cane Goes to W. S. Lorimer, Jr., M.D.," *Tarrant County Physician* Vol. 59 No. 10 (10/87) 37.

47. Lorimer, Personal interview

48. Julia Kathryn Garrett, *Down Historic Trails of Ft. Worth and Tarrant County* (Fort Worth: Dudley Hogkins Co., 1949) 64.

49. John Pumphrey, Personal interview

50. Ibid

51. Ibid

52. Ibid

53. Ibid

54. Ibid

55. *Holy Bible:New Revised Standard Version* (Donelson, TN: Melton Book Company, 1989) Exodus 2.5-6, 49.

56. Kathy Cribari Hamer, "Save the Lives of Abandoned Babies," *North Texas Catholic* Vol. 15, No. 16 (8/20/99) 20.

57. Ann Carey, "New Hope for 'Dumpster Babies,'" *Our Sunday Visitor* Vol. 88, No. 49 (4/2/2000) 12.

58. John Richardson, Personal interview

59. Ibid

60. Ibid

61. Ibid

62. Mary Ann Key, Telephone interview 9/12/2000

63. Ibid

64. Richardson, Personal interview

65. Lou Chapman, *Fort Worth Star-Telegram*, "Doctor Honored for Life's Work," 10/14/94, A25.

66. Richardson, Personal interview

67. Ibid

68. Carolyn Poirot, *Fort Worth Star-Telegram*, "Longtime Physician Honored," 10/14/83 pm, A 17.

69. "Gold-Headed Cane Goes to Mal Rumph, M.D.," *Tarrant County Physician* Vol. 55 No. 11 (11/83) 40.

70. Ibid

71. Art Rutledge, All Saints video

72. Art Rutledge, Personal interview

73. Ibid

74. Ibid

75. Ibid

76. "Gold-Headed Cane Goes to Burgess Sealy," *Tarrant County Medical Society Bulletin* Vol. 47 No. 11 (11/77) 31.

77. Ibid

78. "Gold-Headed Cane to Sealy" *op. cit.* 32.

79. John H. Smith, "Interview with Dr. Burgess Sealy," *Tarrant County Physician* Vol.59, No. 3 (3/87) 48.

80. Burgess Sealy, Personal interview

81. Ibid

82. John H. Smith interview with Sealy, *op. cit.*, 48.

83. "Gold-Headed Cane to Sealy" *op. cit.* 30.

84. "Gold-Headed Cane to Sealy" *op. cit.* 31.

85. Mrs. John T. Tucker, Jr., Personal interview

86. Ibid

87. Author's personal experience

88. Jean Wysatta, *Fort Worth Press*, "Specialist Knows TB From Inside," 11/14/74, A 20.

89. Ibid

90. Kenneth Wiggins, Personal interview

91. Jon McConal, *Fort Worth Star-Telegram*, "Medical Society Here Honors Chest Specialist," 11/14/74 am, A 2.

92. Ibid

93. Mack Williams, *Fort Worth Press*, "Dr. Wiggins' Great Prescription," (In Old Fort Worth Column; Fort Worth Public Library verticla file) 4/16/93

94. Kenneth Wiggins personal papers, "In Memoriam."

CHAPTER 9:
MAY OWEN, MD: FIRST LADY OF FORT WORTH MEDICINE

1. John H. Smith, "May Owen, M.D.," *Tarrant County Physician* Vol. 60, No. 5, (5/88) 12.

2. Ted Stafford, *May Owen, MD: An Authorized Biography* (Austin: Eakin Press 1990) 6.

3. Stafford, *op. cit.*, 3.

4. Ibid

5. Stafford *op. cit.*, 19.

6. Stafford *op. cit.*, 20.

7. Stafford *op. cit.*, 24.

8. Stafford *op. cit.*, 26.

9. Stafford *op. cit.*, 28.

10. Stafford *op. cit.*, 41.

11. David Pillow, Personal interview

12. Ibid

13. May Owen personal papers in Charles Rush's possession

14. Bill Lace, "Dr. May's Seen All the Milestones," *Momentum* Vol. 17, No. 2 (4/83) 3.

15. Stafford *op. cit.*, 138

16. Lace op cit (M Owen per papers; med tech at All Sts.)

17. Lace op cit p. 3

18. John H. Smith, *op. cit..* 12.

19. Stafford *op. cit.*, 93.

20. Stafford *op. cit.,* 104.

21. Stafford *op. cit.*, 143.

22. Stafford *op. cit.*, 144.

23. Stafford *op. cit.*, 151.

24. John H. Smith, *op. cit.*, 12.

25. Jeff Guinn, *Fort Worth Star-Telegram* "Dr. Owen Leaves Legacy of Caring," 4/15/88 pm, Part Two, Section One 1.

26. David Pillow, Personal interview

CHAPTER 10:
WOMEN IN MEDICINE: THE REAL DR. "MOMS"

1. Susan Rudd Wynn, "Women in Medicine Month," *Tarrant County Physician* Vol. 64, No. 9 (9/92) 36.

2. Ibid

3. Barbara Barzansky Ph.D., *et al*, "Educational Programs in US Medical Schools, 1999-2000," *Journal of the American Medical Association* Vol 284, No. 9 (9/6/2000) 1116.

4. "Carlton Establishes Endowment for OMM," *Kirksville Magazine* Winter 1994, 17.

5. Madeline Williams, *The Business Press* "Healing Hands: After 59 Years, Dr. Carlton Has No Plans to Retire," week of 8/29/97, 33.

6. Ibid

7. Catherine Carlton, Personal interview

8. Ibid

9. Nelda Cunniff-Isenberg, Personal interview

10. Angelique Siy, "Dr. Nelda Cunniff-Isenberg," Texas Wesleyan University Alumni Office files, 1998

11. Cunniff-Isenberg, Personal interview

12. Ibid

13. Siy, *op. cit.*

14. Dorothy Patras, Personal interview

15. Ibid

16. Margie Peschel, Personal interview

17. Ibid

18. Ibid

19. Ibid

20. Ibid

21. Ibid

22. Ibid

23. "Gold-Headed Cane Goes to Margie B. Peschel, M.D.," *Tarrant County Physician* Vol. 58, No. 10 (10/86) 37.

24. Margie B. Peschel, "Thanks for the Memories," *Tarrant County Physician* Vol. 67, No. 2 (2/95) 27.

25. Blanche Terrell, Personal interview

26. Susan K. Blue, "Interview with Dr. Blanche Terrell," *Tarrant County Physician* Vol. 56, No. 8 (8/84) 64.

27. Ibid

28. Terrell, Personal interview

29. Ibid

30. Terrell personal papers

31. Blue, *op. cit.*, 64.

32. Susan Wynn, Personal interview

33. Ibid

34. Wynn, "Medicine, Motherhood and Medical Societies," *Tarrant County Physician* Vol. 69, No. 3 (3/97) 7.

35. Ibid

36. Ibid

37. Wynn, Personal interview

CHAPTER 11:
THE GOLD-HEADED CANE AWARD: DOCTORS' DOCTORS

1. William M. Crawford, "Gala Party Planned for the 32nd Recipient of the Gold Headed Cane," *Tarrant County Physician* Vol. 5, No. 9 (9/82) 41.

2. William M. Crawford, "The Gold Headed Cane Speaks," *Tarrant County Medical Society Bulletin* Vol. 43, No. 8 (8/73) 11.

3. Margie B. Peschel, "The Gold-Headed Cane," *Tarrant County Physician* Vol. 70, No. 10 (10/98) 25.

4. John Freese, "The Cane," *Tarrant County Physician* Vol. 54, No. 11 (11/82) 7.

5. Isabelle Newberry, Personal interview

6. Larry E. Reaves, "The Gold-Headed Cane," *Tarrant County Physician* Vol. 71, No. 10 (10/99) 7.

7. Newberry personal papers

CHAPTER 12:
THE GOLD-HEADED CANE HONOREES: 1950 TO 1980

1. Margie B. Peschel, "Our Medical Heritage," *Tarrant County Physician* Vol. 71, No. 10 (10/99) 21.

2. Dolphus Compere, Personal interview

3. Blair Justice, *Fort Worth Star-Telegram*, "Doctor Retires from 'Religion' of Surgery," 11/11/63, 3.

4. Ibid

5. "Rotary Club Hears Doctor Relate 'Surgeons's Religion,'" *Fort Worth Star-Telegram*, 8/30/52 am, 14.

6. Blair Justice, *Fort Worth Star-Telegram*, "Dr. Joe White Acclaimed by Tarrant Medical Men," 12/16/53, 4.

7. Pat Baker, Personal interview

8. Ibid

9. Blair Justice, *Fort Worth Star-Telegram*, "Tarrant's Doctors' Doctor of the Year Got License Before Age to Vote," 12/18/54 pm, 1.

10. Baker, Personal interview

11. Beebee Baker, Personal interview

12. Blair Justice, *Fort Worth Star-Telegram*, "Goldheaded Cane Winner Blazed Trail in Fort Worth as Baby Doctor," 12/19/56 pm, 1.

13. "Dr. Edwin G. Schwarz Gets Goldheaded Cane," *Fort Worth Star-Telegram*, 12/19/56 am, 1.

14. "Dr. Edwin G. Schwarz Gets Goldheaded Cane," *op. cit.* 12/19/56, 4.

15. "Dr. Edwin G. Schwarz Gets Goldheaded Cane," *op.cit.* 12/19/56, 1.

16. Ed Johnson, *Fort Worth Star-Telegram*, "Veteran Physician Honored by City Christians, Jews," 3/8/59, 1.

17. "Dr. Edwin Schwarz," *Fort Worth Star-Telegram*, 10/17/62 pm, Section Five 6.

18. Maggie Droomgoole, *Fort Worth Star-Telegram*, "Pioneer Pediatrician Says First Years Were Not Easy," 3/29/68 pm, A 4.

19. Blair Justice, *Fort Worth Star-Telegram*, "Dr. Louie Oscar Godley Gets Gold-Headed Cane," 12/18/57, 1.

20. UTA Special Collections Library file on L. O. Godley

21. Justice, *op. cit.*, 12/18/57, 1.

22. Justice, *op. cit.*, 12/18/57, 4.

23. L. O. Godley, UTA Special Collections file

24. Droomgoole, *op. cit.*

25. Ibid

26. "Medical Group Honors Dr. Dewitt Neighbors," *Fort Worth Star-Telegram*, 12/17/58 am, 4.

27. Blair Justice, *Fort Worth Star-Telegram*, "Honored Doctor Started on Medical Career at Ranch," 12/16/59 pm, 6.

28. Ibid

29. Jean Wysatta, *Fort Worth Press*, "Doctors' Doctor to Take Over Medical Reins of Local Medical Society," 1/1/61, 6.

30. Margie B. Peschel, "Our Medical Heritage," *Tarrant County Physician* Vol. 71, No. 10 (10/99) 21.

31. "Dr. T. H. Thomason," *Texas State Journal of Medicine* Vol.58, No. 11 (11/62) 968.

32. "Dr. Thomas H. Thomason, Physician Since 1921, Dies," *Fort Worth Star-Telegram*, 10/7/62, 1.

33. Blair Justice, *Fort Worth Star-Telegram*, "Dr. McVeigh Honored by Fellow Physicians," 11/18/61 pm, 1.

34. "Dr. McVeigh Feels Better About Defeat After Calls," *Fort Worth Star-Telegram*, 4/9/53 am. 2.

35. Ibid

36. Seth Kantor, *Fort Worth Press*, "The Good Doctor Deserves It," 1/6/60, 8.

37. Dr. Billy Sills, nephew of West, telephone interview

38. Doug Tatum, Personal interview

39. Thayer Waldo, *Fort Worth Star-Telegram*, "Dr. Walter West Gets 'Gold Cane,'" 10/30/63 am, 1.

40. "Medical Society Installs President," *Fort Worth Star-Telegram*, 1/7/60 am, 2.

41. Guy Draughton, *Fort Worth Star-Telegram*, "Widow Helps with Dedication of Dr. W. B. West Auditorium," 11/26/66, A 4.

42. Bobby Q.Lanier, "Interview with Dr. Sim Hulsey," *Tarrant County Physician* Vol.56, No. 3 (3/84) 44.

43. Ibid

44. Bishop Sam Hulsey, Personal interview

45. Ibid

46. Ibid

47. Ibid

48. "Remarks by Dr. Sim Hulsey On Receiving the Gold-Headed Cane," *Tarrant County Medical Society Bulletin* Vol. 34, No. 10 (11/64) 10.

49. Sam Hulsey, Personal interview

50. Deaton obituary draft, 3/29/55 unpublished, UTA Special Collections Library, Deaton file

51. "Doctors Will Install Deaton As President," *Fort Worth Star-Telegram*, 1/3/56 pm, 22.

52. Jon McConal, *Fort Worth Star-Telegram*, "Dr. Hobart Deaton, Ex-Barber, Medical Society Award Winner," 10/22/65 am, 1.

53. Ibid

54. "Dr. Deaton Gets Gold Cane Award," *Fort Worth Star-Telegram*, 10/22/65 pm, Section Three, 2.

55. Jon McConal, *Fort Worth Star-Telegram*, "County Medical Society Cites Dr. C. S. E. Touzel," 11/4/66, 1.

56. Ibid

57. "The Gold-Headed Cane Award Dinner," *Tarrant County Medical Society Bulletin* Vol 36, No. 11 (12/66) 11.

58. "The Gold-Headed Cane Award Dinner," *op. cit.*, 12.

59. "President's Paragraphs . . . Remarks by Louis Levy, M.D.,"*Tarrant County Medical Society Bulletin* Vol. 36, No. 10 (11/67) 12.

60. Mrs. Louis Levy, Personal interview

61. Jean Wysatta, *Fort Worth Press*, "Dr. Levy, Friend of 2 Football Players, Will Lead Doctors," 10/1/63, 1.

62. Ibid

63. Ibid

64. Mrs. Levy, Personal interview

65. "President's Paragraphs . . . Remarks by Louis Levy, *op. cit.*, 11/67, 12.

66. Louis Levy, "Gold-Headed Cane Presentation 1968," *Tarrant County Medical Society Bulletin* Vol. 38, No. 10 (11/68) 11.

67. Ibid

68. Louis Levy, *op. cit.*, 13.

69. Louis Levy, *op. cit.*, 12.

70. Vernie A. Stembridge speech at Andujar Citation of Merit Awards Luncheon Program, 1/30/99, 3.

71. John Andujar, Personal interview

72. Blair Justice, *Fort Worth Star-Telegram*,"New Head of Medical Society Man of Many Causes, Offices," 1/1/62 am, 3.

73. LaDon Homer, "Interview with Dr. John J. Andujar," *Tarrant County Physician* Vol. 57, No. 8 (8/85) 37.

74. Andujar, Personal interview

75. Stembridge speech, *op. cit.*, 6.

76. Margie B. Peschel, *Tarrant County Physician* Vol. 71, No. 10 (10/99) 22.

77. "Dr. Higgins Planned as a Youth to Be Physician," *Fort Worth Star-Telegram*, 1/3/54 am, Section One 14.

78. "Catholics Honor Doctor For 15 Years of Top Service," *Fort Worth Star-Telegram*, 2/25/60 pm,12.

79. John J. Andujar, "Tarrant County Medical Society, October 30, 1970," *Tarrant County Medical Society Bulletin* Vol. 40, No. 9 (11/70) 11.

80. "Response at Gold-Headed Cane Dinner W. P. Higgins, Jr., M.D., 1970 Recipient," *Tarrant County Medical Society Bulletin* Vol. 40, No. 9 (11/70) 12.

81. Don Fisher, "Humanize Medicine, Honored Doctor Says,"*Fort Worth Star-Telegram*, 10/28/72 am, 1.

82. "Remarks by William M. Crawford, M.D.,"*Tarrant County Medical Society Bulletin* Vol. 42, No. 9 (11/72) 11.

83. W. S. Lorimer, Jr., "Talking with Dr. William Crawford," *Tarrant County Physician* Vol. 61, No. 9 (9/89) 45.

84. Blair Justice, "Doctor Here Owner of Rare Edition of Early Book on Human Anatomy," *Fort Worth Star-Telegram*, 8/27/54 pm, 15.

85. "Presentation of Gold-Headed Cane to Clifton Harold Beasley, M.D. 1973 Recipient," *Tarrant County Medical Society Bulletin* Vol. 43, No. 9 (11/73) 20.

86. "C. Harold Beasley," *Fort Worth Star-Telegram*, 1/13/99, B 11.

87. Frank Cohen, Personal interview

88. Ida Belle Hicks, *Fort Worth Star-Telegram*,"Dr. Cohen Honored by Shanblum Lodge," 9/22/54 am, 4.

89. "Physician Named as Man of Year," *Fort Worth Star-Telegram*,1/22/62 am, Section Three 6.

90. "Pediatrician Cited by Sertoma Club," *Fort Worth Star-Telegram*, Sun. 3/14/65, Section One 12.

91. Bob Lanier, Interview with Dr. Frank Cohen," *Tarrant County Physician* Vol. 55, No. 11 (11/83) 47.

92. Ibid

93. Jon McConal, *Fort Worth Star-Telegram*, "Doctor Who Loves Children Awarded Top Medical Honor," 11/20/75 am, 1.

94. Ibid

95. Grant Begley, Personal interview

96. Ibid

97. "Frank Cohen Presents Gold-Headed Cane to Grant Begley," *Tarrant County Medical Society Bulletin* Vol. 46, No. 10 TCP (12/76) 43.

98. Begley, Personal interview

99. Carolyn Poirot, "Former City Health Official, Dr. W. V. Bradshaw Dies," *Fort Worth Star-Telegram*, 10/2/85 pm, A16.

100. Madeline Williams, "Many Today Owe Lives to Dr. Bradshaw," *Fort Worth News-Tribune* 10/4/85, A 11.

101. "In Memoriam," Bradshaw family personal papers

102. "The Cane, the Gold, the Glitter," *Tarrant County Medical Society Bulletin* Vol. 49, No.12 (12/76) 36.

103. "The Cane, the Gold, the Glitter *op. cit..* 37.

104. Ibid

CHAPTER 13:
THE GOLD-HEADED CANE HONOREES: 1980 TO 2000

1. Margie B.Peschel, "Our Medical History," *Tarrant County Physician* Vol. 71, No. 10 (10/99) 23.

2. Jon McConal, *Fort Worth Star-Telegram*, "Dr. Ware Receives Cane," 10/24/80, C1

3. Margie B. Peschel, "TMA 1993 Distinguished Service Award," *op. cit.*, 48.

4. Ware family personal papers, from Dr. Ware's speech upon receiving TMA emeritus, 1997

5. Carolyn Ondrejas, *Fort Worth Star-Telegram*, "Society Honors Physician," 10/31/81 pm, A24.

6. Ibid

7. "The Gold-Headed Cane, James W. Short, M.D., Presentation by Drue O. D. Ware, M.D.," *Tarrant County Physician* Vol. 53, No. 10 (10/81) 13.

8. Pat Gordon, *Dallas Morning News* "Giving Medicine a Shot in the Arm," 10/21/82 Metro West Section, 1.

9. Moorman, unpublished manuscript, no page numbers.

10. Gordon, *op. cit.*

11. Moorman, Personal interview

12. Ibid

13. "Gold-Headed Cane Goes to Warren W. Moorman," *Tarrant County Physician* Vol. 54, No. 11 (11/82) 44.

14. Ibid

15. Carolyn Poirot, *Fort Worth Star-Telegram*, "Moorman Honored as 'Doctor's Doctor," 10/21/82 am, A 17.

16. Gordon, *op. cit.*

17. Ibid

18. Moorman personal papers

19. Ibid

20. John H. Smith, Personal interview

21. Robb Rutledge, Personal interview

22. Ibid

23. Carolyn Poirot, *Fort Worth Star-Telegram*, "Surgeon Stresses Healing Body, Soul," 10/18/84 am, A 25

24. "Gold-Headed Cane Goes to Dolphus E. Compere," *Tarrant County Physician* Vol. 57, No. 10 (10/85) 33.

25. Compere, Personal interview

26. Ibid

27. Ibid

28. "Gold-Headed Cane Goes to Dolphus E. Compere," *op. cit.*

29. Compere, Personal interview

30. Ibid

31. Carolyn Poirot, *Fort Worth Star-Telegram*, "Fort Worth Urologist Receives Award,"10/2/85 am, A 20.

32. Ibid

33. "Gold-Headed Cane Goes to Dolphus E. Compere," *op. cit.* 62.

34. James Murphy, Personal interview

35. Ibid

36. Grant Begley, "Interview with James D. Murphy," *Tarrant County Physician* Vol. 59, No. 8 (8/87) 41.

37. Ibid

38. Mabel Gouldy, *Fort Worth Star-Telegram*, "TMA President Believes in Idea of Family Doctor," 6/8/66 Section Four 1.

39. Ibid

40. "Gold-Headed Cane Goes to James O. McBride," *Tarrant County Physician* Vol. 61, No. 10 (10/89) 27.

41. Sam Jagoda, Jr., Personal interview

42. "Gold-Headed Cane Goes to James O. McBride," *op. cit.*

43. Margie B. Peschel, "Our Medical History," *Tarrant County Physician* Vol. 71, No. 10 (10/99) 24.

44. Thomas Shields, Personal interview

45. "Gold-Headed Cane Goes to Thomas L. Shields, M.D." *Tarrant County Physician* Vol. 62, No. 10 (10/90) 25.

46. Shields, Personal interview

47. Shields personal papers, "Current News in Dermatology and Syphology, July 1954, 1.

48. Shields personal papers, "'Kissing Bug' Bite," reprinted from the A.M.A. *Archives of Dermatology* July 1956, Vol. 74 pp.14–21.

49. Ibid

50. "Gold-Headed Cane Goes to . . .Shields, M.D." *op. cit.*

51. Rachel Donihoo, "UT Southwestern Establishes Professorship in Honor of Retired Fort Worth Dermatologist Thomas Shields," Shields' personal copy of news release.

52. Stephen Eppstein, Personal interview

53. Carolyn Poirot, *Fort Worth Star-Telegram*, "Tarrant Doctor Tapped to Receive Medical Award," 10/24/91 A 18.

54. "Gold-Headed Cane Goes to Stephen Eppstein, M.D.," *Tarrant County Physician* Vol. 63, No. 10 (10/91) 23.

55. Eppstein, Personal interview

56. John Freese, Personal interview

57. Lou Chapman, *Fort Worth Star-Telegram*, "Surgeon Wins Award from Medical Group," 10/16/92, A 19.

58. "A Passion for Books and Fort Worth History," *Tarrant County Physician* Vol. 62, No. 4 (4/90) 45

59. Chapman, "Surgeon Wins Award . . ." *op. cit.*

60. Lou Chapman, *Fort Worth Star-Telegram*, "Tarrant Group to Honor Fort Worth Physician," 10/5/93, Northeast B 14.

61. G. Douglas Tatum, Personal interview

62. Chapman, "Tarrant Group," *op. cit.* 13.

63. Tatum, Personal interview

64. Lou Chapman, "Surgeon Wins Society Award," *Fort Worth Star-Telegram*, 10/5/95, Arlington Edition A18.

65. Bohn D. Allen, Personal interview

66. Ibid

67. "Gold-Headed Cane Goes to Bohn D. Allen, M.D.," *Tarrant County Physician* Vol. 67, No. 10 (10/95) 9.

68. Allen, "Change, A Sign of the Times," *Tarrant County Physician* Vol. 65, No. 1 (1/93) 5.

69. John H. Smith, Personal interview

70. Dick Ellis, Personal interview

71. Ibid

72. "1996 Gold-Headed Cane Honoree Dick Ellis, M.D.," *Tarrant County Physician* Vol. 68, No. 10 (10/96) 9.

73. Ellis, Personal interview

74. "1996 Gold-Headed Cane Honoree Dick Ellis, M.D.," *op. cit.* 9.

75. "Dick Ellis, M.D, Honored with Gold-Headed Cane,"*Cook Medical Staff News* Fall 96, 26.

76. Ibid

77. "1996 Gold-Headed Cane Honoree Dick Ellis, M.D.," *op. cit.*, 11.

78. Val Borum, Personal interview

79. Val Borum, MD, "Operation Hideout," *Tarrant County Physician* Vol. 69, No. 3 (3/97) 11.

80. Borum, Personal interview

81. Ibid

82. Ibid

83. Borum correspondence to author

84. "TMA Young Physicians Section Honors Dr. Val Borum," *Tarrant County Physician* Vol. 65, No. 7 (7/93) 35.

85. Borum, "Response to Presentation Gold-Headed Cane, Ft. Worth Club 10-30-97" personal papers 1.

86. Ibid

87. Cathy O'Neal, "Sharing Life's Lighter Side: Humor Columnist John Smith, MD, Is Honored for His Integrity and Professionalism," *Tarrant County Physician* Vol. 70, No. 10 (10/98) 27.

88. Ibid

89. John Smith, Personal interview

90. Cathy O'Neal, "Sharing Lifes's Lighter Side," *op. cit.* 28.

91. Laura Vozzella, *Fort Worth Star-Telegram*, "Outspoken Doctor Wins Top Award," 10/28/98, B 4.

92. Ibid

93. M. Dwain McDonald, Personal interview

94. Cathy O'Neal, "The Gold-Headed Cane Award Is Passed to M. Dwain McDonald, MD,' *Tarrant County Physician* Vol. 71, No. 10 (10/99) 14.

95. Ibid

96. Charlotte Huff, *Fort Worth Star-Telegram*, "Doctor of Choice," 10/13/99, B 4.

97. Cathy O'Neal, "The Gold-Headed Cane Award Is Passed to M. Dwain McDonald, MD,' *op. cit.* 14.

98. O'Neal, op. cit, 15.

99. Paul Bourgeois, *Fort Worth Star-Telegram*, "Medical Society to Give Honor to 'Country Doctor' for Work He Loves," 9/18/00, B 4.

100. Jean Wysatta, *Fort Worth Press*, "John H. Richards to Receive Applause of Fellow Doctors,"1/7/64, 3.

101. Ibid

102. John Richards, Personal interview

103. Ibid

104. Paul Bourgeois, "Medical Society to Give Honor," *op. cit.* 9/18/00, 4 B.

105. Ibid

106. "Tarrant County Medical Society Fiftieth Annual Gold-Headed Cane Award Dinner" program, Ft. Worth Club, 10/3/00, 4.

CHAPTER 14:
THE HUMANITARIAN AWARD: CAST YOUR BREAD

1. "Physician's Humanitarian Award Nomination Form," *Tarrant County Physician* Vol. 72, No. 10 (10/00) 19.

2. Cathy O'Neal, "Rebuilding Smiles and Lives," *Tarrant County Physician* Vol. 71, No. 2 (2/99) 15.

3. Betty Cook, "The Doctor Who Fixes Faces," *Scene* Sunday Supplement 2/2/75, 1. Fort Worth Public Library Local History Department vertical files.

4. *Proyecto Huastco Newsletter* 8/21/2000 p. 1

5. O,Neal, *op. cit.*, (2/99) 15.

6. Jan D. Cochrum, Personal interview

7. Ibid

8. *Helps International* brochure, Addison, TX: 15301 Dallas Parkway, Suite 200, no date, 2.

9. Cochrum, Personal interview

10. Glen Stone, "Faithful Service to Guatemala; 2000 Humanitarian Award Recipient Jan D. Cochrum, Md," *Tarrant County Physician* Vol. 72, No. 2 (2/00) 15.

11. Ibid

12. Don Boston, Personal interview

13. Paul Bourgeois, "Life of Service," *Fort Worth Star-Telegram*, 8/22/00 B1.

14. Boston, Personal interview

15. Bourgeois, *op. cit.* B1.

16. Boston personal papers

17. Cathy O'Neal, "2001 Physician Humanitarian Award," *Tarrant County Physician* Vol. 73, No. 2 (2/01) 24.

18. Bourgeois, *op. cit.* B7.

CHAPTER 15: EPIDEMICS AND ADVANCES:
KILLER DISEASES AND DISEASE KILLERS

1. Lynette Iezzoni, *Influenza 1918: The Worst Epidemic in American History* (New York: TV Books, L.L.C., 1999) 44.

2. Federal Writers' Project quoting *Ft. Worth Record* microfiche 11873

3. Federal Writers' Project microfiche 11875

4. Ibid

5. Federal Writers' Project microfiche 11845

6. "Peak of Influenza Epidemic Is Passed, Says Dr. Mahoney," *Fort Worth Record* 10/19/1918, 1.

7. Iezzoni, *op. cit.*, 26.

8. Federal Writers' Project microfiche 11845

9. Nixon, Pat I. *History of Texas Medicine Association: 1853-1953* (Austin: University of Texas Press, 1953) 306.

10. Marinos C. Dalakas, "Post-Polio Syndrome Years Later," *Annals of the NY Academy of Science* p.11

11. Tony Gould *A Summer Plague: Polio and Its Survivors* (New Haven: Yale University Press, 1995) photo between pp 80/81.

12. Judge Lyle, *Fading Family Physician* (Fort Worth: Henry L. Geddie Co., 1965) 65.

13. Dalakas, *Annals, op. cit.* 2.

14. Dalakas, *op. sit*, 5.

15. Eleanor Wilson, "Polio, A Plague Now Defeated, Terrorized Fort Worth for Years Before Salk Vaccine," *In Old Ft. Worth* (Fort Worth: Mack and Madeline Williams, 1977) 89.

16. Isabelle Newberry, Personal interview

17. Morris Fishbein, MD. "Poliomyelitis or Infantile Paralysis," *The Handy Home Medical Advisor and Concise Medical Encyclopedia* (Garden City, NY: Hanover House, 1957) 147.

18. Jean Marx, "New Disease Baffles Medical Community," *Science* Vol. 1217, (8/13/82) 618.

19. C. L.LaGrone, "Update on AIDS: A Resume," *Tarrant County Physician* Vol. 56, No. 7 (7/84) 64.

20. Ibid

21. "AIDS Update," *Science News* Vol. 128 (7/20/85) 40.

22. James Carron, *et al*, "The Epidemiology of AIDS: Current Status and Future Prospects," *Science* Vol. 1229 (12/89) 1352.

23. B. D. Colen, "The New Face of AIDS," *Health* Vol. 21 (12/89) 36.

24. Ibid

25. Hugh Lefler, "Education and AIDS in Tarrant County," *Tarrant County Physician* Vol. 63, No. 1 (1/91) 27.

26. Wetzel, Patricia, "Statement by Patricia Wetzel, MD," *Tarrant County Physician* Vol. 64, No. 5 (5/92): 36.

27. Ibid

28. Charles Oke, "Women with AIDS in Tarrant County," *Tarrant County Physician* Vol. 66, No. 1 (1/94): 16.

29. Sandra Manning, "National Statistical Projections/Trends" *Tarrant County Physician* Vol. 67, No. 3 (3/95): 49.

30. Louis Crampton, editor, *Caring for the Country: A History and Celebration of the First 150 Years of the American Medical Association*. (Chicago: American Medical Association, 1997) 160–161.

31. Val Borum, "Response to Presentation Gold-Headed Cane, Ft. Worth Club 10-30-97," Personal papers 1.

CHAPTER 16:
TCMS: 100 YEARS OF MEDICAL HISTORY

1. Frank G. Sanders, "The Tarrant County Medical Society: Its History, Purposes and Membership," Copy of February 1915 *Tarrant County Medical Society Bulletin*, reprinted in *Tarrant County Physician* Vol. 56, No. 5 (5/84) 65.

2. Sanders, *op. cit.* 66.

3. I. L. Van Zandt III, MD, "History of the Tarrant County Medical Society," *Tarrant County Physician* Vol. 62, No. 2 (2/90) 38.

4. Dolphus E. Compere, MD. "Commemorating 31 Years: A Brief History of the Fort Worth Academy of Medicine," *Tarrant County Physician* Vol. 56, No. 11 (11/84) 63.

5. Bohn D. Allen, "Good-bye Friend," *Tarrant County Physician* Vol. 65, No. 10 (10/93) 5.

6. Robin B. Sloane, "What Does the Medical Society Do For You?" *Tarrant County Physician* Vol. 73, No. 2 (2/01) 9.

7. Brenda Pender "The Way We Were: The Alliance Through the Years," *Tarrant County Physician* Vol. 72, No. 4 (4/00) 29.

8. Pender, *op. cit.*, 34.

9. Bobby Q. Lanier, "Baby Needs New Shoes," *Tarrant County Physician* Vol. 73, No. 1 (1/01) 7.

10. James L. Norman, Personal interview

11. Ibid

12. Ibid

EPILOGUE

1. Mack Williams, "When Every House Had a Water Barrel," *In Old Fort Worth* (Fort Worth: Mack and Madeline Williams, 1977) 103.

APPENDIX A

1. Mack Williams, "Fort Worth's First Medical School," *In Old Fort Worth* (Fort Worth: Mack and Madeline Williams, 1977) 110.

APPENDIX B

By the Way 4/18/96, 1.

APPENDIX C

1902-2001 Presidents of the Tarrant County Medical Society
(from list provided by TCMS)

Bibliography

REFERENCE WORKS

Federal Writers' Project. *Research Data, Fort Worth and Tarrant County Texas* Microfiche. Fort Worth: Texas Writers' Project 1941

Holy Bible: New Revised Standard Version. Nashville, TN: Thomas Nelson, Inc. 1990

Readers' Guide to Periodic Literature. New York: H. W. Wilson Co.

BOOKS

Arnold, Ann. *History of the Fort Worth Legal Community.* Austin, TX: Eakin Press, 2000.

Bobo, Zack. *Ramblings of a Country Doctor.* Dallas: Southwest Offset, Inc., 1977.

Boettcher, Helmuth M., translated from German by Einhart Kawerau, *Wonder Drugs: A History of Antibiotics.* Philadelphia, J. B. Lippincott Co., 1964.

Carpineto, Jane. *On Call: Three Doctors on the Front Lines.* New York: St. Martin's Press, 1994

Crampton, Louis, editor, *Caring for the Country: A History and Celebration of the First 150 Years of the American Medical Association.* Chicago: American Medical Association, 1997

Dalakas, Marinos C., Bartfeld, Harry and Kurland, Leonard, T., Editors, *Annals of the New York Academy of Sciences: The Post-Polio Syndrome: Advances in the Pathogenesis and Treatment, Vol. 753,* New York: New York Academy of Sciences, 1995

Douglas, C. L. *Doctors of the Frontier Days* (Written in collaboration with Mrs. J. W. Poindexter of 1920 Dartmoor Court, Fort Worth, TX) [from a series in the FW *Press*] 1936

Duringer, William C., MD, J'Nelle Pate, editor, *A Pioneer Doctor's Story.* Fort Worth: W. C. Duringer, printed by Paul Printing Co., 1964

Ferris, Sylvia Van Voost, and Eleanor Sellers Hoppe, *Scapels and Sabers: Nineteenth Century Medicine in Texas.* Austin: Eakin Press, 1985

Fishbein, Morris, MD. *The Handy Home Medical Advisor and Concise Medical Encyclopedia.* Garden City, NY: Hanover House 1957

Fisher, Jeffrey A., MD. $R_x 2000$: *Breakthroughs in Health, Medicine, and Longevity by the Year 2000 and Beyond.* New York: Simon & Schuster, 1992

Gallo, Robert, MD. *Virus Hunting: Aids, Cancer, & the Human Retrovirous; A Story of Scientific Discovery.* New York: New Republic Book, Basic Books, a Division of HarperCollins, 1991

Garrett, Julia Kathryn., Mary D. Luke, co-editor *Down Historic Trails of Fort Worth and Tarrant County* Ft. Worth: The Dudley Hogkins Co., 1949

Garrett, Laurie. *The Coming Plague: Newly Emerging Diseases in a World Out of Balance.* New York: Farrar, Straus and Giroux, 1994

Gevitz, Norman. *The D.O.'s Osteopathic Medicine in America.* Baltimore: The Johns Hopkins University Press, 1982

Goggins, Albert M., MD. *Keep Well* Fort Worth: Albert M. Goggins; Bob Ballew & Associates and Main Station Advertising, Inc., 1994

Gould, Tony. *A Summer Plague: Polio and its Survivors* New Haven: Yale University Press, 1995

Iezzoni, Lynette. *Influenza 1918: The Worst Epidemic in American History* New York: TV Books, L.L.C., 1999

Karolevitz, Robert F. *Doctors of the Old West: A Pictorial History of Medicine on the Frontier* New York: Bonanza Books, 1962

Kincheloe, Nancy Butler. *25 Years of Service: One Day at a Time* Fort Worth: Radiation & Medical Research Foundation of the Southwest, 1985

Lyle, Judge M.,MD. *Life of Judge M. Lyle: An Autobiography* Fort Worth: Henry L. Geddie Co., 1964

Lyle, Judge M., MD. *The Fading Family Physician* Fort Worth: Henry L. Geddie Co., 1965

McCollum, Charles H., MD. *Pills and Proverbs* Boston: The Meador Press, 1941

Matathia, Ira & Salzman, Martin, with Ann O'Reilly and the staff of Brand Futures Group. *Next: Trends for the Near Future* New York: The Overlook Press, 1999

Moore, Stephen, and Simon, Julian L. *It's Getting Better All the Time: Greatest Trends of the Last 100 Years* Washington, DC: Cato Institute, 2000

Nail, Riley. *Per Stripes: The John Nail Family in Texas 1839-1995* Private printing, no date, no city

Nixon, Pat Ireland. *A History of the Texas Medical Association: 1853-1953* Austin: University of Texas Press, 1953

Red, Mrs. George Plunkett. *The Medicine Man in Texas* Houston: Standard Printing & Lithographing Co., 1930

Reeves, L. H., MD. *The Medical History of Fort Worth and Tarrant County: One Hundred Years 1853-1953* Ft. Worth: Tarrant County Medical Society, 1955

Russell, Phil R., DO., and Alter, Judy. *The Quack Doctor.* Fort Worth: Branch-Smith, Inc. P.O. Box 1868, 1974

Scott, John David. *True Legacy: The Biography of a Unique Texas Oilman—W. A. "Monty" Moncrief* Fort Worth: (Authorized biography of William Alvin Moncrief, privately published, limited edition, not for public sale.) 1982

Sirica, Coimbra, editor. *Osteopathic Medicine: Past, Present and Future* Proceedings of a Conference Chaired by D. Kay Clawson, MD. New York: Josiah Macy, Jr. Foundation, 1996

Stafford, Ted. *May Owen, MD: An Authorized Biography*. Austin: Eakin Press, 1990

Stokes, C. Ray and Alter, Judy. *Texas College of Osteopathic Medicine: The First Twenty Years* Fort Worth: Texas College of Osteopathic Medicine with the University of North Texas Press, 1990

Williams, Mack. *In Old Fort Worth* Fort Worth: Mack and Madeline Williams, 1977

PERIODICALS

_AAO Journal
Bulletin of the History of Medicine
Christian Journal
Focus
Fort Worth Magazine
Harris Hospital News
Health
JAMA (Journal of the American Medical Association)
Kirksville Magazine
Look Magazine
Medical News
North Texas Catholic
Private Practice
Scanner
Science
Science News
St. Joseph Newsartery
Tarrant County Medical Society Bulletin
Tarrant County Physician
Texas Medicine
Texas State Journal of Medicine

NEWSPAPERS

Dallas Morning News
Fort Worth Gazette
Fort Worth Press
Fort Worth Record
Fort Worth Record-Telegram
Fort Worth Star-Telegram
New York Times
News Tribune
Tarrant Business

Newsletters

By the Way
Cook Medical Staff News
Helps International
Momentum
Our Sunday Visitor
Proyecto Huastico
The Monitor

Personal Papers and Unpublished Works

John J. Andujar, MD

Becky Beasley, PhD

W. V. Bradshaw, MD

Fort Worth Public Library, Southwest and Genealogy Dept.

L. O. Godley, MD at University of Texas at Arlington Library; Special Collections Division

Gold-Headed Cane Dinner Program, October 3, 2000

William T. Harris: John Peter Smith History

Sam Jagoda, Jr., MD (including Bennett Smith's speech at the unveiling of the Flatiron Bldg historical marker, 2/13/71)

Isabelle Brown Newberry

Mrs. Jan Norman

May Owen, MD: Charles Rush, estate administrator

Thomas L. Shields, MD

Texas College of Osteopathic Medicine Oral Tape Transcriptions

UTA Special Collections Library

Mary Helen (Mrs. Drue) Ware

Kenneth Wiggins, MD

Telephone Interviews

Mary Ann Key
Billy Sills

Taped Personal Interviews,
(MD unless otherwise noted)

Allen, Bohn
Anderson, Lee
Andujar, John

Baker, Pat and Harrison, Beebee Baker, daughters of Dr. R. B. Baker

Begley, Grant

Berdan, Barclay, CEO; Harris Methodist Fort Worth

Bernard, Jeffrey, Director of Therapy Services, UT Southwestern Moncrief Cancer Center

Borum, Val

Boston, Don

Carlton, Catherine, DO

Cohen, Frank

Compere, Dolphus

Cothrum, Jan

Craig, William, Executive Director, UT Southwestern Moncrief Cancer Center

Cunniff-Isenberg, Nelda, DO

Darnell, Ruth

Davenport, Emory

Denis, Michael, Executive Director, DFW Area Health Education Center

Ellis, Dick

Eppstein, Stephen

Freese, John

Gracia, Valentin

Guinn, Edward

Hulsey, Bishop Sam, son of Dr. Sim Hulsey

Kleuser, Tom

Levy, Danna, widow of Dr. Louis Levy

Lorimer, William, Jr.

Lutrell, Quay T., Director of Marketing, All Saints Health System

McDonald, M. Dwain

McMillan, Jim, son of James A. "Mr. Mac" McMillan (physicians' answering service)

Moorman, Warren

Murphy, James

Newberry, Isabelle Brown, daughter of Dr. Porter Brown

Patras, Dorothy

Peschel, Margie

Pillow, David

Richards, John

Richardson, John

Rush, Charles

Rutledge, Art

Rutledge, Robb

Shields, Thomas
Smith, John
Stowe, Wanda, secretary to Dr. May Owen
Tatum, G. Douglas
Terrell, Blanche
Terrell, Ted, son of Dr. Blanche and Dr. C.O. Terrell
Tucker, Deedee, widow of Dr. John T. Tucker, Jr.
Ware, Mary Helen, widow of Dr. Drue Ware
Wiggins, Kenneth
Wynn, Susan Rudd

OTHER SOURCES

Milner, John, Former patient of Dr. Abe Greines, personal interview, not taped
Cooks Childrens' Medical Center Website
UNT Science Center Website
UT Southwestern Medical Center Website

Index

PHOTOGRAPHS

Grapevine Public Library
1201 Municipal Way
Grapevine, Texas 76051

ABOUT THE AUTHOR

Dr. Ann Arnold graduated cum laude from Texas Wesleyan University, with majors in history and education. She earned a master's in counseling and PhD in education and psychology from the University of North Texas. She has traveled extensively throughout the United States, Canada, and Western Europe, but her heart is in Fort Worth history.